BRITISH BAT
THE SPANISH
CIVIL WAR

BRITISH BATTLES OF THE SPANISH CIVIL WAR

FIGHTING FRANCO

CHARLES J. ESDAILE

Pen & Sword
MILITARY

AN IMPRINT OF PEN & SWORD BOOKS LTD.
YORKSHIRE - PHILADELPHIA

First published in Great Britain in 2023 by
PEN AND SWORD MILITARY
An imprint of
Pen & Sword Books Ltd
Yorkshire – Philadelphia

ISBN 978 1 52678 281 6

Typeset in Times New Roman 11/13.5 by SJmagic DESIGN SERVICES, India.
Printed and bound in the UK by CPI Group (UK) Ltd.

Pen & Sword Books Ltd incorporates the imprints of Pen & Sword Archaeology, Atlas, Aviation, Battleground, Discovery, Family History, History, Maritime, Military, Naval, Politics, Social History, Transport, True Crime, Claymore Press, Frontline Books, Praetorian Press, Seaforth Publishing and White Owl

For a complete list of Pen & Sword titles please contact

PEN & SWORD BOOKS LIMITED
George House, Units 12 & 13, Beevor Street, Off Pontefract Road,
Barnsley, South Yorkshire, S71 1HN, England
E-mail: enquiries@pen-and-sword.co.uk
Website: www.pen-and-sword.co.uk

Or

PEN AND SWORD BOOKS
1950 Lawrence Rd, Havertown, PA 19083, USA
E-mail: Uspen-and-sword@casematepublishers.com
Website: www.penandswordbooks.com

Contents

For Sinéad with much love

Preface

Life is not without its little ironies. In the summer of 1980, I was, if not for much longer, a third-year undergraduate at the University of Lancaster battling to finish my dissertation, a piece of work that rejoiced in the title of 'Han venido los rusos! The myth and the reality of the International Brigades'. Forty years on or more, what do I find myself working on but a book on exactly the same topic? Admittedly, the focus is different – whereas in 1980 I was looking at the subject *en tout*, now I have rather been looking at one particular group of foreign volunteers, namely the 2,000 men who went out to Spain from Great Britain and Ireland, but the wheel appears to have turned full circle, and all the more so because now both the question that I pose and the methodology which I use to address it are exactly the same. In brief, the issue is one that is dictated by the historiography of the International Brigades, this being something that has in essence altered but little in the intervening forty years. Thus, while it is perfectly true that many works have appeared that I did not have access to at the time that I wrote my dissertation – various memoirs, the writings of Richard Baxell and other specialists, the de facto official history of Bill Alexander, the oral-history anthologies of Max Arthur, Ian MacDougall and Peter Darman, the general history of the International Brigades of Giles Tremlett and, last but not least, assorted studies of the response of Scotland, Wales and Ireland to events in Spain – they have not developed the revisionist dynamic that, in however a naïve, under-informed and, doubtless, half-baked way, I perceived to be necessary. To a very considerable extent we have found out more about such issues as recruitment, motivation and organisation, but a number of key issues, including, most notably, performance on the battlefield, have not been examined in a critical fashion. However, this begs a very important question. According to the introduction penned for one of the anthologies mentioned above by Marxist historian Vincent Kiernan, for example, 'The British battalion of the International Brigades deserves to be reckoned, along with Cromwell's Ironsides, among the bravest and most inspired soldiers that Britain has ever put into the field.'[1] Uplifting as this picture is, however, even the most cursory examination of the detail of the actions of the British battalion cannot but suggest a reality that was very different. Desperate to protect the reputation of their heroes, apologists for the International Brigades have taken refuge in an obvious tactic, namely to lay the blame for what amounts to a record of persistent military failure on the overwhelming material superiority of the Nationalist forces.[2] The problem with this, however, is that it is clear that the forces of General Franco were not nearly as well equipped as has often been argued, and, further, that the control of the air of which so much has often been made was not something on which they could rely until the winter of 1937 at the very earliest.[3] From this it follows that what is needed is a new study that is prepared to address the subject in a much more critical spirit, and, to return to my undergraduate self, revisit the conclusions advanced in 'Han venido los rusos!', namely that, in reality, the International Brigades were not an élite force, but rather a set of formations that were in most respects utterly indistinguishable from the rest of the army of which they were a part, and, by extension, alas, of little real military capacity.[4]

The Spanish Civil War being a subject on which it is possible to write almost without cease, I have made a conscious effort to keep this work within manageable parameters. Absent, then, are many issues ranging from the political background to the conflict and the details of the revolution of 1936 to the role of the many Britons, especially those employed as doctors and nurses, who served in non-combat situations. This is not reflective of any belief that such matters are irrelevant, but rather of a recognition of the demands of practicality, not to mention the fact that they can easily be accessed in the pages of many other works, all of which are listed in the Bibliography. If something is needed to place what I have written in this book in context, as good a place as any is my *The Spanish Civil War: a Military History*, not that this will ever take the place of Hugh Thomas' magisterial *The Spanish Civil War*.

Last but not least, as usual, I owe thanks to many people: to Martin Blinkhorn, professor emeritus of the University of Lancaster, for all the kindness and encouragement he lent not just me, but many other students; to Rupert Harding at Pen & Sword for his steadfast faith in my abilities over many years; to Tara Moran, who took over the editorial role in the wake of the former's well-earned retirement; to Alison Flowers for her careful sub-editing; to Antonio Bardiel Jadía for sharing with me his intimate knowledge of the battlefield of Quinto; to Alan Warren, Antonio Requena and Bob Maycock for their help with photographs of the sites that, courtesy of Covid, I have been unable to visit for myself; to the Imperial War Museum, the University of Swansea, the University of California San Diego and the Marx Memorial Library for permission to use various images in their collections; to all the staff of the Sydney Jones Library at the University of Liverpool, but, most especially, Katy Hooper and Catherine Macmanamon, for their unfailing patience; and, above all, to Sinéad for everything.

Charles J. Esdaile
Liverpool, July 2023

Maps

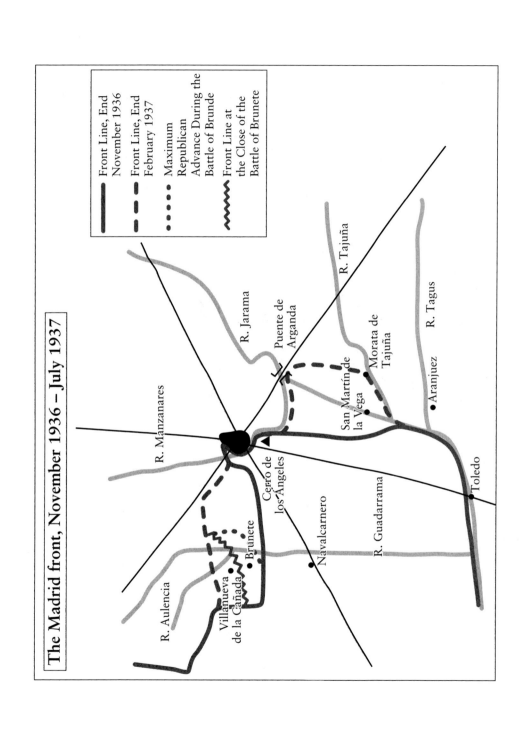

The Madrid front, November 1936 – July 1937

Front Line, End
November 1936

Front Line, End
February 1937

Maximum
Republican
Advance During the
Battle of Brunde

Front Line at
the Close of the
Battle of Brunete

R. Manzanares

R. Jarama

R. Tajuña

Puente de
Arganda

San Martín de
la Vega

Morata de
Tajuña

R. Tagus

Aranjuez

Cerro de
los Ángeles

Navalcarnero

R. Guadarrama

Toledo

Brunete

Villanueva
de la Cañada

R. Aulencia

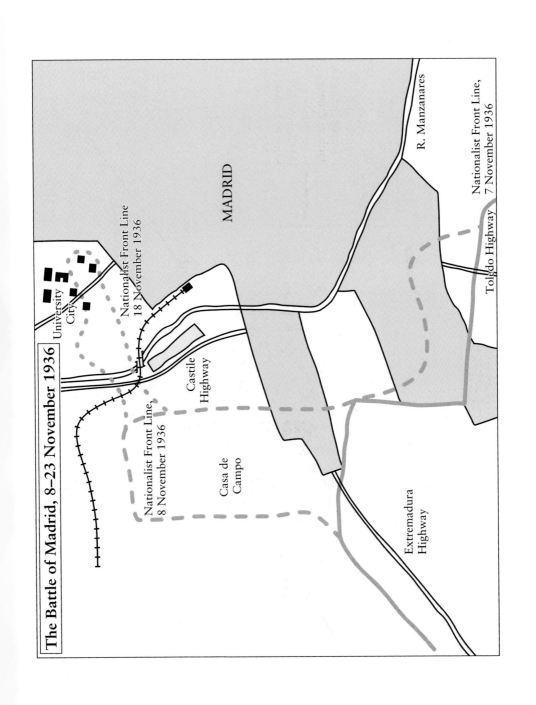

The Battle of Madrid, 8–23 November 1936

MADRID

University City

Nationalist Front Line 18 November 1936

R. Manzanares

Nationalist Front Line, 7 November 1936

Toledo Highway

Castile Highway

Nationalist Front Line, 8 November 1936

Casa de Campo

Extremadura Highway

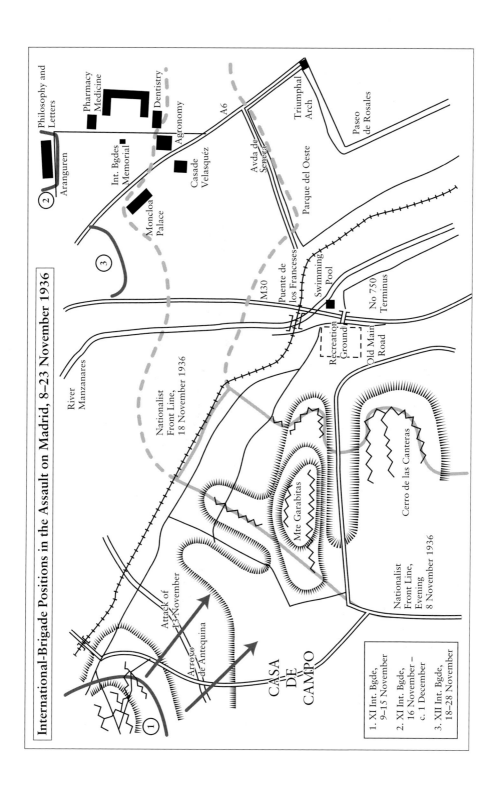

International-Brigade Positions in the Assault on Madrid, 8–23 November 1936

Philosophy and Letters

Pharmacy
Medicine

Dentistry

Agronomy

Aranguren

Int. Bgdes Memorial

Casade Velasquéz

Moncloa Palace

A6

Avda de Seneca

Triumphal Arch

Parque del Oeste

Paseo de Rosales

M30

Puente de los Franceses

Swimming Pool

No 750 Terminus

Recreation Ground

Old Main Road

River Manzanares

Nationalist Front Line, 18 November 1936

Attack of 13 November

Arroyo de Antequina

CASA DE CAMPO

Mte Garabitas

Cerro de las Canteras

Nationalist Front Line, Evening 8 November 1936

1. XI Int. Bgde, 9–15 November
2. XI Int. Bgde, 16 November – c. 1 December
3. XII Int. Bgde, 18–28 November

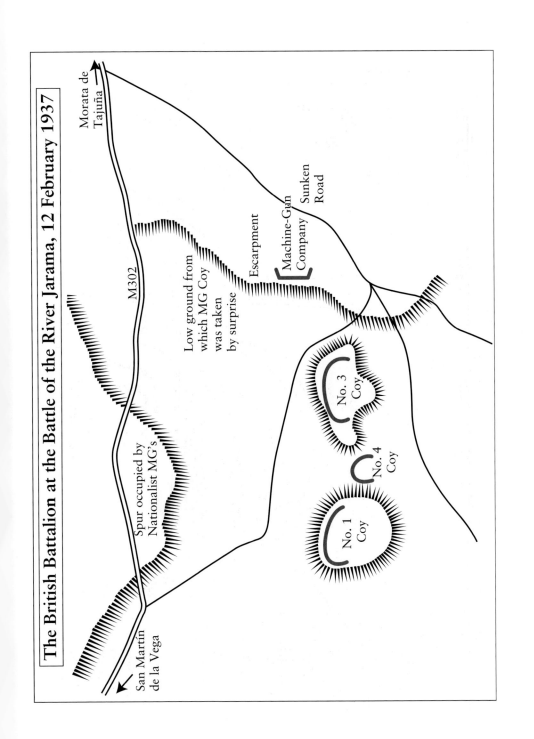

The British Battalion at the Battle of the River Jarama, 12 February 1937

Morata de Tajuña

M302

Low ground from which MG Coy was taken by surprise

Escarpment

Machine-Gun Company

Sunken Road

Spur occupied by Nationalist MG's

No. 3 Coy

No. 4 Coy

No. 1 Coy

San Martín de la Vega

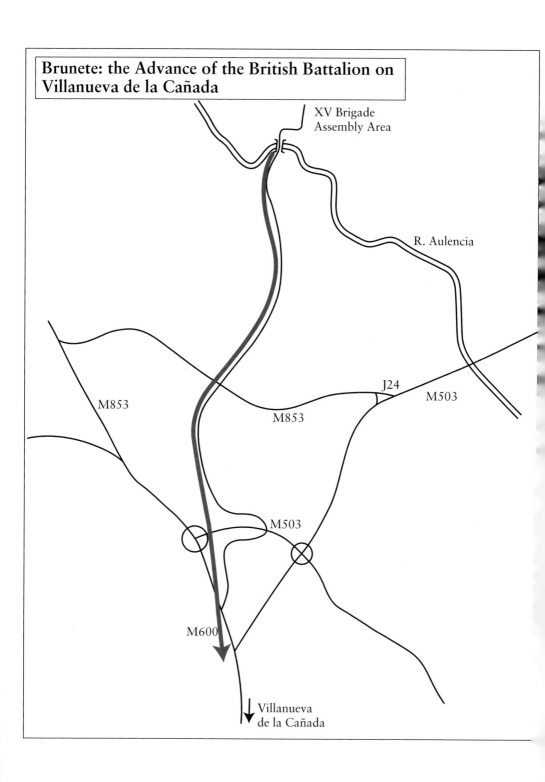

Brunete: the Advance of the British Battalion on Villanueva de la Cañada

XV Brigade
Assembly Area

R. Aulencia

J24

M503

M853

M853

M503

M600

Villanueva
de la Cañada

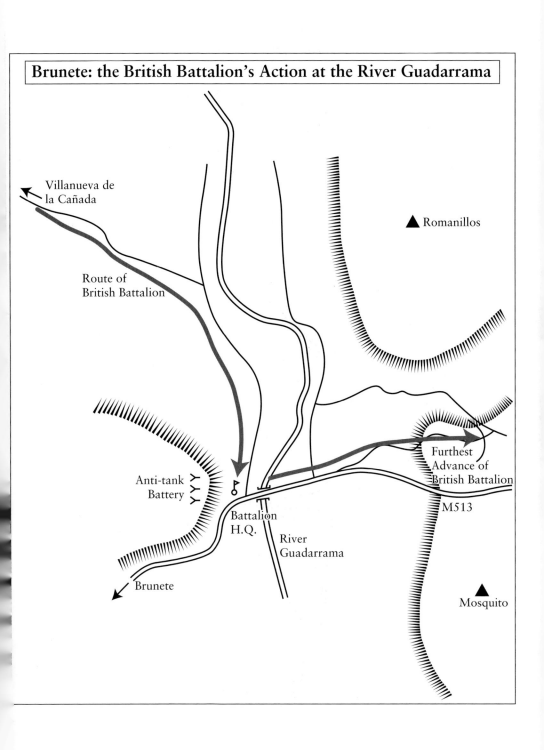

Brunete: the British Battalion's Action at the River Guadarrama

Villanueva de
la Cañada

Romanillos

Route of
British Battalion

Anti-tank
Battery

Furthest
Advance of
British Battalion

M513

Battalion
H.Q.

River
Guadarrama

Brunete

Mosquito

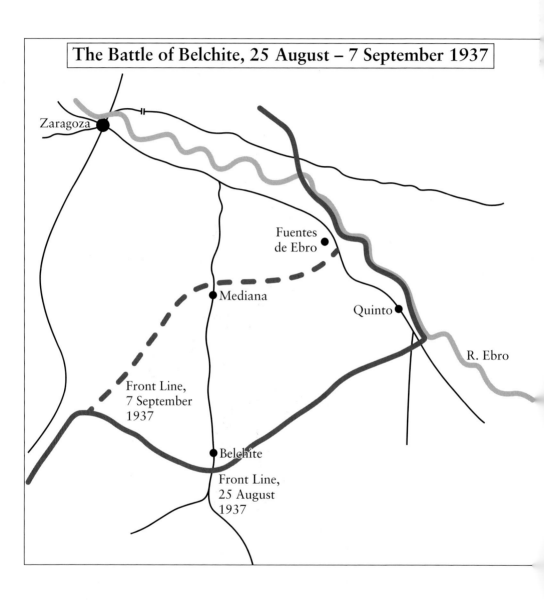

The Battle of Belchite, 25 August – 7 September 1937

Zaragoza

Fuentes
de Ebro

Mediana

Quinto

R. Ebro

Front Line,
7 September
1937

Belchite

Front Line,
25 August
1937

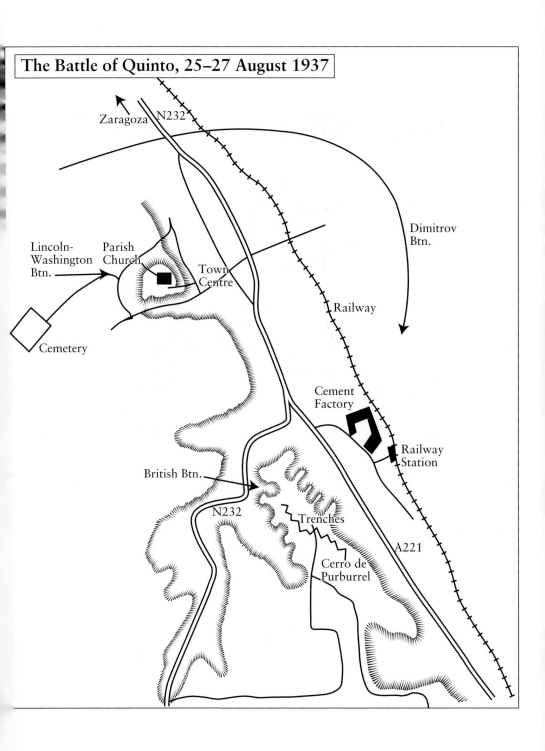

The Battle of Quinto, 25–27 August 1937

Zaragoza
N232

Dimitrov
Btn.

Lincoln-
Washington
Btn.

Parish
Church

Town
Centre

Railway

Cemetery

Cement
Factory

Railway
Station

British Btn.

N232

Trenches

A221

Cerro de
Purburrel

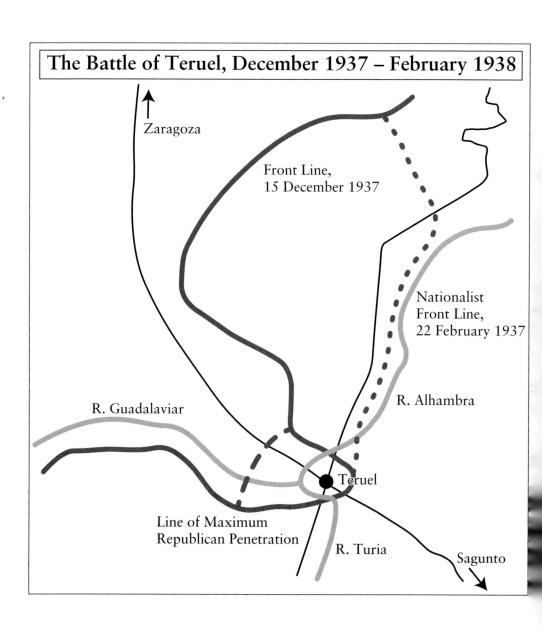

The Battle of Teruel, December 1937 – February 1938

Zaragoza

Front Line,
15 December 1937

Nationalist
Front Line,
22 February 1937

R. Guadalaviar

R. Alhambra

Teruel

Line of Maximum
Republican Penetration

R. Turia

Sagunto

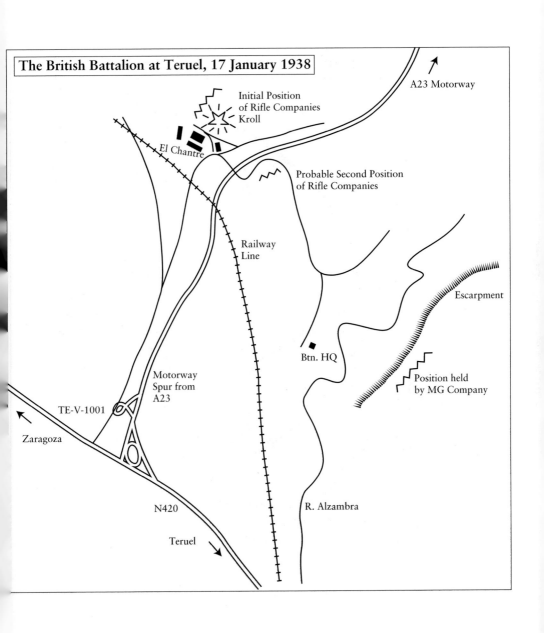

The British Battalion at Teruel, 17 January 1938

A23 Motorway

Initial Position
of Rifle Companies
Kroll

El Chantre

Probable Second Position
of Rifle Companies

Railway
Line

Escarpment

Btn. HQ

Position held
by MG Company

Motorway
Spur from
A23

TE-V-1001

Zaragoza

N420

R. Alzambra

Teruel

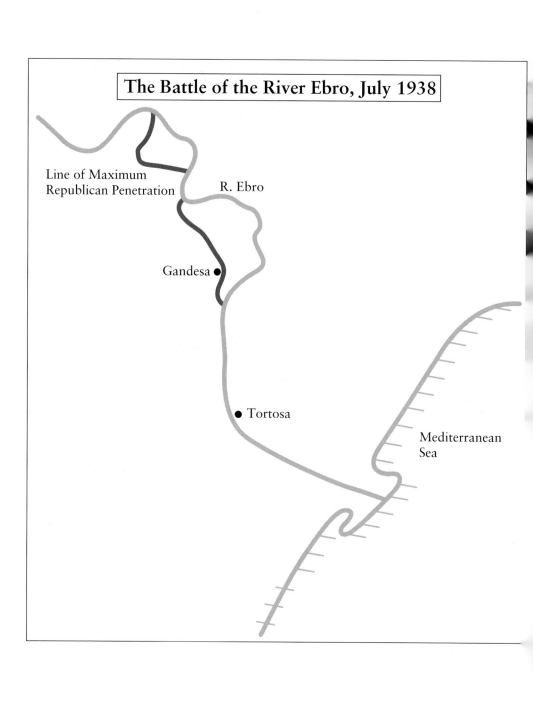

The Battle of the River Ebro, July 1938

Line of Maximum
Republican Penetration

R. Ebro

Gandesa ●

● Tortosa

Mediterranean
Sea

Chapter 1

The International Brigades
in History

It was a dark and rainy dawn in the Spanish capital and few people were on the streets. However, it was not just the piercing cold and persistent drizzle of a Castilian winter that kept so many of the inhabitants indoors. It was 8 November 1936, and, the day before, the spearhead of the forces advancing on Madrid under the command of Francisco Franco, the portly general who had seized command of the Army of Africa in the course of the military uprising that had convulsed Spain some five months earlier, had reached the southern suburbs of Leganés and Carabanchel Alto. Having swept all before them in the course of their long march from Seville, they appeared unstoppable, and that despite a desperate counter-attack the morning before which had checked them for a few hours and prevented them from penetrating the extensive city forest known as the Casa de Campo. With many of Franco's troops Moorish auxiliaries who were reputed to castrate their prisoners, and stories spreading of massacres in every town that the rebel forces had occupied, the population was in a state of complete panic: far from rushing to the barricades in the manner demanded by the strident propaganda posters covering every square inch of wall, the defiant voice of the capital's radio stations and the inflammatory speeches of numerous Anarchist, Socialist and Communist leaders, the denizens of the districts south of the River Manzanares had for the past two days or more been pouring across the Puente de Toledo and heading up the steep slopes towards the city centre. Still worse, sheltering in the fleeing crowds could be seen hundreds of militiamen bent only on seeking shelter from the storm. In short, the picture was one of complete despair, the coalition government headed by the Socialist leader, Francisco Largo Caballero, having only increased the sense of crisis by taking flight for Valencia in the face of the enemy attack.

So confident were the Nationalists – the name by which the rebel coalition that had launched the rising had become known – of success that some of the hundreds of journalists who had rushed to cover the fighting were busily penning reports to the effect that Franco was already victorious: were the rebel commanders not in receipt of copious aid from Nazi Germany and Fascist Italy? Madrid, however, was not alone: tanks and armoured cars supplied by Soviet Russia had already been doing battle with the oncoming Nationalists, while the first formations – mixed brigades as they were called[1] – of the new regular army that was being formed to supplant the all but useless political militias that had formed the backbone of the Republican forces since the summer were moving into position west of the capital. Nor were these troops the only reinforcements that had been sent to help the defenders. On the contrary, as the guns rumbled in the distance, a series of trains had arrived in the railway terminus of Atocha and disgorged some 2,000 men, most of them dressed in black berets and leather jerkins. Yet, unlike all the other forces manning the defences, these new combatants did not speak Spanish, the station yard rather resounding to the sound of a medley of French, German and Polish voices with here and there a handful of English ones as well. Organised though they were as just one more mixed brigade, they were rather foreign volunteers who had come to assist the Republic in its fight against fascism, while they belonged not to the Republican army proper, but rather an entirely separate force run by agents of the Communist International from a base in Albacete, a provincial capital 100 miles to the south-east of Madrid.[2]

Volunteers of the XI International Brigade in Madrid, November 1936. (Alamy)

Originally titled the International Column but now renamed the XI International Brigade, the new force had yet to see action. This event, however, seemed unlikely to be much delayed. Cold, tired and miserable, the motley crowd of men slung their blanket-rolls and haversacks across their soldiers and set off along, first, the north-south boulevard known as the Castellana and, then, the Gran Vía, the street that barely twenty years before had been driven through the narrow streets of Chueca and Malasaña from the Castellana to the imposing Plaza de España, a route that could be construed as taking them directly to the sector of the front that was most threatened by Franco's forces. One of the men tramping through the dawn was John Sommerfield, a machine-gunner in the French Commune de Paris battalion:

> There was a sense of unhappy apathy everywhere, a feeling of almost hopeless exhaustion … Ours was no triumphant entry: we were a last desperate hope, and, as … we marched through the windswept streets, past the shuttered shops and the food queues, I thought the hurrying people on the pavements looked at us as if we were too late and had come only in time to die … But soon my own unfortunate circumstances banished these melancholy reflections: I was carrying the St. Etienne and, heavy as it was, the burden of the weight was rendered worse by the pressure of its ridges on my shoulder … After twenty minutes … all of us who were carrying the guns … were drenched with sweat and trembling with exhaustion … I didn't care about the war or Madrid; there was only one thought and desire in my mind – to be able to lie down.[3]

It was hardly an auspicious début, and all the more so as the Commune de Paris battalion did not go straight into action, but rather took up a reserve position in the so-called 'University City', a complex of imposing, if widely spaced, buildings making up the campus of Madrid's brand-new university, the only excitement being some long-distance shelling that, as a volunteer called Knight remembered, caused a general panic. Thus:

> We heard a sound which most of us knew only from the movies as the sound of approaching shell fire. The aim was good and the explosions took place among our ranks. The ground did not offer any cover and most of us simply scrambled forward over the edge of a bank which took us down into a sort of valley which at least got us out of sight … Down on the lower ground we sorted ourselves out and most of us realised ruefully that we had left our weapons behind.[4]

Yet, very soon the determination of the Communists to derive maximum advantage from the International Brigades – a force which not only owed its origins to the Comintern but was wholly under its control – had coupled with the fevered imagination of certain journalists to generate the makings of a legend that continues to resound down to the present day. First in the field, as might be expected, was the leadership of the International Brigades themselves. Here, for example, is the version of events penned by their supreme head, the French Communist André Marty:

> In combat uniform, the brigade marched along the Gran Vía. Solemn, severe and martial in aspect, it was a real army … a single disciplined whole, whose officers had but to give the word for the mass to set off, to halt or to change formation … It was the first time that Madrid … had seen with its own eyes what a regular army ought to look like, how, indeed, the people-in-arms ought to be organised, the crowds comprehending very well how invincible the same organization and discipline would make the thousands of men in the trenches … Having completed its route, the brigade was sent to the point of greatest danger, namely an area where some enemy soldiers had managed to get across the Manzanares by surprise. The next day the Commune de Paris … and Dombrowski battalions took up positions blocking the way to the University City. Meanwhile, the Edgar André battalion … counter-attacked the Puente de los Franceses, Initially, the fight was very bloody, but in the end the volunteers cleared the Western Park of Moors and secured the bridge. With their opponents thrown back across the river, they then entered the Casa de Campo where they proceeded to beat off the attacks of the enemy for the next six days.[5]

However, satisfying the notion of the XI Brigade marching directly into action in the fashion described by Marty, this whole passage was mendacious in the extreme. Thus, while there was indeed a skirmish involving the Edgar André battalion, what happened was much more complicated than Marty claimed. In brief, having been ordered to occupy some trenches in the Parque del Oeste, one of its companies spotted some Moors on the other bank of the river and immediately waded through the shallow water to attack them, only immediately to be driven back by heavy fire. Not satisfied with this, the Moors then charged across the river in their turn, the result being a sharp fight in which the Republicans only gained the upper hand with some difficulty. To the extent that the Parque del Oeste was eventually cleared of interlopers, Marty is correct, but the idea that the Edgar André battalion established itself on the western bank of the river is clearly nonsense.[6] Yet, it was not just Marty and his fellow apparatchiks who were prepared to exaggerate the truth. An eyewitness to the events of 8 November, for example, was Geoffrey Cox of the *News Chronicle*:

> The next morning I was drinking coffee in [a] bar of the Gran Vía when I heard shouting and clapping outside. I walked out to the pavement edge … Up the street from the direction of the Ministry of War came a long column of marching men. They wore a kind of khaki uniform and loose brown Glengarry caps [i.e. berets] like those of the British tank corps. They were marching in excellent formation. The tramp, tramp of their boots sounded in perfect unison. Over their shoulders were slung rifles of obviously modern design … Each section had its officers, some carrying swords and revolvers … The few people who were about lined the roadway, shouting almost hysterically, 'Salud! Salud!'[7]

As time went on, meanwhile, more and more writers picked up on the story. Here, for example, is the novelist, Manuel Chaves Nogales, a Republican sympathiser who remained in Madrid throughout the Nationalist assault who published an account of the battle in 1938. Thus:

> The situation became ever more anguished … Protected by the fire of their artillery, the rebel columns reached the University City, the best troops of the Republic, the veterans of Lister, Galán, Barceló and Mena, having no option but to give way … The collapse of the front … could have been decisive. Thus, the masses of untrained militiamen would have abandoned the field in a state of complete disarray had not a new force of veteran troops of which the enemy were completely ignorant arrived in Madrid that same day … Though they were just 3,500 strong, many of them veterans of the Great War … who knew how to fight in the open field, it was them who, whether in the Casa de Campo … or the University City, heroically flung themselves to the ground and saved Madrid.[8]

And, finally, here is Arturo Barea, a Socialist militant who had been posted to the bureau of censorship that had been established in the ultra-modern headquarters of the telephone company on the Gran Vía, but had been attending a meeting at the War Ministry on the morning of 8 November and therefore missed the sight of the XI International Brigade marching in serried ranks (or otherwise) past his very window:

On that Sunday, the endless 8 November, a formation of foreigners in uniform equipped with modern arms paraded through the centre of the town: the legendary International Column ... had come to the help of Madrid. After the nights of the sixth and the seventh when Madrid had been utterly alone in its resistance, the arrival of those anti-fascists from abroad was an incredible relief. Before the Sunday was over, stories went round of the bravery of the international battalions in the Casa de Campo, of how 'our' Germans had stood up to the iron and steel of the machines of the 'other' Germans at the spear-head of Franco's troops, of how our German comrades had let themselves be crushed by those tanks rather than retreat.[9]

Curiously, it was not just in the Republican zone that the myth of the International Brigades was fomented. On the other side of the lines the failure of the direct assault on Madrid was something that caused general consternation and therefore had to be explained away, one useful means of doing this being to emphasise, and, indeed, exaggerate, the role of the International Brigades. To quote Harold Cardozo, a British newspaper correspondent friendly to the Nationalists who had joined the advance on Madrid:

The attempt to rush [the capital's] defences ... failed because the Reds, instead of falling back from the 'open city' of Madrid when they had been defeated before it, [took] refuge in its maze of streets and ... lined the barricades with foreign volunteers and with foreign arms ... Before the end of November it was estimated that at least 10,000 Red volunteers, nearly all men with previous military training, had passed through Perpignan alone. Thousands of others had ... landed direct at Barcelona or Valencia ... The Reds had evoked this foreign aid much earlier than had the Nationalists as was evidenced by the presence of Red foreign-infantry units in the line at the end of October. Had the Nationalists marched straight on Madrid at the end of September, they would not have found any of those foreign units ... and, most probably, the Spanish capital would have fallen at the first assault.[10]

As early as 1937, if not before, then, the International Brigades had established themselves as a prominent feature in the reportage of the war, this being a tendency that was reinforced as time went on by a number of different factors of which the most important was undoubtedly the combat record of their five chief representatives: whereas most formations in the Republican army spent the bulk of their service on one front only, the International Brigades were constantly being transferred from one front to another, the result being that their list of battle honours was as long as it was impressive, embracing, as it did, not only Madrid, but also Boadilla, Jarama, Guadalajara, Brunete, Belchite, Teruel and the Ebro. To explain this situation, it is necessary to turn to the politics of Civil-War Spain, and, more especially, the origins of the Spanish Civil War. So far as these last are concerned, they are far too complex to admit of discussion in a work of this nature, but, in brief, the conflict rose out of a situation in which the progressive forces that had secured the establishment of the Second Spanish Republic in 1931 had eventually come to mount such a challenge to the established order that powerful elements of the latter chose to rise in revolt with the aid of elements in the army who sympathised with their cause while yet having particular grievances of their own. Underpinning the government in power when the revolt took place, there was a strategy known as that of 'popular front', in brief, the notion that all men and women of good will and progressive views should come together to oppose the threat of fascism. In so far as the Spanish version of this idea was concerned, it was essentially the fruit of negotiations between the Socialist party and two parties representing the left and the centre of the Republican movement, but outside Spain the picture was very different in that the notion of 'popular front' originated in Moscow. In brief, after years of denouncing its Socialist rivals as crypto-fascists and actively working for revolution, at Stalin's instigation the Comintern – the governing body of world Communism – suddenly initiated a dramatic change of policy. Driven by fear that Hitler, like all fascists, was a catspaw of capitalism, and that Germany could therefore be expected sooner or later to attack Soviet Russia, it now switched to the self-same policy that was currently shaping events in Spain. On the international front, then, the task of Soviet diplomacy would be to get Britain and France in particular to line up with Russia in an alliance against Germany, while on the domestic one the Communist parties were to make every effort to secure the election of governments favourable to the idea of a partnership with Moscow, something that would in turn require the negotiation of alliances with the other parties of the left and centre.[11]

When Spain erupted in revolt in July 1936, the pursuit of this policy had reached a critical moment. Thus, in France an electoral alliance with the Socialists and the Radicals had just two months before secured the formation of a Popular-Front administration in Paris, but in Britain the Communists' change of heart had yet to secure any concrete benefits. For Stalin, then, events in Spain were very awkward. Had it just been a matter of one more coup, the Comintern could simply have seized upon them as one more piece of evidence that fascism – a word that in the Communist lexicon referred to any authoritarian right-wing movement or regime – was on the march, but such was not the case. On the contrary, in part motivated by the fear that revolution was nigh, the rising had precipitated just such a development, in that, everywhere that the rebels were defeated, power passed to self-appointed committees whose make-up varied in accordance with the balance of forces in any given area but whose policies were everywhere directed towards either challenging the existing order or bringing it down altogether, the situation being rendered still more dramatic by the onset of a 'Red Terror' which eventually cost the lives of some 40,000 people including nearly 7,000 members of the clergy. For Stalin, scarcely anything could have been more unfortunate, for he knew that the turmoil in Spain would inevitably be blamed upon him personally, thereby wrecking his efforts to secure the support of Britain and France. Still worse, in the first instance, at least, there was very little that he could do to remedy matters, for the Spanish Communist Party was dwarfed by the Anarchists and Socialists who together had ever been the main representatives of the Spanish Left. Some increase in Communist influence, true, had been secured by a species of entrism whereby the Party had forged alliances with the Socialists' youth movement and Catalan section alike, but in no region of the Republican zone was it even remotely possible to put an end to the chaos. Something needed to be done, then, and that directly, for otherwise Russia would once again be left facing the full weight of German military power.[12]

However, bleak though this situation was, all was not lost, the fact being that there were several factors which were open to exploitation by the Communist leadership. In the first place, there was the large section of the Republican population that was not composed of the urban and rural proletariat, but was rather drawn from the peasantry and the middle classes, groups which had nowhere to go under the existing state of affairs and would therefore be glad to turn to a party which seemed to be ready to defend their interests. And, in the second, there was the war: the political militias that formed the backbone of the Republic's defence in the wake of the outbreak of civil war quickly proving all but useless in military terms, any party that stood four-square in favour of the creation of a new army in with a chance taking on the insurgents would be bound to garner much support, including that of the many officers who had rallied to the government rather than support the uprising. Never far from opportunistic, the Spanish Communist Party leapt to take advantage of the opportunities all this represented. Only a few short months before fervently revolutionary, it now switched its position entirely: in speech after speech Party luminaries such as its only female deputy, Dolores Ibárruri (the famous 'Pasionaria'), denounced the revolution, offered full backing to the government and called for the formation of a new army, a pattern for which was established by the party militia known (for reasons too arcane to go into here) as the Fifth Regiment that was hastily put together by the Party's military specialists, Juan Modesto and Enrique Lister, both of them manual workers who had risen far enough in the former's ranks to secure access to training in Moscow. Outside Spain, meanwhile, other measures were afoot, it being here that we first come upon the International Brigades. Thus, on 18 September 1936 a meeting of the Comintern sanctioned the formation of a force of volunteers willing to fight for the Republic.[13] As for the aim of this policy, on the surface it was presented as an open-handed gesture of proletarian solidarity, but the reality was far more complex in that forming an 'international column' – the term first used – would at one and the same time provide a concrete example of the policy of 'popular front' in action, demonstrate the advantages of militarisation and provide Moscow with a potential means of military intervention against the Spanish revolution (not for nothing does Richardson entitle his work on the subject *Comintern Army*, one thing that is particularly striking being the manner in which the International Brigades, as the new force became known, were not integrated with the rest of the People's Army, but rather given a completely separate command structure that was wholly made up of agents of the Comintern.)[14]

Once the decision had been taken to form the Brigades, it was not long before a stream of volunteers – perhaps 25,000 by the end of the year – had begun to head for Spain, most of them eventually entering the country via an adventurous crossing of the Pyrenees. Having arrived, meanwhile, they joined forces with the considerable number of athletes with left-wing views who had boycotted the Nuremberg Olympics in favour of the Communist-organised People's Olympiad that had been scheduled to open in Barcelona the very same weekend that the conspirators rose in revolt. The popular image, of course, is one of complete spontaneity, of decent human beings concerned about the rise of fascism giving up everything to go and risk their lives in defence of democracy. There were, indeed, some individuals who conformed to the stereotype, just as there were also some individuals who conformed to the equally common stereotype that portrays the International Brigades as a collection of poets and writers in arms. However, in both cases such figures were the exception rather than the rule, the fact being that the vast majority of the volunteers were working class, and up to two-thirds members of the Communist Party.[15] Some of the recruits had military experience in one or other army, but most were too young to have served in the First World War, while such were the economic travails of the inter-war period that many were in poor physical shape.[16] Commitment, however, was not lacking: some of the men may more-or-less secretly have harboured dreams of adventure in the sun while others were refugees from unemployment, but there were very few who were not possessed by a sincere sense of mission or were anything other than genuine volunteers (at least in the sense that they were not forced to go: particularly once the flow of volunteers had started to dry up, some Communist militants seem to have been asked to go by officials of their local branch, but they always had the option of refusing even if it should be noted that to do so was to risk falling into disfavour with the leadership).[17] And, finally, if many were Communists answering a call that was in the end above all about serving the Party's best interests, this did not mean either that they were not decent human beings or that they were any less than genuine in their desire to fight fascism: in Germany and Italy alike, Communists had been among the first victims of Hitler and Mussolini, while, as one Scottish volunteer who was never a member of the Party remembered, 'They were at that time a devoted and idealistic and disciplined group of people: I had a great admiration for … members of the Communist Party'.[18]

By the beginning of 1937, then, it had been possible to form five International Brigades, each of three or four battalions composed of three rifle companies and one machine-gun company. In so far as possible, meanwhile, recruits were grouped together by nationality, language or ethnicity: of the thirty battalions that were eventually formed, one was primarily Austrian, two American, one British, one Bulgarian, one Canadian, one Czech, seven Franco-Belge, two Italian, three German, one Polish, one Latin-American and nine mixed East-European.[19] As for the officers, appointed by the Party authorities, at the lower levels these came from the same ethnic groups as their men, but the higher ranks were disproportionately East-European thanks to the presence in the Red Army of some 500 erstwhile Austro-Hungarian prisoners of war who had turned Communist and offered their services to the Bolsheviks in the wake of the October Revolution. To take just one example, the first commander of the XI Brigade, Lazar Stern, who took the *nom de guerre* 'Kléber', was in reality a Jew from the erstwhile Habsburg territory of Bukovina.[20]

If the International Brigades were both a Communist-Party initiative and, in large part, a Communist-Party organisation, it was also the Communists who, at least for the first year of their existence, dictated where they should be used, for, with the Soviet Union the only power willing to supply arms to the Republic, the latter's representatives and adherents could scarcely fail to secure much influence in the counsels of the Republic. Hence, of course, the fact that the International Brigades were given such a prominent role in the fighting, this being aimed at, on the one hand, exploiting their propaganda value to the full and, on the other, making use of their supposedly much greater combat potential. In reality, as we shall see, this combat potential was much exaggerated: the International Brigades were in fact both of limited military value and not much better than the rest of what eventually became the People's Army of the Republic. However, for the Communists, such truths were irrelevant, all that mattered being to uphold the reputation of their creation, and all the more so as doing so served to denigrate the militia system and, by the same token, justify the need for its militarisation.

Long before the war had ended, then, a powerful legend was already in the making, the chief pillars of which were first established by *The Book of the XV Brigade*, a blatant work of propaganda edited by Frank Ryan, a Left-leaning Irish Republican activist who rose to a position on the XV Brigade's staff before being captured by Franco's troops in March 1938. Thus, two messages come through above all from the collection of more-or-less brief articles written by veterans of the British battalion of which the work consists, namely the crucial nature of political unity in the face of the menace of fascism and the heroism and military contribution of the men who had gone to Spain to fight Franco. For example, to quote one passage, 'The unity of international democracy which finds its most emphatic expression in the International Brigades ... must be maintained and extended. The road of that unity is the only road to peace and progress.'[21] Equally:

> The battle-honours of their kith and kin who comprise the XV Brigade are cause for justifiable pride to the peoples of the United States, Great Britain, Canada and Ireland ... Breaking through the barriers of narrow nationalisms, smothering the animosities of politics and parties, they spontaneously united and realised in one bound the age-old ideal of the unity in arms of international democracy. Fired with that ideal, they rallied to the aid of the Spanish people. Hastily organised, ill-trained, their first task was to hold back the fascist hordes and thus give a breathing space in which the People's Army could be organised.[22]

Much the same message, meanwhile, was conveyed in a work published the following year entitled *Britons in Spain: the History of the British Battalion of the XVth International Brigade*. Penned by William Rust, a leading Communist journalist who served as the first editor of the *Daily Worker* and went on to become the latter's chief correspondent in Spain, this proclaimed the secret of the volunteers' success to be their 'absolute anti-fascist unity'; boasted that the XV Brigade 'gallantly carried its flag through some of the greatest actions of the war and established an unbroken record of heroism and military prowess'; and for good measure threw in a dazzling array of lies and half-truths (we learn, for example, that the International Brigades were organised by the prominent centrist politician Diego Martínez Barrio, at the orders of Prime Minister Francisco Largo Caballero; that the Brunete offensive 'considerably strengthened' the Republican front; and that the Battle of Belchite was no more than 'an attempt to seize a highly fortified area and to strengthen the pressure on Zaragoza').[23]

Pride of place among the litany of praise, however, must come the words of Dolores Ibárruri. As she proclaimed in a speech delivered at the last parade of the International Brigades, an emotive ceremony that took place in Barcelona in October 1938:

> You are history! You are legend! You are the heroic example of democracy's solidarity and universality ... Crossing over frontiers bristling with bayonets and watched for hungry dogs anxious to tear at their flesh, these men reached our country as crusaders for freedom. They gave up everything ... and they came and told us: 'We are here: your cause, Spain's cause, is ours. It is the cause of all advanced and progressive mankind.'[24]

Such rhetoric, meanwhile, was also a feature of the autobiography Ibárruri published in exile in Russia after the war. For example:

> Acting on the fraternal sentiments that people all over the world were expressing, the Comintern called on all democrats and anti-fascists to help the Spanish people. It urged them to form brigades of volunteers to fight for their own countries' liberty on Spanish soil ... North and South Americans, British, Belgians, Norwegians, Finns, Danes, Swedes, Austrians, Swiss, Albanians, Yugoslavs – volunteers from fifty-four countries – fought the war in Spain, shedding their blood unhesitatingly in deeds of inspiring bravery ... the International Brigades, small in number, immense in historic importance, brought us their own native peoples' traditional love of liberty to merge with the heroic traditions of the Spanish people in heroic fraternalism.[25]

Whither such as Dolores Ibárruri led, the men who had actually fought in the International Brigades could not but follow. In the first place, there was the physical and emotional impact of what they had been through: not only had many of the survivors been wounded, in some instances several times over, but they had all endured terrible privations and lost countless friends, the result being a desperate desire to legitimise themselves that was rendered all the stronger by the prejudice and suspicion with which they were viewed after 1939. In the second, there was the impact of defeat in that, in the words of an anonymous Australian writer, 'This sorrow, the lament of a chance lost, [was] magnified by a concurrent magnification of the almost mystical sense of moral righteousness felt at the time.'[26] And, in the second, there was the issue of loyalty. Many of the volunteers, of course, were Communist stalwarts, and democratic centralism alone was therefore sufficient to keep them in line and persuade them to remember the war as the Party wished it to be remembered, a tendency that can be witnessed in two types of publication. First of all, then, we have the various works of history published by survivors of the fighting such as the Americans Arthur Landis and Robert Colodny, the Irishman Michael O'Riordan and the Englishman Bill Alexander. Typical enough of the spirit in which they approached their writing is the extraordinary parting shot offered by the first of these authors. Thus: 'A final summation of the achievements of the men of the Abraham Lincoln Brigade [sic] … would suggest that … they might easily surpass any other group of fighting men in the military history of the United States'.[27] About the best that can be said of this piece of bombast is that it is not alone. On the contrary, here we have Colodny waxing lyrical in respect of the International Brigades' contribution to the defence of Madrid:

> The blood shed by the International Brigades had a double exchange value. It stopped Varela's army at the moment when the militia's lines were stretched to breaking point. In dying scientifically, the volunteers showed the Spaniards how to save their own lives … General Kléber's XI International Brigade … provided … the moral spark, the firepower and the blood [needed] to hold Madrid.[28]

Next in line comes Irish Communist Michael O'Riordan, who in 1979 published a work on the Irish volunteers under the title *Connolly Column: the Story of the Irishmen who Fought for the Spanish Republic, 1936–1939*, the Connolly Column being the name given to the contingent of Irishmen who reached Spain in December 1936 and were immediately sent into action on the Córdoba front before being absorbed into the ranks of the British battalion. Consisting in large part of uncritical borrowings from *The Book of the XV Brigade*, and, in particular, the contributions thereto of Irish Communist Frank Ryan, O'Riordan's work is predictably unstinting in its praise of the International Brigades and Communist strategy alike. Thus:

> The effect of the arrival of the International Brigades in Madrid was that the fascists, to their consternation, were flung back … Appearing in Madrid at such a crucial moment, the International Brigades were a great demonstration of international solidarity at a time when fascism was rampant throughout Europe … In this situation the Spanish people had dared to light a torch of freedom, and, to the world's surprise, many hands from many lands came to help keep that flame alight despite the overwhelming odds against them.[29]

And finally, there is Bill Alexander, a sometime commander of the British battalion who survived the Civil War and went on to become possibly the very first self-proclaimed Communist ever to obtain a commission in the British army. In his work, *British Volunteers for Liberty: Spain, 1936–39*, then, he is as staunch as he is forthright: 'Not every volunteer was a hero; not everyone maintained faith and pride in the cause for which they volunteered. But the overwhelming majority ... showed enormous resources of talent and stability under stress, and emerged [both] stronger and willing and able to support those less tempered.'[30]

Of course, the number of International-Brigaders who tried their hand at history was very few. That said, there were many who wrote memoirs relating their experiences, published hastily scribbled diaries or made themselves available for interview to others working on the Civil-War period: hence the second category of publication referred to above. Needless to say, whether one is speaking of the wider struggle against fascism or the details of this or that battle in Spain, the general tone of such material is wholly positive. With regard to the former, then, we have one volunteer proclaiming, 'To me, it has always been misleading to call the war in Spain a civil war at all when you think of the amount of material help which reached Spain from the Axis powers: Spain was an opening round in the Second World War'; another, 'By fighting against fascism in Spain, we would be fighting against it in our own country and every other'; and, yet one more, 'Although the war was fought exclusively on Spanish soil, I never saw it as a domestic conflict. To this day, I cannot view it except as part of the struggle between the forces of fascism and democracy that was being fought throughout Europe.'[31] As for events at the front, there is much grandiloquence or, perhaps, self-delusion. Very occasionally one comes across a voice full of doubt and cynicism – as one of the last British volunteers to reach Spain, John Bassett, writes, for example, 'The years have passed and I have changed with them, but events and disclosures have often given me cause to wonder if our struggle [was] any less futile than that of Flanders, if we had only given Hitler a little more time to practise, if we had only been struggling to replace one tyranny by another.'[32] But such introspection is very rare. Much more common are passages such as the following effort from the pen of Walter Gregory in respect of the last gasp of the Republican Aragón offensive:

> The British Battalion began to advance up the Ebro valley toward Zaragoza. Our objective was Fuentes de Ebro, and, if we had taken it, we would have been able to see Zaragoza in the distance. With such a prize almost within sight, our morale and excitement were quite terrific: we felt that we were at last making significant inroads into fascist-held territory as we overcame all of the resistance we

encountered. The list of our victories was beginning to lengthen: Purburell Hill, Quinto, Mediana, Belchite ... Inspired by our progress ... our spirits soared and our determination to win hardened still further.[33]

All too typically, these remarks are little short of nonsense. Thus, the triumphant advance on Fuentes de Ebro is a fiction, the British battalion simply being sent to take up positions outside the town that had been in the hands of Republican troops for the past month; the assault on the Cerro del Purburrel, as we shall see, a distinctly inglorious affair; and the capture of both Quinto and Mediana nothing to do with Gregory and his comrades. As for Belchite, while the British did indeed fight there, the capture of one small town defended by fewer than 2,000 men should not have taken twelve days of fighting, what had occurred therefore being, at best, a hollow victory. Just as ridiculous, meanwhile, are the claims of the second commander of the British battalion, Tom Wintringham, that the abortive Lopera offensive of December 1936 drew troops away from the Madrid front on the grounds that 'the appearance of one of our brigades down there on the straight road to Seville, Franco's base, must have made him detach troops from his Madrid army to cover his own "goal"'.[34] However, it was not just the volunteers who were guilty of such exaggeration. Also guilty were the cloud of writers and other intellectuals who attached themselves to the Republican cause and were all too ready to lionise the International-Brigaders, not least, one suspects, because they felt guilty at their failure to fight the good fight themselves. An obvious example is Ernest Hemingway who lived in Madrid for many months, often visiting the front and offering much welcome hospitality to those American volunteers who managed to obtain leave and spend a few days in the Spanish capital.[35] Equally, far away in England, the poet W.H. Auden and the composer Benjamin Britten both produced hymns to the heroism of the International-Brigaders in the form of the poem 'Spain' and the choral work 'Ballad of Heroes'.[36] Finally, last but not least, we might cite the case of the author Peter Elstob, a colourful character, to say the least, who endeavoured unsuccessfully to enlist in the International Brigades and in 1960 worked out his frustrations through the publication of a novel entitled *The Armed Rehearsal* whose centrepiece was a graphic description of the experiences of the British battalion in the Battle of the River Jarama. Once again, the keynote was triumphalism. For example:

By the middle of the morning of the second day it was apparent that a near-miracle had taken place. Despite heavy losses ... somehow the survivors had been brought together, rallied, rearmed and encouraged to go back into the fight. A few towering men had accomplished this, even, in many cases, without being able to speak the language of the men they were rallying. The long ragged defence line … only just held, but it held.[37]

Yet, the fact that the literature we have examined thus far is full of the sort of errors, exaggerations and downright falsehoods quoted in these pages has not deterred the International Brigades' many admirers from constructing a version of their history that does not draw upon much else. In some instances – good examples are constituted by such works as I. MacDougall's *Voices of the Spanish Civil War: Personal Recollections of Scottish Volunteers in Republican Spain, 1936–1939* (Edinburgh, 1986), P. Darman's *Heroic Voices of the Spanish Civil War: Memories from the International Brigades* (London, 2009) and M. Arthur's *The Real Band of Brothers: First-Hand Accounts from the Last British Survivors of the Spanish Civil War* (London, 2009) – the books concerned are simply compilations of the recollections of assorted volunteers presented without anything in the way of annotation, the result being that legitimation is given to stories that in many instances have little in the way of foundation. Little better, meanwhile, is Judith Cook's 1979 *Apprentices of Freedom*, a work written in the context of what at the time appeared to be the rebirth of fascism in Britain that stresses the conviction felt by surviving volunteers that their struggle in Spain had been worthwhile, the finest moments of their lives even, and relies entirely on the words of the veterans themselves. Not surprisingly, then, the tone is not just admiring, but redolent of hero worship. For example:

> There has been nothing like [the British battalion] since and the overwhelming advance of military technology will ensure that there is nothing like it again. It was almost the last time, at least in Europe, that men thought they could go out on the streets and fight tanks with their bare hands and win … Their cry of 'No pasarán' – 'They shall not pass' – comes down to us to this day.[38]

Meanwhile, in others, if there is more of an argument, the aim is essentially to sing the praises of working-class culture, and, more especially, its response to events in Spain in one or other region of the United Kingdom, such coverage there is of the fighting relying heavily (and uncritically) on the accounts, whether written or oral, of the Brigaders themselves, in which category we find H. Francis, *Miners against Fascism: Wales and the Spanish Civil War* (London, 1984), D. Gray, *Homage to Caledonia: Scotland and the Spanish Civil War* (Edinburgh, 2008), p. 223 and G. Davies, *'You are Legend': the Welsh Volunteers in the Spanish Civil War* (Cardiff, 2018).

Such works are clearly too romanticised to be of much use in analysing the history of the International Brigades, but unfortunately much the same is true even of many books that look at the volunteers from a wider perspective. Let us take, for example, Vincent Brome's *The International Brigades*. Dating from the 1960s, this was for a long time standard reading on the subject, but there is much in its pages that is little more than the fruit of invention pure and simple. As a good example, one can cite the book's account of the attack launched by the XI International Brigade and other troops in the Casa de Campo on 12 November 1936. In reality, this was beaten off with some ease, but Brome's version of events is entirely different. Thus:

> The German battalions [*sic*] suffered heavy casualties, but such was the impetus of sheer idealism that they overran one position after another. Time and again it was hand-to-hand fighting in the old 1914–1918 tradition with bayonet charges of a bloodily brave kind … with Moors encountering machine-gunning as skilled and accurate as their own.[39]

What shines forth here is not knowledge but rather a monumental ignorance of the events which Brome is purporting to describe. In fairness to the author concerned, he was writing at a time when little was available on the history of the International Brigades other than the torrent of propaganda emanating from the Communist movement, but even contributions to the historiography that appeared much further on in time have proved unable to free themselves from the shackles of the myth, a myth perpetuated by the dozens of monuments to the 'volunteers for liberty' that have appeared in Britain and elsewhere. In the case of the most recent history of the brigades as a whole, for example, the journalist Giles Tremlett is far more inclined to stress the positive than he is the negative. Thus:

> The Brigaders are normally viewed as experiencing defeat … This ignores the full nature of what they were fighting for; the destruction of world fascism … They continued the struggle when the Second World War broke out five months after the war in Spain ended, playing a remarkably important role in resistance movements across Europe … and the defeat of Hitler and Mussolini became their final victory.[40]

As for attempts to challenge the monolith of memory, they do not face an easy time. For example, there is the telling anecdote given us by Gerben Zaagsma, the author of a monograph on the Jewish presence in the International Brigades:

*The International Brigades
heroicised (1) – London.*
(Wikimedia Commons)

The extent to which dispassionate debate on these issues can be fraught, even among academics, was well illustrated during a Spanish-Civil-War conference held in Bristol in 2006 where one (non-academic) contributor advocated a 'history, not homage' approach to … the International Brigades … The call was critically received, not only by relatives of volunteers, but even by some of the professional historians who were present.[41]

Despite such reluctance, there has yet been a certain amount of progress. Beginning with Richard Baxell's *Unlikely Warriors: the British in the Spanish Civil War and the Struggle against Fascism* (London, 2012), this is by far the most detailed analysis of the British battalion of the International Brigades ever to have seen the light of day. For all his close association with the International-Brigades Memorial Trust (the self-appointed custodian of the Brigades' historic memory), meanwhile, Baxell does not shy away from many issues that contradict the all-too-familiar image of dedication to the struggle: there is, for example, considerable coverage of the serious slump in morale that followed the Battle of Brunete, as well as an admission that at least some of the volunteers were of poor quality in terms of their physique or motivation. All this is very much to the author's credit, and yet one cannot but feel that his efforts fall a little short. Take, for example, the issue of Communist control of the International Brigades and their status as a 'Comintern army' whose chief *raison d'être* was to draw the teeth of the revolution that broke out in the Republican zone in the immediate aftermath of the rising of July 1936. Despite acknowledging the fact that some volunteers consented to act as agents for the Servicio de Información Militar (the de facto branch of the NKVD that was set up in Spain to crush anyone with the temerity to challenge the Party line), not to mention his acceptance that the majority of the volunteers stemmed from the

The International Brigades heroicised (2) – the battlefield of the River Jarama. (author's collection)

ranks of the Communist movement, Baxell claims that recruitment was motivated by nothing more than the twin desires to defend democracy and fight fascism. Well perhaps, but the evidence that there was widespread approval of the suppression of, first, the 'Trotskyite' POUM and, second, the Anarchist-controlled Council of Aragón cannot but suggest that, whatever their thoughts had been at the hour of enlistment, the men of the British battalion would have been unthinking in their obedience to orders designed to use them against so-called wreckers and fascist spies. As Baxell writes:

> Trapped in their trenches on the Jarama front, the men in the British battalion were informed by their political commissars of events in Barcelona ... According to battalion commander Fred Copeman, 'The Brigaders were outraged. "Why, men asked, was it possible that these people could obtain arms ... so far in the rear when the front line was starved of ammunition?"' It is not surprising that many in the British Battalion reacted with such hostility, overwhelmingly reliant as they were on Communist propaganda; 'How were we to know any different?' asked one ... volunteer.[42]

Baxell's book is, of course, an example of the now not-so-new 'new military history' and is therefore inclined to subordinate discussion of battles and campaigns to other issues, but, if so, this not the case with the next work which we must consider in this review essay, this being B. Hughes, *They Shall Not Pass! The British Battalion at Jarama, the Spanish Civil War* (Oxford, 2011), a detailed discussion of the British battalion's baptism of fire at the Battle of the River Jarama in February 1937 in a four-day action that saw about half of its strength killed, wounded or taken prisoner. An episode that is covered exceptionally well in the memoir literature – for a particularly good account, see Jason Gurney's *Crusade in Spain*[43] – this saw the 500 men who made up the unit flung into the front line in a desperate attempt to plug the gaps left by the launch of the Battle of Jarama, an attempt on the part of the Nationalists to envelop Madrid from the south in the wake of their failure to take the city head-on the previous autumn. Equipped with Russian Moisin-Nagant rifles that they had scarcely ever fired and three types of machine gun, of which only one, the unwieldy Russian Maxim M1910, proved serviceable and even then not until the original ammunition it had been issued with had been replaced with bullets of the correct calibre, the volunteers advanced into an area of scrub-covered hills overlooking the valley of the River Jarama, only to be raked with both artillery and machine-gun fire and driven back to a line of knolls where they were even more exposed than before: so bad was the situation, indeed, that one of them acquired the nickname 'Suicide

Hill'. By sunset 125 men were dead and many others wounded, while the next two days saw not just many further casualties but also the capture of part of the machine-gun company in a surprise attack. As one Scottish volunteer less inclined to romanticism than many of his comrades recalled, 'It wasn't a battle at all: it was a bloody slaughter as far as we were concerned … The International Brigades got a real beating.'[44]

According to International-Brigade legend, the last day of the action concluded with a gallant counter-attack that drove the Nationalists back to the verge of the Jarama valley. However, though Hughes faithfully retells the story, this event is almost certainly overblown in the manner in which it has usually been presented: the trenches that mark the line held by the battalion at the end of the battle can still be traced today, and they are nowhere near the knolls which the volunteers had tried to hold on 12 February.[45] Nor is this the only occasion where he is less than critical in his approach to the narrative. Thus, a major feature of the traditional account is that the machine-gun company was captured on account of the cowardice of a company commander called Overton, and this is the version of events followed in *They Shall Not Pass!* However, it is now widely believed that Overton was scapegoated in an attempt to shield his superiors, and it would have behoved Hughes at the very least to have been a little cautious in his presentation of the usual story. Worst of all, however, he completely misunderstands the context of the action and therefore falls into the trap of acquiescing in the idea that the British battalion turned back the Nationalist offensive and thereby saved Madrid. Such is the proud claim advanced by many letters, memoirs and reminiscences, yet, as intimated above, the axis of the Nationalist advance did not run directly through the sector held by the British volunteers, but rather much further to the north. With the British positioned, as they were, at the shoulder of the salient and Franco's troops were driving ever deeper into Republican territory, they had to be subjected to suppressive fire and driven off any ground from which they could harass the Nationalist forces pushing forward across the empty steppes to the north, but it is quite clear that they were never attacked full-on, and, by extension, that, if they were still holding the line on the evening of 14 February, it was because such an attack had never come. To quote Hugh Thomas, 'The legionaries and Moroccans, despite initiative and good leadership, were … driven into a defensive posture once they had captured the heights beyond the Jarama'.[46]

Better on the military detail than most other works though it is, *They Shall Not Pass!* is yet a considerable disappointment. For a more realistic appreciation of the Brigades, it is therefore necessary to turn to more scholarly treatments of the subject. As might be expected, as well as being free of the millstone of personal participation in the conflict, professional historians are less inclined to be swayed by propaganda, and the result is a much more considered approach, and one that is in general critical of the record of the International Brigades, if not downright hostile. The earliest of the works concerned, namely R.D. Richardson's *Comintern Army*, did not challenge their military record: on the contrary, indeed, Richardson's view was that the volunteers had played a key role in the defence of Madrid, especially, and given much good service elsewhere as well.[47] But he did suggest that said record had been exaggerated at the expense of the Spanish forces who had fought beside them, and, more particularly, other aspects of Russian aid to Spain, namely the modern tanks and aircraft that were supplied to the Republic from November 1936 onwards, and at the same time argued, not just that the International Brigades were a Communist creation, but also that they were set up with the specific intention of at the very least creating the possibility of turning Spain into a 'people's democracy'. At the same time, if the Brigades were more efficient than the rest of the Republican forces, it was in part because Communist control ensured that discipline was much tougher than it was in the rest of the Republican army, in part because Communist predominance among the volunteers themselves ensured that they were more motivated than many other troops, and in part because, as creatures of the Communist movement, they got the best of the arms and equipment sent from Russia. To quote Richardson's peroration then, everything revolved around the fact that 'the International Brigades remained what they had been from the beginning, an integral part of the Comintern's interlocking directorate in Spain'.[48]

Richardson's findings have not gone unchallenged by the historical community. In his *Spanish Civil War: Reaction, Revolution and Revenge*, for example, even if his reasons for doing so – the belief that the failure of the direct assault on the Spanish capital centred on 'a heroic effort that involved the whole population' – are misplaced Paul Preston states baldly that 'the role of the International Brigades in the defence of Madrid should not be exaggerated', and yet he is fierce in his condemnation of 'anti-Communists in the United States [who] have presented the International Brigaders as the dupes of Moscow'.[49] Equally, in response to Richardson's claims that discipline within the Brigades was maintained by a reign of terror, for example, Peter Carroll, the most recent chronicler of the Abraham Lincoln battalion, has insisted that stories of mass executions of deserters and political dissidents are simply untrue. In his words, then:

> Even if all the … charges of assassination proved true, the total number of Americans killed outside combat would total less than ten … The rarity of these killings undermines the notion … that the International Brigades enforced discipline by terror. No-one, it should be emphasised, was punished for political dissent, and numerous … deserters were permitted to return to the ranks without penalty or stigma.[50]

Notably, however, Carroll does not back up Richardson's inclination to extoll the military record of the volunteers: on the contrary, his account of such actions as the attack mounted by the Abraham Lincoln battalion on 27 February 1937 during the Battle of River Jarama is one of a day of dismal failure in which the courage of the Americans availed them none at all given their lack of training and firepower, while he also questions the Communist mantra that the attack was actually a great success on account of the manner in which it supposedly persuaded the Nationalists that the Jarama front was too strongly held to merit further attacks.[51]

In still other works, meanwhile, the pendulum has swung even further against the International Brigades. In the wake of the decision of the post-Franco Spanish régime's decision to grant Spanish citizenship to the survivors of the International Brigades, it is scarcely surprising to find the leading apologist for the Nationalist cause, Ricardo de la Cierva, publishing a book that rubbished every aspect of the International Brigades' military and political reputation, and that in defiance of the long-term right-wing convention that their contribution should rather be exaggerated so as to delegitimise the Republican cause and magnify the extent of Franco's victory.[52] However, particularly as a specialised military historiography has begun to appear, so similar conclusions have been reached by observers approaching the subject from a stance that is much more objective. Thus, in his recent *The Spanish Civil War: a Military History*, the current author has ventured the following opinion:

> Readers of this work will have to come to their own conclusions, but it is difficult to escape the sensation that, militarily, the International Brigades contributed very little – whether at Madrid, Boadilla, the Jarama, Brunete, Belchite, Teruel or the Ebro, they performed no better than the Spanish units around them – and that, politically, the situation was not much better: there is little firm evidence that, even in Madrid in November 1936, the presence of the International Brigades inspired a single Republican soldier to fight harder.[53]

Still more damning, meanwhile, are the views of Edward Hooton:

> The *brigadistas* were portrayed as the republic's shock troops but … inadequate training and poor leadership meant that their operations became massacres of the innocents … For all their heroism, [they] represented one of the most cynical publicity stunts since the Children's Crusade, providing cannon-fodder to publicise the Republican cause. As one commentator observed, 'They cannot be said to have given an example of discipline or military ability to the

Spanish troops, nor was their achievement greater than that of the Republican army or, at least, its best fighting units.'[54]

To conclude, then, it is evident that there is room here for yet another book on the Spanish Civil War. Between the triumphalism of the legend and the cynicism of the new history there is a yawning gulf, and with it much material that remains open to discussion, the object of the current work being to explore this dichotomy via the combat record of the British battalion. That said, what is at issue is not courage, but rather contribution: while there is no doubt that many of the volunteers showed great bravery and commitment, the extent to which their presence made any difference to the fortunes of the Spanish Republic is something that remains open to exploration at a level that has as yet been but little attempted.

Chapter 2

Baptism of Fire

Although the British battalion of the International Brigades was not formed until February 1937, from the very beginning there were British participants in the fighting. By sheer happen-stance, the military rising had coincided with the People's Olympiad, an Olympic Games organised in Barcelona by the Comintern as an alternative to the official event which was, of course, in 1936 being held in Berlin. These 'people's games' having brought many left-wing activists to the Catalan capital, the latter to their astonishment suddenly found themselves in the middle of a war. Wildly excited at being thus presented with the chance to fight 'fascism', a number of them rushed to enlist in the militias that were being raised to fight on the Aragón front, and within a few days the war had therefore claimed its first British victim in the person of a London-based artist named Felicia Brown. At the same time, a trickle of volunteers began to arrive from England, all of them middle-class young men who possessed sufficient wherewithal to get to Spain under their own steam, the most prominent among them being John Cornford, a 20-year-old Cambridge student who had turned Communist and was beginning to make his name for himself as a poet. However, while a few individuals chose to remain with the militias, within a short time the authority of the Comintern had made itself felt, the result being that the bulk of the Barcelona volunteers soon found themselves heading for Albacete, the south-eastern provincial capital that had been chosen as the base for, as it was then called, the 'International Column'. At their destination, meanwhile, they were joined by fresh volunteers who had come out from Britain, among them seven men whom Cornford had managed to persuade to join up in the course of a hasty trip back home.[1]

Having reached Albacete, the British were initially fed into a largely French battalion that had been given the name Commune de Paris. United with two other battalions – the German Edgar André and the Polish 'Dombrowski' – it was this force that marched along the Gran Vía on the morning of 8 November 1936. Whether it could have made much of a show is at best doubtful, the parade-ground drill which was all that the instructors at Albacete had been able to offer had all been performed according to the French model, the result being that the

British Communists who found themselves in Barcelona in July 1936 on account of the People's Olympiad and immediately formed an infantry unit called the Tom Mann Centuria. First and second left are London garment workers Sid Avner and Nat Cohen, and, fourth from left, Tom Wintringham. Avner was one of ten British volunteers killed fighting with XII International Brigade at Boadilla on 20 December 1936. (Southworth Collection)

many men who had experience of other armies ended up thoroughly confused.[2] What, however, was the military situation at this point? In brief, the military rising had left the Nationalist forces in control of a broad stretch of territory north of Madrid that encompassed everything from the Portuguese frontier in the west to the Aragónese cities of Zaragoza, Huesca and Teruel in the east with the exception of a narrow strip of territory along the northern coast embracing the provinces of Asturias, Santander, Vizcaya and Guipúzcoa. In the south, however, the situation was very different in that the rebels had secured no more than a few pockets of territory surrounding the cities of Seville, Granada and Cádiz, while, in general, they were very much on the defensive. That said, they did hold a major trump card in that they controlled the whole of the Spanish colony of Morocco and with it the best troops in the armed forces in the form of the Foreign Legion and the numerous regiments of Moorish auxiliaries. Battle-hardened by long years of fighting against the rebel forces of Abd el-Krim and from the start of the uprising commanded by the intensely ambitious Francisco Franco, the Legion and the Moors had no sooner reached mainland Spain courtesy of Junkers and Savoia bomber transports supplied by Hitler and Mussolini than they had sliced through the police detachments and ill-armed militias that were all that Andalucía's loyalists could deploy in defence of the Republic, linked up Seville, Granada and Cádiz and driven north to take the key city of Badajoz, thereby making contact with the Nationalist forces in northern Spain.[3]

A view of Toledo that is but little changed from the one the besieging Republican forces would have enjoyed in 1936; the alcázar *dominates the skyline top right.* (author's collection)

Nationalist soldiers fighting in the suburbs of Madrid, November 1936. (Wikimedia Commons)

There followed the famous 'march on Madrid'. Driving eastwards along the valley of the River Tagus, the mobile columns into which Franco's men were organised swept all before them and by the end of September they had relieved the *alcázar*, a mediaeval fortress situated in the heart of the city of Toledo that had been seized by the Nationalists at the start of the war and then subjected to a long siege by large numbers of militiamen sent down from Madrid. Turning north, they had then headed for the capital, though a combination of exhaustion and stiffening resistance ensured that progress was much slower than before. Even so, the first days of November saw the rebel forces reach the southern suburbs of the city and launch the attack that produced the air of crisis that we encountered at the beginning of the previous chapter.[4] In a desperate attempt to save the capital from the triumphant enemy, the Republican high command rushed in every man it had to hand, including, of course, the XI International Brigade. At this point, however, the reality parts company from the legend. If the reality of the parade along the Gran Vía was at best prosaic, this was even more true of the brigade's role in the fighting. As we have seen, the only unit to see any fighting immediately on its arrival was the German Edgar André battalion, the rest of the brigade being sent not to the front line, but rather to a reserve position in the University City where it suffered little mishap other than some light shelling which caused no casualties. From there the volunteers were sent across the river to defensive positions that had been dug in the northern fringes of the Casa de Campo, and it was only here that the British volunteers received their baptism of fire. Like the fight of the Edgar André battalion in the Parque del Oeste, however, this was not the most auspicious of affairs. In brief, in the small hours of 11 November a fighting patrol consisting of the 115-strong company of Lieutenant Blanche was sent out into the scrubland ahead of the XI Brigade, together with a four-man machine-gun team drawn from the English-speaking section. Almost immediately discovered by the enemy as a result of their own carelessness, they were subjected to withering fire, and were soon fleeing in panic, leaving behind them over half their number, including New-Zealanders Griffith Maclaurin and Steven Yates who were both shot dead and a man originally from Somerset but resident in London named Robert Symes, who was carried to safety but later died of his wounds.[5]

On 13 November there followed a more serious affair in the form of a full-scale attack designed to slice through the communications of the Moors and Foreign Legionaries holding the foothold on the western bank of the Manzanares which

The trenches occupied by the XI International Brigade in the northern fringes of the Casa de Campo. (author's collection)

The area of the Casa de Campo which witnessed the Republican counter-offensive of 13 November; the centre of Madrid can be seen on the skyline to the left, while Monte Garábitas is the high ground to the right. (author's collection)

the Nationalist forces had obtained on the very day that the XI Brigade had arrived in the city after a rapid advance that had seen them sweep right across the Casa de Campo. Among the men who experienced the fighting that followed was John Sommerfield. Thus:

> As soon as we … came out into the open we were under fire, but there was plenty of cover … Some of the light armoured cars went up ahead of us, firing … The enemy was invisible, presumably far away, and the attack being on so long a front, it was impossible for us to get any idea of what was happening … There was more firing now and it was more accurate. Then the first shells began to arrive: it was only small stuff and they hadn't got our range until … aeroplanes came over and had a look … Ahead was a patch of bare flat ground and then trenches … There was no-one in the trenches, but it wasn't easy getting there – a hundred yards' dash with no cover … We tumbled in and lay gasping in the loose earth at the bottom … When there was a little lull, a few

of us went over the top ... We went forward in short rushes. Big shells were landing now, and shrapnel ... Eventually we landed breathlessly up against a dung-heap at the back of [a] farmhouse.[6]

The farmhouse mentioned by Sommerfield almost certainly being an isolated building whose ruins can still be seen on the eastern flank of Monte Garábitas, the Commune de Paris appears to have done quite well in this attack, but by the end of the day, along with all the rest of the Republican forces involved, they were back in their starting positions. Although the English-speaking volunteers had lost no further casualties, the brigade as a whole had been hard hit, and so that same night it was pulled back to the village of Aravaca to rest and refit. On 15 November, however, a fresh crisis erupted in that the Nationalist forces launched a heavy attack that had soon taken them across the Manzanares and into the first buildings of the university campus, XI International Brigade therefore hastily being sent in to help plug the gap that same night. In the fighting that followed, however, the Commune de Paris played only a limited role. Thus, while the Edgar André and Dombrowski battalions were sent to contest the Faculty of Medicine and the French cultural institute known as the Casa de Velásquez, it was kept in reserve at the Faculty of Philosophy and Letters, a massive building of ultra-modern design that overlooked the pocket of territory that the Nationalists had occupied in the wake of their passage of the Manzanares, but had not attempted to occupy. Subjected, as they were, to little more than sniping and occasional shellfire, the battalion therefore had a comparatively easy time of it.[7] To quote John Cornford:

[We found ourselves] in a really comfortable position in the Philosophy-and-Letters building. This was our best front-line period: comfortable; above all, warm; and supplies regular. [Philosophy and Letters was] a great gutted building, with broken glass all over, and the fighting consisted of firing from behind barricades of ... books at the fascists ... in the Casa de Velásquez opposite ... The afternoon of the second day, I think I killed a fascist. Fifteen or sixteen of them were running from a bombardment. I and two Frenchmen were firing from our barricades with sights at 900: we got one, and both said it was I that hit him.[8]

Also involved in the fighting, was Sommerfield:

We came to a high-up room with big windows ... A few hundred yards away was the Casa [de] Velasquez whose riddled baroque turrets were still pointed at the raining sky ... We were shelled, but

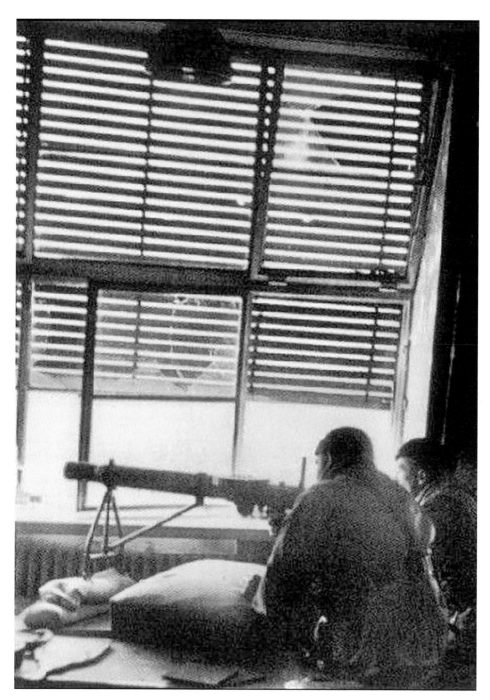

A light machine-gun team of the XI International Brigade ensconced in the Faculty of Philosophy and Letters of the University of Madrid. (Wikimedia Commons)

The Faculty of Philosophy and Letters today; Cornford and his comrades manned the windows facing the camera. (Antonio Requena)

not much and not very accurately. Some [projectiles] hit the building, but it was so huge and so strongly built that little damage was done ... I found a big arm-chair, put it behind my loop-hole, and sat for hours with my feet against the wall, sniping ... They tried to attack with tanks, but they were driven back: the little figures ran and tumbled and lay still.[9]

Suffer heavy casualties in the fighting though the XI International Brigade as a whole did, this was scarcely the stuff of legend, the same observer even going so far as to question whether he and his fellows actually achieved anything at all. Thus:

I have never been quite certain why we were kept in the Philosophy Building all that week. Opposite was the mouth of a little ravine and the story was that it was through there that the fascists would have to come to attack: a few did come out one night, but we drove them back after an hour's shooting. In my opinion the only thing we did that week to earn our keep was one afternoon when we put a fascist machine-gun out of action.[10]

Much the same, it has to be said, was true of the next group of British volunteers. Consisting of twelve men who had reached Albacete too late to join Cornford and his comrades in the Commune de Paris, this was absorbed into a company of a German-speaking battalion named after the German Communist Ernst Thaelmann that was currently being put together as part of a new XII International Brigade.[11] As for the venue for its *mise en scène*, this proved to be the Cerro de los Angeles, a prominent conical hill just a few miles to the south-east of Madrid that had been abandoned without a fight as the Nationalists closed in on the city. We here return to the counter-attack of 13 November, the idea of this having been not just an advance in the Casa de Campo, but rather a double-envelopment that would see substantial Republican assault columns hit both flanks of the Nationalist array and threaten the front-line troops with encirclement. The initial targets, then, included not only Garabitas, but also the Cerro de los Angeles, the isolated hill that served as the anchor that secured the right flank of the troops attacking the capital. Topped by a monastery and the shattered remains of a large statue of Christ which had been dynamited by the militia in the aftermath of the uprising (a famous photograph shows it being 'executed' prior to the explosion by a *miliciano* firing squad), the hill was well defended, and in consequence the Republicans made little progress. A company of T26 tanks sent to encircle the hill came under heavy artillery fire and beat a hasty retreat, leaving two of their number in flames, while the infantry, all of whom were drawn from XII International Brigade (there were several other brigades involved in the eastern prong of the Republican offensive, but all of them were fighting in sectors further to the south), became ever more scattered and disorientated. Nor was this surprising. Only 1,500-strong, the brigade had been organised with even more haste than its predecessor, and went to the front in a state of complete disorder. Indeed, according to the few survivors of the events of the next two months, their training was not just sketchy, but positively non-existent. In the words of Middlesbrough clerk David Marshall, who was to be shot in the foot in the action that followed, 'We hadn't even fired the rifles before we went into action.'[12] A 19-year-old Communist militant from Glasgow named Phil Gillan describes what happened. As he later recalled:

We went for a concentrated six-weeks' training at a wee place called Villafranca. We got up the next morning and went out into the fields … but we got no training whatever … Round about midday two motorcyclists came flashing out to the fields where we were. They

had a quick word with our commander, and we were withdrawn …
and put into lorries. We went to a place called Chinchón [and] arrived
there about four o'clock in the afternoon … Woken up about two in
the morning, we travelled … to a place called the Hill of the Angels
where we engaged in our first action.[13]

One participant in the fiasco that was the inevitable result was Esmond Romilly
(an upper-class rebel who was a nephew, no less, of Winston Churchill):

On both sides west and south-west of the fort [*sic*] came the flashes
and explosions of rifle and machine-gun fire. My dominant feeling
was of excitement: then the smack of a bullet in the earth near
modified this feeling. Jeans … told us … that the present orders
were for the machine-gun to be prepared for action in a position for
continual firing; the rest of us were to take up positions a few hundred
yards ahead … I dug with my bayonet to make a position near the
machine-gun. After a lot of clinking and arguing and cursing, I heard
the rat-tat-tat of our light-machine-gun … The effect of this fire
was startling and disagreeable. We were suddenly in a hurricane of
bullets … I remembered I was supposed to be doing some protection.
Unfortunately I could discern no figures at whom to direct my fire:
I discharged five rounds, putting the sights at 1000 metres. It was the
first time I had discharged a rifle in my life.[14]

Fighting alongside Romilly was Gillan. Utterly committed to the cause though he
was, he was later candid enough to admit that Communist dogma was not proof
against human fear: 'I was just plain scared, and I'm not afraid to admit it …
The air was full of machine-gun bullets. Did I duck? You bet I did!'[15] Diving to
the ground, Gillan found that it was three minutes or so before he could summon
the strength to conquer his nerves and get back on his feet. At least he did so,
however: not all the men concerned were quite so enthusiastic. Another volunteer
was London journalist Keith Watson. Increasingly possessed by second thoughts
about coming to Spain (he was to flee to Barcelona the very next day), he had
contrived to slip away in the first moments of the advance and was now skulking
in the rear, only to discover that cowardice was no guarantee of safety:

Zwiss, zwiss: leaves flew from the bush I sheltered behind … I felt a
deadly cold fear inside my stomach … The whining noises became
more frequent. I was convinced each bullet had a personal venom …
The spoil spurted up in little clouds all round me. Zwiss, zwiss, zwiss:

the machine-gun bullets screamed just above my head. Sobbing with relief, I flung myself under a tree. Sweat soaked me … The cover was good … There I lay firing from behind my tree until darkness fell.[16]

Mere long-distance sniping was not going to shift the Nationalists, however, while matters now went from bad to worse. Exhausted and hungry, an entire company of the Thaelmann battalion broke and ran. By nightfall, indeed, the entire brigade was in a state of complete disarray. A White exile who was hoping to work his way back to Russia via service in the International Brigades, Alexei Eisner was an aide-de-camp of the brigade's commander, Mata Zalka (known in Spain as Lukacz):

When night fell, the offensive was abandoned. As the combat had unfolded so the defects of our improvised organization had begun to reveal themselves, but the coming of darkness multiplied them many times over. The commander of the brigade and his general staff had no idea where the first-aid posts, the field kitchens and the other second-line units had got to, while the difficulties were redoubled by the fact that we had no regular contact with the individual battalions, just as these in turn had no contact with their constituent companies.[17]

Mercifully enough, British casualties were light: Watson and two other men were missing (it was later discovered that they had deserted) while Marshall had been wounded, but that was all.[18] Restored to order over the next few days, meanwhile, the men of XII International Brigade were next taken by truck to the northern outskirts of Madrid and flung into battle once again, this time on the fringes of the University City. Entering the line on 18 November, they remained there for the next ten days, engaging in a number of bitter skirmishes around two buildings which the memoirs and other recollections of the volunteers invariably refer to as the 'Red House' and the 'White House', both of them suburban villas belonging to representatives of the propertied classes. Here the battle raged back and forth for days with both sides seeking to improve their positions while at the same time holding back the attacks of the enemy. Very much in the thick of things was Phil Gillan:

There was quite a substantial number of corpses all over the place … One of the sort of awe-inspiring scenes that we saw were three Moors who had been climbing over these railings … and had been shot and killed. They had fallen over, but … their feet had caught on top of the spikes and they were hanging down like big bats … The bulk of the troops we were fighting was the African army, the Moors. If we advanced, they would disappear rapidly, and, if they were advancing, we would disappear back the other way as quickly as we could … It was something like *All Quiet on the Western Front* ... where they both kept going backwards and forwards.[19]

For an account of one such attack, we can turn to Esmond Romilly:

> Four tanks moved up the road. Rebel artillery was active all the time and occasionally the shells sent up great clouds of smoke near the road, but the tanks chugged slowly on. We watched them out of sight round the bend. Then the poum-poum-poum of their guns showed the attack was in full swing. The suspense was maddening. I remembered reading books about the war and for the first time the expression 'going over the top' had some meaning. Jeans shouted, 'Fix bayonets! Everyone ready!' The Italians were lying ready on the ridge. They would cover us with rifle fire. Behind the road four machine-guns started up. 'Forward! Rush ten yards, drop, wait for the next advance, everyone to fire at the windows', shouted Jeans. We reached the wall of the White House. It was a mad scramble … A few of the Germans dropped on the way: it was like seeing people killed in an American film.[20]

Two days later Romilly found himself facing a heavy Nationalist counter-attack. As he recorded in his memoir *Boadilla*:

> I was lying flat on my stomach. We shoved in clip after clip of cartridges until the breaches and barrels of our guns were red-hot. I never took aim … never looked up to see what I was firing at … never saw the enemy, never knew for certain where they were … My head was in a whirl: I was almost drunk from the smell of powder … It was a mad scramble: pressing my elbows into the earth, bruising them on the stones to get my rifle to my shoulder, pressing the trigger, rasping back the bolt, then shoving it home.[21]

On 28 November the XII Brigade was pulled out of the line. Amazingly enough, all the British volunteers had come through the fighting unscathed, but losses in the brigade as a whole had been very heavy. There was, however, little chance of a rest: within a few days, the Thaelmann battalion, at least, was back in its old

Republican militia holding a barricade on the outskirts of Madrid, November 1936. (Wikimedia Commons)

positions. This time, however, there were no heroic charges, no enemy attacks to repel. On the contrary, what followed for Romilly and his fellow volunteers was day after day of the cold, fear and boredom of trench warfare. Eventually, the increasingly weary battalion was pulled out and given a period of rest in a luxurious country club in the countryside behind the lines. It was, however, the lull before the storm. Thus, on 29 November, Franco's forces had launched a fresh offensive, this time in the area immediately to the west of the Casa de Campo, the aim being to broaden the narrow finger of territory leading to the Nationalist positions in the University City. For the next two weeks attack was followed by counter-attack, but by the middle of December the Nationalists had taken the key villages of Pozuelo, Húmera, Aravaca and Boadilla del Monte. Once again, the two International Brigades found themselves in the thick of the fighting. Put into line in the latter stages of the battle, on 14 December they were sent to counter-attack Nationalist forces that were threatening Boadilla. Sent to discover the whereabouts of the battalion on the Thaelmann's flank, Romilly suddenly found himself exposed to the full power of the enemy's artillery. Thus:

> The sound of the … guns wasn't so bad: you heard it in threes – wang, wang, wang! – [but then came] the shrieks and [shell-]bursts, one after the other. The third one … seemed meant for us. I thought

it must be on top of us when we heard [the explosion]; then, thirty seconds later, I realised something had hit my helmet. We stretched out our hands, picked up some of the wicked little bits of metal and dropped them quickly: they were red-hot.[22]

With the winter day far advanced, the fighting soon ground to a halt. Thanks to thick fog that blanketed the battlefield overnight, the next day was one of complete inaction, but, on 16 December, a day of bright winter sun that brought out the enemy aviation in force, the volunteers advanced once more. Hardly had it done so, however, than the XI Brigade ran into serious trouble. As recent Cambridge graduate and future agent of the Office of Strategic Services and Harvard professor Bernard Knox later wrote:

> The storm burst as John [Cornford] was taking us up to relieve a Spanish machine-gun post. We found ourselves under fire from the heights where we meant to relieve [the Spaniards], and, a few minutes later, as we squeezed and strained ourselves into the earth, the remains of our front line came crawling back … shouting excitedly, 'Los fascistas! Los fascistas!' As if we didn't know … For the rest of the morning we held the road to the village, firing at close range into lines of attackers that were crossing our line of fire to outflank us. The most disturbing feature of the situation was the withdrawal of the infantry companies on our right and left flanks … Things looked pretty desperate. So far as I could see, our two … machine-guns (one of them badly jammed) was the only thing between Boadilla and the Fascists … Aeroplanes came over and added to the confusion … We sighted four fascist tanks coming up the road towards us, and just at that moment big shells began to fall on the village.[23]

Caught in what was fast becoming a hopeless position, the British machine-gun section hastily fell back through the village and eventually reached safety, though not before Knox was felled by a bullet to the throat, and two other men – Irish volunteers William Barry and Thomas Patton – shot dead. Not very far away, meanwhile, the volunteers serving in the Thaelmann battalion were in even worse trouble. By now, thanks to wounds, desertions and transfers, there were just twelve of the original eighteen-man English-speaking squad left. Stationed in the open woodland characteristic of much of the Spanish countryside, they stood little chance of resisting the oncoming Nationalists. 'We were firing all the time', wrote Esmond Romilly. 'I copied the others and fired in the same direction

Republican militia pictured during the Battle of Boadilla. (Wikimedia Commons)

till the barrel was red-hot. And always … there was the deadly cross-fire … There were bombing planes over us and shrapnel bursting behind.'[24] Casualties, meanwhile, were heavy: the section commander, Arnold Jeans, a Latvian exile who, extraordinarily enough, had been a tutor to the family of the then queen, was killed instantly when he was shot in the head; 22-year-old Southampton clerk Raymond Cox, research scientist Lorimer Birch and Joe Gough fell at their Lewis guns trying to cover the retreat; London Jew Sid Avner, ex-soldier and Folkestone cafe proprietor Harry Adley and Edinburgh student Martin Messer were all lost to machine-gun fire or explosions as they tried to escape; and Phil Gillan was wounded in the neck by a bullet that miraculously passed through from one side to the other without inflicting any major damage. Apart from Gillan, the only survivors were the Irishman Bill Scott, the Australian volunteer Richard Whatley, Esmond Romilly and Arthur Ovenden, a First-World-War veteran who was co-proprietor of the same cafe run by Adley.[25]

For all the tragedy, the war went on. Shocked and in poor physical shape, Romilly and Ovenden were sent back to England, but the six British Commune-de-Paris volunteers who were still on their feet – Cornford, Jock Cunningham

*Jock Cunningham,
George Nathan and
Ralph Campeau,
December 1936.*
(Southworth
Collection)

(an ex-regular who had been imprisoned for leading a mutiny and was to play a leading part in subsequent events), Joe Hinks, Jock Clarke, Edward Burke and University-of-London student Sam Lesser – were now transferred to the XIV International Brigade, a new unit that was still in the process of formation and included a full British company, most of them Communists who had made their way to Spain via the 'underground railway' that had now been set up by the Comintern (by contrast, Cornford, Romilly and the other men who had fought at Madrid and Boadilla were generally either middle-class students, intellectuals and blue-collar workers who had been able to fund their own travel to Spain or, more rarely, representatives of the working classes who had been funded to attend the ill-fated 'Popular Olympiad' in Barcelona). Little better trained and equipped than its two predecessors, the new brigade soon found itself heading for the distant Córdoba front, an area which had been chosen as the site of one of three widely separated attacks designed to take some of the heat off the Madrid front. The British company, 145-men strong, was part of the largely French Pierre Brachet battalion, while it was headed by George Nathan, a charismatic Jewish homosexual whose courage in the First World War had earned him the rank of sergeant major in the Guards. Among the British was a band of fifty Irishmen, the so-called Connolly Column, that had been put together by the Irish Communist Party under the command of leading activist Frank Ryan, one of whose men was Dubliner Joe Monks:

> Captain Nathan … was hard-working and full of enthusiasm, We had no guns so our training concentrated on the relationship that exists between the infantryman under fire and the kindly earth to which he must cling for most of the time if he wishes to go on living.

It was [get] up, plunge forward and [get] down faster than one got up. Nothing, according to Nathan, was beneath notice … He had a great eye for country: hills and hummocks, trees and bushes, all had messages for him.[26]

Someone else who was much impressed with Nathan was erstwhile naval rating Fred Copeman, a man whose good opinion counted all the more because of his deprived upbringing, pugnacious nature and background as a mutineer. Thus:

Another outstanding member of the group was George Nathan, an ex-army officer, efficient, capable with loads of courage: above all, the typical British officer; fair, yet one who, when giving orders, left those receiving them under no illusions as to what was required. Nathan dressed as I would expect – his riding boots shining like a new pin, every button polished, hat at the right angle and riding-crop in hand – and even … ran a batman. At first I thought him a snob, yet … he stood out as the most capable officer.[27]

Arriving at the front on Christmas Day, the XIV Brigade was ordered to attack the village of Lopera but its commander, the Pole Karol Swierczewski (known in Spain as 'Walter'), delayed moving until he had sent out patrols to discover the whereabouts of the enemy positions. Nor did it help, meanwhile, that the Nationalists possessed complete air superiority, the troops being repeatedly strafed even as they headed for the front. One such attack was recorded by Manchester volunteer Maurice Levine. Thus:

Suddenly out of that cloudless blue sky a plane was diving down, spitting bullets. Nat Segal, a London East-Ender, was killed instantly. More planes came over, and we left the road to disperse into the olive groves. Someone told us to get rid of our mess-tins, as the bright aluminium, reflecting the sun, might reveal our presence to the enemy planes. Most of us did so only to bitterly regret it later.[28]

As a result, the battle did not begin until late in the afternoon of 27 December by which time the handful of Nationalist troops who had initially been stationed in Lopera had received substantial reinforcements and dug themselves in on two low hills known as the Cerro de San Cristobal and the Cerro del Calvario that overlooked the ground over which the XIV Brigade would necessarily have to advance. That said, despite the fact that they were armed with nothing better than single-shot Steyr rifles dating from the 1880s and Chauchat light machine guns – a 'bargain-basement' First-World-War development which suffered from numerous design faults and could rarely fire more than a handful of rounds without malfunctioning[29] – the British and Irish volunteers were sent on ahead as an advanced guard. From the beginning, however, it was clear that Nathan's efforts to instil the tactics of fire and movement, let alone the principles of military discipline, in the men under his command had not borne much in the way of fruit. In the words of Joe Monks:

> All were excited … as we moved off … Ahead of us there was the crackle of rifle fire and the long whinings of bullets passing by … Nathan, taking counsel with Colonel Delasalle, ordered … the four sections so that the company would go forward … diamond shaped … Reacting to the situation psychologically, many tended not to stay in the extended-cum-blob formation, and got themselves into crowds. Nathan shouted, ordering them to get back into extended order … Sharper invective was hollered by him at those who tended to fall behind and be stragglers … Naturally, they found the fault in the captain and not in themselves: one of them in later years spoke of Nathan as a vainglorious drunk.[30]

Vainglorious or not, Nathan certainly proved he was an effective leader. To quote the same observer once again:

> Low on the next down-slope … Nathan stopped. From [his] crouched running position, he rose to his full height, and, by spreading his arms, called upon the [men] to halt. 'Cheer!' he commanded. 'Give them something to fear!' Standing in ordered sections, they did raise a mighty cheer. 'Charge!' Following him and the stick he swung above his head, they went in a dash over the intervening hollow, and, moving at speed, started climbing the next slope.[31]

Also among the men moving forward was a plasterer from Dublin who had fought in the Irish Civil War named Donal O'Reilly:

> The company … moved to the attack … through an olive grove … with the zing-zung of the bullets playing a tune; occasionally, [there was] a snick as a bullet clipped off a cluster of leaves. Out from the friendly trees, [we advanced] down a short valley … and then [it was] up, up, among the hills … tough work with our tremendous load … The fire was terrific; the language was terrific.[32]

Helping to deliver covering fire as a Number Two in a Chauchat team was another Manchester volunteer, namely Walter Greenhalgh:

> Yelling like a load of dervishes, we dashed up this hill. They just sat up there and waited and fired their machine-guns at us. Every now and then, Paddy lay down and fired the gun three or four times, but then it would jam … I'd take the thing apart and sort it out, and then he'd fire another three or four rounds. It was all very slow, but we did finally reach the top without too many casualties and actually chased the fascists away.[33]

This success, alas, proved short-lived. The rest of the Pierre Brachet battalion (and, indeed, the rest of the XIV Brigade) lost all cohesion as it made its way through the dense olive groves which cloaked the area of its approach march while the volunteers were constantly assailed by fire from the Nationalist troops dug in on the hills ahead as well as hit by repeated air attacks. Progress, then, was minimal, and all the more so as the limited Republican artillery support proved completely ineffectual. With dusk falling rapidly, Nathan and his men therefore found themselves in an invidious position. Among the growing number of casualties was Joe Monks:

> Suddenly, it was night: the planes were gone; the artillery exchange ceased. Looking at the flashes … of the rifles and machine-guns that were in front of us, we were ordered … to concentrate our fire on what appeared to be a spire in Lopera … Nathan assured us that we would have the fascists out … within ten minutes as he moved about from section to section. He was close by when a bullet apparently aimed at the flash of my rifle went through me. Its impact felt like the kick of a mule … The captain had me pulled down off the rim of the ridge; he took my rifle and threw it over to Donal O'Reilly because the breach of Donal's rifle had earlier burst asunder … Blood was pouring … from under my shoulder and from the exit hole in my back.[34]

With his command under such heavy fire, Nathan was eventually left with no option but to withdraw. According to legend, the Guards veteran continued to show great courage, steadying a number of men who had started to fall prone to panic and getting those volunteers still in action to fall back by sections.[35] However, the reality was almost certainly very different: 'It was all total confusion', recalled Walter Greenhalgh. 'We had to retreat and the fascists advanced, and we even lost that bit of hill we'd taken.'[36] Some of the wounded, it seems, were abandoned (though not Joe Monks, the latter being safely got away to the rear). As Sam Lesser recalled long afterwards:

> There were heavy casualties and I was wounded. I didn't know at the time where … [but] when I tried to get up I couldn't … Our people had to retreat and I was lying there unable to move, and there was no possibility of a stretcher bearer coming for me. We were badly equipped … in respect of … medical equipment, which was very, very sparse.[37]

Shot in the back and legs alike, Lesser was eventually rescued by fellow veteran of the Madrid front Jock Cunningham, who dragged him to safety the following morning after a long search of no man's land; typically enough, it later transpired that he had been hit by friendly fire coming from the rear. Still other men who had gone to ground in improvised 'scrapes', among them Maurice Levine, never realised that their comrades were retreating and woke next morning to find themselves all alone amidst the debris of battle.[38] The whole affair, in short, had been a complete fiasco, though the responsibility was for the sake of convenience laid at the door of the commander of the Pierre Brachet battalion, Gaston Delasalle, a handy scapegoat who was court-martialled and shot.[39]

As for the cost, it was very heavy: of the 145 members of the British company, just 67 survived unwounded, while the total number of dead in the XIV International Brigade as a whole appears to have been about 300 (all told, by contrast, Nationalist casualties were no more than 100 dead and 100 wounded).[40] Among the fallen, meanwhile, were John Cornford and Ralph Fox, a fervent Communist writer who had been appointed to the post of Brigade Political

Cambridge graduate John Cornford and his girlfriend Margot Heinemann. (International Brigade Memorial Trust)

Commissar, while another volunteer from Cornford's group, Edward Burke, had been mortally wounded, later dying in hospital in Madrid. In respect of Cornford, in particular, meanwhile, various stories did the rounds as to how he fell, but the version told by the one man who witnessed the event in person should probably be regarded as definitive. Thus:

> We were all lying in a long straight line on the brow of the hill … John Cornford … had a bandage round his head: he looked like Lord Byron. The bandage was very white and he wouldn't wear a hat … We were waiting for this artillery barrage to open up [but] nothing happened: everything was quiet, and we could see the fascists coming out of the village … We waited and waited, and finally John … climbed up to the brow of the hill to look over. The early sun just caught his bandage, and that was it: he got one straight through the head.[41]

As inauspicious as all this was, following the Lopera offensive, XIV Brigade was briefly sent to the Madrid front where a fresh battle had broken out thanks to a renewed Nationalist offensive in the Boadilla sector (so much for hopes that the Lopera operation would cause Franco to switch some of his forces away from the Spanish capital). However, by the time that they had arrived, the guns had fallen silent, so the brigade was sent back to Albacete for a period of rest and re-organisation. Several hundred British volunteers having now reached that city, the decision was taken to form them into a full battalion on the basis of the men who had survived Lopera. Thus was born the unit with whose many misfortunes the rest of this book will chiefly be concerned. All in all, however, the first British battles in Spain (not that they had really been British battles at all) do not make for impressive reading. Some of the volunteers had been brave enough, on occasion, indeed, even suicidally so, but others had quickly decamped in the face of the realities of war, while the litany of failed attacks against opposition that was in reality quite limited in terms of both numbers and firepower does not suggest much in the way of military competence. Nor were things much better when they were fighting on the defensive: if the University of Madrid's Faculty of Philosophy and Letters was held without difficulty, the reality was that it scarcely came under attack, while Boadilla had seen them comprehensively outmanoeuvred and outfought. As for the wider claim that the arrival of the XI and XII International Brigades somehow saved Madrid, this is demonstrably false, the fact being that the two formations could add little in the way of either experience or firepower to the defence of the city. And, for all this, the price had been very high: by the end of December 1936 no fewer than ten of the original twenty-six British volunteers were dead and another two wounded.

The Battlefields Today

1. The Casa de Campo
Thanks to over eighty years of urbanisation, the Madrid of today bears little resemblance to that of 1936. That said, it is still possible to trace some of the movements of Cornford, Romilly and their fellows. To begin with the XI Brigade, setting aside the Gran Vía, a major thoroughfare that continues to be lined by many of the same buildings – most obviously the crucial observation post constituted by the Telefónica building (in 1936 Madrid's only skyscraper) – that witnessed the arrival, grand or otherwise, of its three component battalions, visitors should first seek out the trenches in the northern fringes of the Casa de Campo whence was launched the attack of 13 November. This necessarily involves a long walk (allow 2–3 hours), but the expedition concerned does at least offer the advantage of a partial tour of the Casa de Campo, a sprawling area of woodland which has changed little since the Civil War (that said, patches of non-native vegetation, mostly quick-growing conifers, mark areas of ground where the native ilex trees and stone pines suffered particularly badly from fire or explosions). In order to reach the sector of the front where the XI Brigade went into action, the visitor should take a No. 75 bus from the Plaza de Callao to the end of its line beside the River Manzanares. From the bus stop walk along the bank of the river to the end of the street, noting on the way the Puente de los Franceses (though now only used by suburban trains, in 1936 the lines which cross it were part of the main route from Madrid to the French frontier; meanwhile, firmly held by the Republicans throughout the battle, the bridge completely dominated the area a few hundred yards to the north where the Nationalists crossed the river en route to the University City and, with it, the improvised footbridge that was their only means of communication with the troops in the Clinical Hospital and its fellows). At the end of the street turn left and take the footbridge across the motorway: at the far side will be found a fragment of what was prior to the coming of the Republic the main road from Madrid to northern Spain and, just beyond it, a small piece of brickwork that is all that remains of a Republican front-line pill box. The Nationalist positions, meanwhile, lined the slopes to the left just beyond the treeline.

From the vicinity of the pill box angle to the right across the football field and then pick up the track that runs along the side of the railway embankment. Follow this for several hundred yards until a Y-junction a little way beyond an electricity sub-station situated beside the railway. At this point, take the track to the left and follow this more-or-less due north-west parallel with the railway, though this last is now hidden behind the rising ground to the right. Still following the track, the visitor will now find that it rises quite steeply towards a crest just past a manhole marked by yellow posts. At said crest turn to the left and follow it into the trees: within a very short distance will be found a line of trenches, these representing the positions from which the Nationalists repelled the attack of 13 November. Returning to the track, turn left and at the bottom of the slope turn right along the valley until the railway line is reached. At this point turn left and follow the track beside the railway for perhaps three-quarters of a mile to a spot marked by a bridge across the line. At the bridge take the more minor of the two tracks leading off to the left and follow it into the trees. Several hundred yards further on a knoll will be encountered on the left-hand side that offers a commanding view of Monte Garábitas (the hill surmounted by a watchtower) and, with it, the area advanced across by XI Brigade on 13 November. This knoll marks the site of the Republic front line in the northernmost fringes of the park and is ringed by trenches and graced by the remains of a Republican artillery position, while the area on the other side of the track will be found to be pitted with the remains of dug-outs and support trenches. Just to the left of the knoll, meanwhile, a sap will be found running down the hill towards the Nationalist front line: communicating, as it does, with what was evidently a rather rudimentary fire trench, the area through which it passes might well represent ground taken in the attack.

From the fire trench walk forward until a metalled road is reached. At the road turn right and follow it across the bridge and up the hill on the other side. On reaching the T-junction just beyond the summit, turn left and follow the road to the bottom of the hill whereupon the footbridge across the motorway will be spotted on the other side of the football pitch. However, more adventurous visitors may care to explore the summit of Monte Garábitas, surrounded as this is by a whole network of trenches and dug-outs. On the other side of the road, meanwhile, will be found the Cerro de las Canteras, a spur running down towards the river of which the end is marked by a typical First-World-War-style 'redoubt' (roughly speaking, a cluster of trenches and dug-outs offering all-round defence). Available from both Garábitas and the Cerro de las Canteras, meanwhile, are extensive views of the city centre and the University City alike. Finally, to return to the bus stop from which the walk began, follow the road downhill and walk across the football field in the direction of the footbridge across the motorway.

2. The University City

To return to the specific doings of the International Brigades, the next spot to visit is, of course, the University City. This is best approached on foot from the Moncloa metro station. From said metro station, take the Avenida de la Victoria, noting the triumphal arch erected by Franco to commemorate the entry of his forces into Madrid in March 1939. On the left, meanwhile, is the Western Park – from November 1936 to March 1939 the no man's land separating the two armies – and on the summit of the rising ground to the right the Clinical Hospital, this, like the rest of the University, having been rebuilt according to the same design as the original. After a short distance a road (the Avenida de Seneca) runs down the slope to the left: this essentially marked the southern side of the pocket of territory occupied by the Nationalists in the University City though their forward-most positions were actually just inside the park.

At the roundabout, a short walk straight on will lead the visitor to the Casa de Velásquez: all but totally destroyed in the fighting, this was again rebuilt along much the same lines as it had enjoyed before 1936. However, to reach the Faculty of Philosophy and Letters turn right at the roundabout and walk northwards along the Avenida de la Complutense. On the left, will be seen the Faculty of Agronomy (an important Nationalist bastion on the northern side of the pocket) and across the road to the right the Republican stronghold represented by the Faculties of Dentistry and Medicine, while a monument to the International Brigades is situated in the square opposite the Ciudad Universitaria metro station; here and there it is possible to see the marks of bullets and shrapnel. To reach the Faculty of Philosophy and Letters, at the next major road junction turn left on to Calle Profesor Arangurén and it will be shortly encountered on the right: while the building is not open to all, there is nothing to stop interested individuals from taking a coffee in the ground-floor bar or, perhaps, wandering some of the corridors (NB only the right-hand half of the building dates from 1936, the remainder being a post-war extension). In and around the entrance, meanwhile, there are a number of inscriptions commemorating the Nationalist soldiers that fought in the area and the re-opening of the building by General Franco in 1943.

3. Cerro de los Angeles

A well-known religious monument and recreational site, the Cerro de los Angeles can be reached from the centre of Madrid (take the No. 447 bus from the Plaza de Legazpi). Today the slopes are covered in pines, but in 1936 they were almost completely bare other than for some rough scrub. Also new to the site, meanwhile, is a large seminary and a Carmelite convent (at the time of the Civil War the only building was the eighteenth-century basilica of Nuestra Señora de los Angeles), while the towering monument to the Sacred Heart is a Franquist reconstruction of the similar monument inaugurated in 1919 that was destroyed by left-wing militia in the immediate aftermath of the uprising (however, it occupies a new position: as witness the remains of the plinth on which it once stood, the original monument was situated at the northern end of the esplanade). On the slopes below may be seen the remains of trenches dug by one side or the other during the fighting of November 1936, together with a number of pill boxes constructed later in the war (for a useful map, see <https://www.scribd.com/doc/117355837/Fortines-Cerro-

de-Los-Angeles-Madrid>, accessed 5 November 2019). Unusually, particularly on the southern and western flanks of the hill, having been erected by the Republicans prior to the assault on Madrid, some of the concrete works were in existence at the time of the events described in this chapter.

4. Lopera

Though a long way from Madrid, the battlefield of Lopera is well worth a visit, especially as recent years have seen a considerable effort to commemorate the battle on the part of the local authorities (the town's castle houses a museum to the Civil War, while a monument to Fox and Cornford may be found in the Jardín del Pilar Viejo).[42] There is no bus direct from the capital, but Córdoba, Jaén and Andújar all offer frequent alternatives, and are linked with Lopera by local services. To reach the battlefield, walk eastward out of town on the Arjonilla road (the JV-2032). A few hundred yards beyond the Precocinados de la Esperanza plant, take the second track leading off to the north (the Cañada del Calvario). The hill to the left is the Cerro del Calvario, while that straight ahead is the Cerro de la Casa, it being the area between the two which saw the British company suffer most of its casualties (there are, it seems, far more olives than there were in 1936, the heavy losses suffered by the volunteers in part being the result of having repeatedly to cross patches of open ground; according to local tradition, meanwhile, if the local olive groves have flourished, it is because of the blood that soaked the soil in which the new trees were planted). Follow the track across the crest of the Cerro de la Casa, and, at a left-hand rectangle bend, turn west. Continue to follow the track and after three successive right-angled bends (right-left-right), it will eventually bring the visitor out onto the Andújar road (the J-2031). At this point turn right: within a short distance a deep ravine will be come across at right angles to the road; known as the Arroyo de las Casillas, the obstacle which this created undoubtedly did much to disrupt the initial Republican advance, providing, as it did, numerous opportunities for volunteers who had lost their nerve to go to ground. Finally, from the ravine walk back along the J-2031 to Lopera, noting the Cerro de San Cristobal en route (this is the high ground crowned by an industrial estate). Finally, do not be deceived by the various concrete defence works that litter the area: while these may serve to indicate the approximate position of the Nationalist defenders, like most of those elsewhere, they date from well after the battle.

Chapter 3

The Battle of Jarama

Following the disastrous Córdoba offensive, the next episode in the story of the British volunteers was the major Nationalist push known as the Battle of Jarama. Had Boadilla and Lopera occurred a few earlier weeks earlier, it is possible that the formation of a British battalion could have been seriously delayed, for it is quite clear that, for all the efforts of the Party machine to put a favourable gloss on events, the combination of heavy casualties on the one hand and an evident lack of progress on the other was soon to have a deleterious effect on recruitment. However, the first three months of the life of the International Brigades had been instilled with a strong sense of hope that Madrid, as the phrase went, would be the tomb of fascism, and this had produced a flood of recruits from Europe and the wider world (most notably, Canada and the United States). By the end of 1936, then, the barracks that had been requisitioned for the new force at Albacete was bursting with fresh volunteers, including about 500 from Britain and Ireland. With the return of the survivors of Lopera, then, enough men were available to form a full battalion consisting of three companies of riflemen and one of machine-gunners. The story of the new unit's organisation, composition and training having been told at length elsewhere, such matters will therefore not be treated more than extremely cursorily in the current work.[1] In brief, however, militarily speaking, the picture is scarcely a satisfactory one. Dispatched to the poverty-stricken village of Madrigueras for basic training, the volunteers, the vast majority of whom were not the students and writers of the autumn of 1936 who had made their way to Spain by dint of their own resources, but rather ordinary members of the working classes who had been drawn in via the mechanisms of the Communist Party, were soon disillusioned. All the more was this the case as so many of the men – perhaps as many as 50 per cent – had served at one time or another in the highly exacting ranks of the British army, and were therefore genuinely stunned at what they perceived as nothing more than sheer slovenliness. Thus, the training was rudimentary and the conditions even worse: not only were the billets filthy and the food unpalatable, but little was done to keep the men entertained other than to stage endless lectures on the correct nature of the policy that had been adopted by the Comintern in Spain. Not surprisingly, then, drunkenness was rife, while bitter disputes broke out between the British recruits and their Irish counterparts: many of the latter being veterans of the Irish War of Independence, they were outraged to discover that both the first commander of the battalion, one Wilfred Macartney, and the hero of Lopera, George Nathan, had served with the hated Black-and-Tans. As for attempts to improve matters, they often served only to make things worse, a good example being the decision to end the friction with the Irish by replacing Macartney with Tom Wintringham: for all that Wintringham was a mild-mannered individual who was well liked and had established a solid reputation for himself as a regular contributor to the Communist press, his military experience was limited to having been, first, a mechanic in the Royal Flying Corps, and, later, a motorcycle dispatch rider. Nor did it help matters that stories were soon spreading that all was not quite right in respect of Macartney's departure: officially, this last was caused by an accident in which he was shot in the arm by the most senior British Communist in Spain, Peter Kerrigan, but, according to rumour, the latter had deliberately shot him as a means of getting him out of the way without the Party having to admit that it had made a mistake (commissioned in the Royal Scots in the First World War, Macartney had at least seen front-line service, but he was by all accounts a figure of little or no competence who had far more taste for drink and pretty girls than he did for the business of soldiering, while at the same time being something of a fantasist).[2]

Fortunately or unfortunately, as the case may be, the Madrigueras interlude did not last for very long. In the middle of January, Franco's forces having taken all their objectives, the series of battles of which the struggle at Boadilla had been a part had come to an end with the troops in positions that were to remain

unchanged to the end of the war. Both along the highway to La Coruña and around the University City and in the Casa de Campo,

Some prominent personalities from the early days of the British battalion: from left, Wilfred Macartney, Douglas Springhall, Peter Kerrigan, Tom Wintringham and Frank Ryan. (Imperial War Museum)

Nationalists and Republicans alike began to construct elaborate trench lines that were eventually to turn the whole zone into a miniature version of the Western Front complete with bunkers, pill boxes and dense wire entanglements. Inside the city, meanwhile, the primitive barricades of November were supplemented by the conversion of entire city blocks into fortresses by knocking holes in the walls separating each apartment from the next and blocking doors and windows alike with massive sandbag walls. That said, Madrid was still very much in danger. Now that their flank and rear was secure, the Nationalist troops massed before the capital could turn their attention to cutting the vital Valencia highway, this having long since become the beleaguered city's only practicable source of food, munitions, arms and reinforcements. On 6 February, then, 19,000 Nationalist troops commanded by José Varela, an officer who was rapidly establishing a claim to be the very best of Franco's generals, the vast majority of them either Moors or Foreign Legionaries, left their positions south of the city and struck due east towards the River Jarama.[3] Supporting them were around 60 Panzer I tanks, almost all of them crewed by Spaniards, and no fewer than 101 guns, including 6 batteries of the Schneider M1917 155mm howitzers that had equipped the pre-war army's regiments of heavy artillery, together with much of the newly organised Condor Legion, the Italian Legionary Aviation and the rather more exiguous resources of the Nationalist air force (as well as planes, the Condor Legion appears also to have contributed the services of its 4 batteries of 88mm FLAK18s). Impressive as this array may have seemed, however, there were distinct limits to its striking power, all the field guns and howitzers being, at best, weapons of First-World-War vintage, and the Panzer I tanks puny affairs armed with nothing better than a pair of machine guns.[4]

At first, progress was rapid. No more than 3,000 Republicans were deployed in the area hit by the Nationalists while the terrain consisted of rolling uplands which offered no obstacle to the attacking forces. In just five days, then, the Nationalists were approaching the River Jarama, leaving the defenders in shreds, while they had also gained the dominant ridge known as La Marañosa, this last being an ideal position on which to emplace their heavy guns. At this point, however, the situation got more difficult, not least because the eastern bank of the river was dominated by a steep escarpment, the southern part of which – the ground over which the British battalion was to fight – was dominated by a prominent hill known as Pingarrón. Behind the river, meanwhile, were substantial reserves, the Republicans having themselves been massing for an attack on the insurgent positions south of Madrid. All of them dependent on the commander of the Army of the Centre, Sebastián Pozas Perea, these consisted of XI, XII and XIV International Brigades, I Shock Brigade and I, XVII, XVIII, XIX, XXI, XXIII, XXIV, LXV, LXVII, LXIX and LXX Mixed Brigades.[5] Hastily rushing up from Albacete, meanwhile, was yet another formation in the form of the XV International Brigade, a new force composed of the British battalion, the Slavic Dimitrov battalion, the largely French Sixth-of-February battalion and the American Abraham Lincoln battalion, which had been thrown together in response to the Nationalist offensive.[6]

To return to the course of the battle, on 12 February the first Nationalist troops got across the Jarama both near the village of San Martín de la Vega and at a more isolated spot some miles to the north, the crossings in both cases being the result of bridges falling into their hands more-or-less intact thanks to the carelessness of the defenders. What concerns us here, however, is only the fighting that took place in the vicinity of San Martín. To understand this, it is necessary to begin with the rarely visited Nationalist perspective on events. As we have seen, aimed at cutting the Valencia highway, the offensive launched on 6 February had initially taken an easterly direction, but, once the line of the Jarama had been obtained, the axis of the advance shifted to the north-east as to do otherwise would have required the attacking forces to drive a much deeper salient into the Republican positions than was actually necessary. With San Martín de la Vega on the extreme right of the Nationalist thrust, what this meant was that any action there was likely would be extremely limited, the task of any troops committed therefore being, not to push on at all costs, but rather to establish a defensive line covering the flank of the units to their left driving to cut the road.

As we shall see, all this was to put a very different complexion on events from the one conveyed by the traditional accounts. Having taken the bridge at San Martín, then, the troops who had reached the Jarama at that point crossed the river and ascended the hills beyond the river on the other side. From the bridge a country road headed eastwards in the direction of the rather larger settlement of Morata de Tajuña, but, inviting though this route was, it was absolutely of no interest to the attackers – to be precise, elements of the Fourth Brigade of the 'Reinforced Division of Madrid' commanded by Carlos Asensio Cabanillas[7] – these last rather making their way onto the empty plateau that stretched northwards from the road in the direction of the Valencia highway. Left to themselves, Asensio Cabanillas' men would simply have dug in, but they were suddenly assailed by Republican forces in the shape of the XV International Brigade, which had just been brought up to the area of Morata de Tajuña by lorry and ordered to advance westwards astride the road to San Martín. Sent forward into the line with little or no knowledge of the enemy positions and the most inadequate of armament – the rifle companies, for example, were armed with a mixture of Colt M1895 and Chauchat M1915 machine guns, but the canvas ammunition belts supplied with the former (survivors of some of the very large consignments supplied to Russia in the First World War) proved to have perished, while, as the fighting at Lopera

The River Jarama near San Martín de la Vega. (author's collection)

had shown all too well, the latter simply could not be depended on – the volunteers were cut to pieces.[8] First to feel the full weight of Nationalist firepower were the Dimitrov and Sixth-of-February battalions as they were deployed to the north of the road and therefore in direct line with Asensio Cabanillas' men. Unfortunately for the volunteers, the ground over which they had to advance was devoid of cover, the result being that they were quickly forced to fall back to the shelter of the slopes overlooking Morata. Illustrative of the experience is the diary of a French volunteer named Galli:

> We are in contact with the enemy … The machine-guns are firing fiercely … I can see comrades running from one tree to the next and already there are a few forms lying quite still … The fascists have the advantage of numbers and of arms. Their machine-gun fire is devastating our ranks. Nearly a whole company has been wiped out. I learn that our machine-guns are out of action … The sound of cannons begins to mingle with that of the machine-guns: a rain

The erstwhile wayside inn from which the British battalion started its advance on the morning of 12 February 1937. During the battle that followed it was to become the battalion's cookhouse and hospital. (author's collection)

of steel is falling along the whole front occupied by our brigade … The fascists are increasing the intensity of their fire. We are giving way: it is necessary to retire. Slowly we move backwards … The machine-gunners are struggling along with their useless guns … but it is hard work in the powerful mid-day sun … Ever more frequently we hear the shells whistling through the air. The machine-gunners can no longer see us, and they have stopped firing, but the shelling goes on.[9]

To the left of their two fellow battalions, by contrast, the British enjoyed the cover afforded by extensive groves of olives while they were faced by no enemy troops whatsoever. Alarmed by clear signs that the Sixth-of-February and the Dimitrovs were in trouble, Wintringham halted his men at the first crest he came to with the intention of waiting until such time as the situation had become clearer, only to receive a message from the brigade commander, a Hungarian Communist named Janos Galiscz who was yet another of the erstwhile Habsburg officers who Stalin had dispatched to Spain to run the International Brigades, to the effect that they should advance at once. Left with no option but to obey, having set up a command post in a sunken lane just to the rear, Wintringham therefore sent his three rifle companies down the steep slope at whose crest he had halted and into the broken ground beyond: on the left was No. 3 Company commanded by erstwhile London bus driver William Briskey; in the centre No. 4 Company commanded by Stockton volunteer and Scots-Guards veteran Bert Overton; and on the right No. 1 Company commanded by sometime naval rating and member of the IRA Kit Conway (in theory, Conway's place should have been filled by Jock Cunningham, but the latter had been struck down by an attack of influenza and had only the day before reported sick). No maps were available other than a hasty sketch of the surroundings put together by Jason Gurney, a London-based South-African sculptor who was one of the battalion's very few middle-class recruits and had secured a job for himself as a cartographer, but the general layout of the area was clear enough. Morale, meanwhile, was high, not least because some Nationalist planes that appeared over the battlefield were chased away by a flight of Republican Polikarpovs with the loss of two of their number, one and all also taking comfort from the fact that No. 2 Company – the battalion's vital heavy machine-gunners under the command of a tall Scot from Edinburgh named Harry Fry – were busily ensconcing themselves in a commanding position on the high ground the riflemen had just left. In the words of Walter Gregory, a young brewery worker from Nottingham who was attached to Briskey's company: 'We looked magnificent; we felt magnificent; and we felt that, if only our colleagues back home who had made it possible for us to be there could see us now, how proud they would be.'[10]

The track along which the rifle companies of the British battalion advanced en route for Suicide Hill on the morning of 12 February 1937. (author's collection)

The site of the British battalion's baptism of fire on 12 February 1937; Suicide Hill is out of picture, but the knoll held by No. 1 Company can be seen on the left, together, in the distance, with the spur from which the volunteers were enfiladed with machine-gun fire. (author's collection)

Sadly, the feeling of elation was instantly shattered. Positioned as they were on the plateau to the north, the Nationalists quickly spotted the British volunteers and rushed a machine-gun company to a steep-sided knoll just to the south of the Morata de Tajuña road. Currently intent on crossing two low hills that stood between them and the river, of which the closest was to go down in the battalion's lexicography as the 'conical hill', and the one beyond and somewhat further to the left as either 'Casa-Blanca Hill' or 'Suicide Hill', the volunteers were suddenly assailed by a storm of fire. James Prendergast, a factory worker from Dublin who later became a political commissar, was No. 1 Company's runner:

> We … were beginning to deploy. I had been told to look out for a bridge, our objective. Just then we came under direct fire. Men were hurriedly seeking cover among the scrub, but, once we lay down, we saw that we had no view ahead. For a while we fired from standing

The summit of the knoll held by No. 1 Company on 12 February 1937; the lack of even the most vestigial cover ensured that the casualty toll was extremely heavy. Suicide/Casa-Blanca Hill is the tree-covered skyline in the distance. (author's collection)

positions ... but the fascist fire, front and flank, was now pretty heavy. Men were being hit all around ... [Sean] Goff tumbled over, his hand to his head, his face white. It was a narrow shave: his helmet was dinged [*sic*] ... The fire on us had grown so heavy now that ... fear was not felt any more, because it was no use feeling afraid.[11]

Also well to the fore was the sometime sailor Fred Copeman, who had been commissioned and attached to No. 1 Company as a supernumerary:

At that moment I saw my first real casualty: Davidovitch, a young Jewish lad ... had received one in the stomach and it wasn't a nice sight ... Cries could now be heard in every direction; the casualties were coming in very fast. I ran down to Kit Conway who was well in front striding through the undergrowth ... He ordered that my company should dig in at the top of the [conical] hill and give covering fire for the remainder of the battalion ... Just then I came across George Bright. George was a carpenter, over sixty years old ... [who] had been well known to me during the unemployed struggles in London. I asked him what the hell he was doing there, and, just as he opened his mouth to answer, there was a very quiet plop and a small red hole appeared in his forehead: he died instantly.[12]

In principle, the front-line troops should not have been on their own. On the contrary, they were expecting to receive the support of the machine-gun company's eight Russian Maxim M1910s. Unfortunately, they were now dealt a major blow in that the lorry that was supposed to be bringing up the machine guns had not turned up. We come here to a saga that was all too typical of the chaos that dogged the Republican war effort. Seemingly terrified by the proximity of the dreaded Moors, the truck driver concerned had simply unloaded his precious cargo some hundreds of yards east of the sunken road and hastily retired without letting anyone know what he had done. Eventually, the guns and their attendant ammunition were located by a squad of men sent to the rear and dragged up to the front line under heavy fire. Thomas Hyndman was a sometime British soldier who had volunteered for the job because he did not trust his rifle to be serviceable: 'The enemy fire was increasing ...The dead and wounded were everywhere ... I lost my partner: bullets got him in an almost straight line down his back. I pushed him off the gun, moved forward a few feet with it and went back for the cases.'[13] However, this was not the end to the story. When the guns were finally got into position, it transpired that the wrong ammunition had been supplied for them, so that a second expedition had to be dispatched to get the right type, a supply of this last eventually being located in a truck found overturned in a ditch. Even then, the travails of the machine-gun company were not at an end, for the new bullets were not loaded into belts, but rather loose, the net result being that, with enemy shells bursting all around them, the gunners were forced to strip all the ammunition out of the old belts and replace it with the supply that had just been brought up. Thus disadvantaged, all Fry could do was to dispatch a squad to the edge of the plateau with orders to direct their fire on the Nationalist machine-gun positions across the valley. However, this move availed the men chosen for the task nothing more than a few casualties of their own, the three rifle companies in the meantime having no option but to go to ground. Appointed Briskey's runner, Walter Gregory was detailed to carry a report on the situation to Wintringham: 'Shells were dropping all around me and I weaved about in the hope of gaining added protection ... The carnage was horrendous. There were not only dead and dreadfully wounded men lying all over the ground, but there were bits of bodies thrown all over the hillside.'[14] Another witness to the slaughter was Albert Charlesworth, a Manchester volunteer serving with Bert Overton's No. 4 Company. Thus: 'Over to our left on the top of a hillock [i.e. Casa-Blanca/Suicide

Hill] was a white house, and, as the battle progressed, we could all see bodies rolling down from this … position, sixteen or twenty I must have seen roll down there.'[15] Among the casualties spotted by Charlesworth may have been Richard White, an oddity among the British volunteers as he came, not from London, the South-Wales coalfields, the industrial north or Scotland, but rather rural Dorset:

> I dropped down behind a tree with my rifle in front, and, just as I dropped down, I felt as though a locomotive had run over me and put a bullet through both legs … A numbness set in, but, while I was trying to think, another one hit me through my left shoulder. I just lay there and one of my comrades … made a run over to join me to see what he could do … I almost immediately got another bullet through my left hip … I said to him, as far as I was able to talk, to get the hell out, get away, which he did. There was nothing anyone could do.[16]

Badly armed as they were – even the rifles with which the men were armed could not be fired with any degree of accuracy due to the fact that the volunteers had stripped them of the spike bayonets with which they had arrived without realising that the sights were calibrated to take account of the extra weight which the former exerted[17] – the British battalion had no chance. An anonymous eyewitness attached to Wintringham's headquarters remembered:

> From Morning to dusk it was a battle between our riflemen and a numerically superior enemy well equipped with automatic rifles, machine-guns, artillery and tanks … The close-range fire of the fascist light machine-guns and the heavier guns firing over their heads was more intense than any of the veterans among us had experienced: "Worse than the Somme" was the opinion of the men who had survived that battle. Grass fell in swathes before it; men lifting their heads to fire were shot through the face.[18]

There is, of course, considerable exaggeration here, but the fact that the rifle companies were badly shaken cannot be doubted. Another volunteer watching from the rear was amateur cartographer Jason Gurney:

> Clouds of smoke and dust … gradually spread right along the line of our forward positions. The barrage continued for about three hours. From my position in Harry Fry's trench, I could see the chaos on Casa-Blanca Hill, where some of the men were working away with bayonet and tin helmet in an attempt to produce some sort of fox-hole in which to hide. None of the Colts or [Chauchats] were firing and very few rifles.[19]

Isolated on the so-called 'conical hill' in the centre of the line in full view of Nationalist machine-gunners ensconced on the knoll beside the Morata Road, No. 1 Company endured a particularly dreadful beating, not least because its position boasted even less cover than there was on Suicide Hill. Among the men caught on the summit was James Prendergast:

> I settle into a new firing position: my rifle is soon burning hot. Kit comes over: I notice his face [has] lines of sweat running through the dust. He hands me a note: it is from Brigade HQ telling us we must hold out at all costs. He tells me to transmit these instructions to the [company] on our left flank ... What's left ... are around the white house, I am told ... On the way it seems as if a thousand bees are buzzing past my face ... I get to the yard and shout: no reply. I clear the low wall and go in: yes, they are there all right – all dead. I shiver as I move back ... I reach the hill-crest ... Kit is directing fire ... using a rifle himself and pausing every while to give instructions. Suddenly, he shouts, his rifle spins out of his hand and he falls back.[20]

The dead men seen by Prendergast had belonged to Overton's company, but, if this force was suffering heavy losses, to its left the position of the British battalion was being challenged still more dramatically. Initially positioned, as they were, in lower ground that was to some extent masked by Suicide Hill, the men posted to hold this sector – Briskey's No. 3 Company – had been relatively safe from the fire of the enemy, but, all of a sudden, they were over-run by a fierce Moorish bayonet charge, among the casualties of which was Briskey himself. Making his way back from headquarters, Walter Gregory had reached the low ground in the lee of the British front line, only to see his commanding officer fall before his very eyes:

> Suddenly the shelling stopped ... What was happening? The answer came immediately. Pouring down from the Casa-Blanca hill, shrieking loud enough to awaken the dead, came score after score of Moorish soldiers ... They were coming straight towards me, yelling their battle cries to terrify their enemies and to bolster their own courage ... Where the company had been when I left it, there were now enemy troops in considerable strength. I was surprised to see ... Bill Briskey charging across the exposed ground clearly intent on reaching me. Why Bill tried to reach me I shall never know, for, when we were separated by but a few yards, he suddenly doubled up and wrapped his arms around his chest before pitching forward. In seconds I was bending over him, but he was already dead.[21]

Also wounded at this time was No. 1 Company's political commissar, a Communist youth organiser from London named Ralph Campeau, while Conway's replacement, a Scot named Kenneth Stalker, was killed instantly by a rifle bullet that struck him in the head, yet another of the many dead or mortally wounded being the same Sean Goff who had had such a lucky escape when the Nationalists first opened fire. Among the men detailed to assist with the growing number of casualties was medical orderly Tom Clarke:

> The call went out for stretcher-bearers, and I was one of the unfortunates on the stretchers. So we went up and the first lad we took out was a lad called Campeau … Great big fellow he was: I think he must have weighed about fifteen stone. There were only two of us on the stretcher, and the bullets were coming just like bees … We got him across [the valley], but he died … in hospital … It was really just a slaughter.[22]

With Briskey's command falling back in disorder and Conway's rapidly being shot to pieces, the one unit that was still relatively intact was Overton's No. 4 Company, most of the survivors of which had sensibly enough taken shelter in the lee of the knoll which they had occupied. All too soon, however, a Nationalist column having advanced far enough along the Morata road to direct fire upon the men concerned from their right rear, the situation of this force also went into freefall. To quote Charlesworth again:

> It must have been late afternoon, when, over to the right … I could see a battalion … advancing up the road led by a tank. They advanced to a position approximately level with us … and opened fire. We were dead ducks … because they were … looking down on us. We had to evacuate … and scramble back up the hill [i.e. the escarpment crowned by Fry's machine guns] as best we could. I got over the hill and … took up my position in the firing line and stayed there until [an] order came to fall back to the sunken road … There were not many left to go back.[23]

By this time the troops on the hillocks were also falling back. Casualties had been very heavy, the 400 men in the 3 rifle companies having lost 100 dead and 125 wounded since midday. As Gurney later admitted in his memoirs:

> At this particular moment we were a broken battalion … Seventy per cent of those who had been holding the forward positions were either

The sunken road to which the survivors of the British battalion retired at nightfall on 12 February 1937. (author's collection)

killed or wounded ... All their automatic weapons had been lost or abandoned, and many of them had no weapons at all ... They were all in a state of greater or lesser shock, hungry and suffering from a tremendous thirst.[24]

Eager to exploit their success, the Nationalists advanced on the ridge that overlooked the positions that had been defended by the broken rifle companies. A considerable number of the latter's members having failed to stop at the crest, preferring instead to keep retreating in the direction of the inn where they had been served breakfast, ahead of them lay nothing more than the hitherto helpless machine-gun company and the handful of men who constituted Wintringham's headquarters. Fortunately, just at this very point, Fry's eight Maxim guns had finally been readied for action, the triumphant Moors therefore receiving an unexpected bloody nose. 'For the first time ... we opened fire in earnest, the strategically placed Maxims giving devastating cross-fire', recalled David Hooper, an unemployed Londoner who had volunteered to serve in Spain in the wake of the failure of his marriage. 'I could see dead men all over the place ... To be honest, I was bloody scared, but I kept on firing. Then we stopped ... and we could hear the wounded enemy's moans and groans [but] no-one came to help them.'[25]

It was not just the Moorish wounded who suffered. Already scarred by its experiences during the day, the British battalion now found itself assailed by complete logistical collapse. No food was served out until dawn the following morning and there was no drinking water, while those casualties who survived found themselves

facing a dreadful ordeal. Together with Prendergast, Charlesworth and Gregory, all three of whom were wounded in the course of the afternoon, Conway and Campeau were all given such rudimentary treatment as was available and evacuated to the rear, but many others were less lucky. Sent out by Wintringham to report on the situation, Gurney came across a shocking site. Thus:

Fred Copeman, a redoubtable sometime naval rating who made a name for himself at the Jarama and subsequently rose to the command of the British battalion.
(Imperial War Museum)

In a hollow by the side of the road I found a group of wounded
men who had been carried back from Casa-Blanca hill ... to a non-
existent field dressing station ... There were about fifty stretchers,
all of which were occupied, but many of the men had already died
and most of the others would by morning: they were chiefly artillery
casualties with appalling wounds from which they could have had
little chance of recovery ... I went from one to the other, but was
absolutely powerless to do anything other than to hold a hand or to
light a cigarette.[26]

Luckier than all of these men – he had only had the thumb of his right hand
shattered by an enemy bullet – Gregory has left us an excellent picture of the
chaotic scenes endured by the British wounded:

Some distance from the front, a passing ambulance gave me a lift for
the remainder of the journey to the dressing station. [This] presented
an awful sight: there were wounded troops lying all over the place
with more arriving all the time ... The first day of that battle brought
home to me ... the problems that the International Brigades faced
in coping with their casualties. Although the medical staff we had
were excellent, they were too few and ... were not sufficiently well
equipped. For example, when the British battalion went into action
for the first time, [it] had a battalion doctor, an ambulance which ...
operated a shuttle service between the front line and the dressing
station, and four or five stretcher bearers ... Two problems became
immediately obvious: first, the distance from the front line to the
dressing station was about four or five kilometres – a long way for
even a superficially wounded man to travel under his own steam;
secondly, four or five stretcher-bearers ... for a battalion of 600 men
engaged in heavy fighting was far too few.[27]

Even for the men who had survived unwounded, it was a dreadful night. To shock,
fear, hunger and thirst was added bitter cold, for the February night was icy, while
many men had discarded such blankets and warm clothing as they had possessed
in the course of the advance to contact. Still worse, no sooner had the new day
dawned, indeed, than it transpired that, far from being relieved or even given
a chance to re-organise, the battalion was being expected to launch a counter-
attack, the aim of which was nothing less than to throw the Moors and legionaries
backs across the river. Aerial and tank support were promised, true, but, even
so, Wintringham was horrified: with his command in shreds, it would be hard

put to it even to hold its positions, let alone drive the better armed Nationalists from the ground they had conquered. Nevertheless, comforted by an early incident in which a company of Moorish reinforcements that was ill-informed enough to march in column of fours along the Morata road was forced to scatter by Fry's machine guns, loyal Communist as he was, Wintringham managed to put together a strike force of about 100 men and settled down to wait for the support that he had been promised. This, however, proved disappointing: a single T26 tank put in an appearance, only almost immediately to retire again; a flight of Republican planes made a brief raid on the Nationalist positions around the Casa Blanca; and the XV Brigade's exiguous artillery battery – it had but one Armstrong-Whitworth 60-pounder and two Schneider 75mm field guns – for the first time put in an appearance, only for the fire it laid down to prove utterly ineffective.

With the task facing him looking utterly hopeless, Wintringham was now even more unhappy than before, but, completely out of touch with the situation as they were – the field telephones linking them to the various battalions were of such poor quality that conversation on them was impossible – Galiscz and his staff were doing nothing but demand that he advance post-haste. If that were possible, however, the situation now went from bad to worse in that the Nationalists suddenly seized the initiative. Thus, observing that the right flank of Fry's position rested on a re-entrant that drove some way back into the plateau, a substantial force of infantry succeeded in reaching the shelter that it offered, and, having driven off the few volunteers – all of them drawn from Overton's company – assigned to protect it, they suddenly swarmed over the lip of the depression and took the machine-gunners from the flank and rear, quickly overrunning Fry's badly isolated men and taking about a third of them prisoner, including, not least, Fry himself. To this incident there attaches one of the many legends surrounding the history of the battalion in that it has often been claimed, not least by veterans of the battle, that the machine-gun company was overcome by the enemy advancing in column with their fists upraised in the Communist salute singing 'The Internationale', but this version of events was later indignantly denied by men who had been on the spot, such as the company commissar, Edinburgh Communist Donald Renton.[28] The fact that no such subterfuge was attempted does not mean that confusion did not play a part in events, however. Herewith, then, are the details of the scrimmage retailed by Renton's close friend, George Watters:

> They came in from both sides. Someone had cried out that it was our own fellows that were coming up from the rear, so we didn't pay attention … All I know about it was that I got hit on the head with … the butt end of a rifle … When I came to they [i.e. Watters' fellow gunners] were all standing … with their hands up.[29]

So far, so good: at bottom what happened is clear enough. However, a variety of factors – most notably, a general desire to camouflage the shortcomings of the British battalion – led to the emergence of a narrative that sought to pin the blame on Overton, the latter being an easy target, not least because, on the third day of the action, over-wrought beyond endurance, he had fled the field. That he was a genuine case of shell shock is fairly clear – at all events he was immediately hospitalised – but it was evidently decided to make an example of him, and he was therefore reduced to the ranks and posted to a labour battalion in whose ranks he was subsequently killed at the Battle of Brunete.[30] To return to the course of the fighting, whoever was responsible for the disaster, Wintringham reacted with commendable energy. Thus, already besieged by messages from Galiscz to the effect that he should launch an immediate assault on the Nationalists and drive them back across the river, no sooner had he received word of the capture of Fry's company than he sought to lead the few men that made up his headquarters in a counter-attack. Among the participants was a Jason Gurney much shocked by the turn that developments had taken:

Some of the men of the machine-gun company captured at the Jarama on 13 February 1937. (Southworth Collection, Special Collections, University of California San Diego)

> The sheer weight of noise was tremendous … Wintringham stood up to lead the charge [but] was almost immediately shot through the thigh and collapsed … Aitken [the battalion commissar] and about ten others jumped to their feet … and charged. Very, very reluctantly I followed them … By the time that I had run about sixty yards I realised that there was no longer anyone in front or alongside me, and I dived for cover under one of the small hills built up around the foot of every olive tree.[31]

Hidden behind his olive tree, Gurney stayed down for a while, and then made a desperate dash for the shelter of the sunken road. On arrival he found a scene of absolute pandemonium. As he later wrote:

> All that was now left of the battalion was a handful of men rushing up and down … in a state of utter confusion. This was only increased when two Russian tanks appeared from the main road and started to bombard the Moors in the machine-gun trench. Their fire was erratic and there was a moment of panic when we thought that they were shooting at us … One unfortunate individual … was rushing round in a cocoon of insulated wire and crying, 'I have captured the fascist communications! I have captured the fascist communications!' Eventually he leapt up on to the parapet and was shot dead by a burst of machine-gun fire.[32]

Reduced to a state of complete incapacitation, Gurney fled to the rear, and was to remember the next few days as little more than a blur which he only got through by dint of the care of friends at the XV Brigade's headquarters. Luckily for the battalion, however, the enemy made no attempt to follow up their success, and so a makeshift line was put together consisting of those few men of the rifle companies who were still on their feet and had not joined the ever growing crowd of fugitives who had, like Gurney, drifted back to the so-called 'cookhouse' or even further afield; those machine-gunners who had eluded the Nationalist *coup de main*; and a squad that had been detailed for the task of protecting brigade headquarters. Morale, however, was paper thin, and, as darkness fell, a sudden explosion in the sunken road – the work, it seems, of a stray enemy flare that ignited a box of hand grenades – produced a general panic that soon had most of the men fleeing through the olive groves in a desperate attempt to reach safety. Fortunately enough, however, the Nationalists did nothing to press their advantage other than spraying the battalion with machine-gun fire, the result being that the battalion commissar, George Aitken, a well-liked figure who had already distinguished himself the previous night, was able to restore at least a degree of order, in which task he was much aided by a Fred Copeman who was still on his feet despite the fact that he had twice been hit by bullets in the course of the previous day.[33]

During the night, meanwhile, further assistance turned up in the person of Jock Cunningham, the latter having shrugged off his condition and rushed up from the rear to join the fighting. Beyond doubt a brave man, Cunningham managed to instil his men with sufficient fighting spirit to launch a surprise attack that recovered several of the missing Maxims. Having thereby gained a little time, he then ordered his men to fall back from the sunken road, a position that was desperately vulnerable to enfilade fire, to a fresh line a few hundred yards to the rear. In this, however, he was over-ruled by a message from Galiscz, and very soon the British once again found themselves back where they had started. Exactly as Cunningham had foreseen, however, the insistence on holding the sunken road almost immediately led to fresh disasters. Exactly what happened is unclear – one story is that a Nationalist thrust from beyond the British left flank overran the last men in the line[34] – but, whatever the cause, the remnants of the battalion broke and ran. Behind the lines, meanwhile, the scene was one of complete disintegration with groups of fugitives either commandeering every vehicle that they could find or simply fleeing on foot. Sent across from brigade headquarters to see what was going on, the Irish leader Frank Ryan was stunned by the sight with which he was now confronted:

> Dispirited by heavy casualties, by defeat, by lack of food, worn out by three days of gruelling fighting, our men appeared to have reached the end of their resistance. Some were still straggling down the slopes from what had been, until an hour ago, the front line … All, as they came back, had similar stories to tell, of comrades dead, of conditions that were more than flesh and blood could stand, of weariness they found hard to resist.[35]

Here again we simply do not know what happened. According to the usual version of events, Ryan and Cunningham managed to rally the fugitives with the assistance of Galiscz, who at this point at last put in a personal appearance, and then led a gallant counter-attack that began with the survivors of the battalion marching up the road in columns of four singing 'The Internationale' and soon had the astonished Nationalists falling back in disorder. Originating in the account of Frank Ryan, this story is accepted without question by Hughes and Baxell, but it is deeply lacking in verisimilitude, the reality almost certainly being far more prosaic. Thus far more likely is that, assuming they had attacked at all, the Nationalists did no more than occupy the area originally defended by Harry Fry, leaving the British battalion to creep up the slopes and take up a new line well short of the sunken road. That said, some combat did take place. Liverpool volunteer Jack Edwards was shot in the foot, while a rather vague passage in the memoirs of Frank Thomas, a Welsh sympathiser with fascism of lower middle-class origins who had travelled out to Spain to fight for Franco and enlisted in the Foreign Legion, speaks of a British bayonet charge that appears to refer to this action.[36]

By one means or another, then, the situation was stabilised, but, if this was so, it was hardly surprising. For all the hyperbole about the British battalion stopping Franco in his tracks and saving Madrid, nothing of the sort had occurred. As more than one volunteer observed, by the end of the battle, the Nationalists could have broken through without the slightest difficulty, while even on 12 February a full-scale assault would have smashed Wintringham and his men beyond repair. However, such an assault never came. Thus, what the myriad accounts of the British battalion's gallant stand ignore is the fact that, positioned where it was, the battalion was not in the Nationalists' direct line of march, but rather on its flank, the result being that, to commit more resources to the sector held by the British battalion and, indeed, the rest of XV Brigade, would have been to weaken the north-easterly drive on the Valencia highway that was the chief axis of the offensive. Break through at Morata, the Moors and Legonaries most certainly could have done, but to reach the Valencia road they would have had to clear the broad valley of the River Tajuña and then ascend another line of heights similar to the ones they had fought across on the far side while all the time exposing their flanks more and more to Republican counter-attacks. Far from being the Pingarrón massif, then, the crucial point on the battlefield was rather the Puente de Arganda – the multi-spanned girder bridge that carried the highroad across the River Jarama 10 miles to the north. If anyone stopped Franco, it was therefore the various brigades that fought in that sector. Heroic though Wintringham and his men may have been – Thomas admits that his 600-strong *bandera* had lost two-thirds of its strength by the time that the Nationalist assault ground to a halt, and, further, that, of his own squad, just one man was left other than himself[37] – they had clearly not stopped the enemy advance, perhaps the most succinct comment that can be made on their contribution to the fight being that the most detailed military account of the war available – that of Martínez Bande – says little about the sector of the line south of the road to Morata de Tajuña, makes no mention of the British battalion whatsoever and devotes but a single paragraph to the activities of the XV Brigade as a whole.[38]

The Battlefield Today

The site of the first action of the British battalion is one of the most evocative of all Spanish Civil-War battlefields. For those visitors with access to a car, the best approach is from the direction of Madrid via the M301 to San Martín de la Vega. Just before this settlement is reached, turn left onto the M506 following signposts to Arganda. After a distance of perhaps 1 mile turn right onto a track signposted as leading to a picnic area running southwards along the river bank: very shortly there will be encountered the remains of a road bridge. All but brand new at the time of the Civil War, this was the crossing seized by Asensio Cabanillas' men on the night of 11 February, though its destruction dates not from the Civil War, but, rather, a disastrous flood in 1947.

Having visited the bridge, return to the M506 and cross the river. On the other side turn right at the road junction onto the M302 following signs to Morata de Tajuña and then take the first left (unnamed) and the second right (Calle Halcón). After a few hundred yards, this deteriorates into a track unsuitable for anything other than four-wheel-drive vehicles. Ascending this track will bring the visitor to a summit that offers excellent views of the whole of the Jarama valley (including, some 2 miles to the north, the Pindoque railway bridge), the heights west of the Jarama captured by the Nationalists in the first few days of the battle and, last but not least, the area of rough terrain immediately south of the Morata road that saw the British battalion lose such heavy casualties.

Return to the M302 and turn left towards Morata. After some 2 miles turn right onto a broad unmade road heading roughly south-west through a wide expanse of olive groves. This is the 'sunken road' that played so prominent a part in the battle, not that it is anywhere more than 2ft deep. Continue along the track for approximately 1 mile until a track is reached branching off to the right. Immediately to the left will be found a convenient stretch of open ground which can be used as a parking space. Just at the western edge of the open ground will be found a small cairn commemorating the British battalion while the track that leads northwards along the edge of the olive groves will take the visitor very close to the position taken up by the machine-gun company, though to reach the latter it is necessary to push on ahead and to the left until a deep ravine is reached running roughly parallel with the Morata road: it was the Nationalists' penetration of this area that enabled them to overrun Fry and his men.

Return to the parking area and take the track running roughly westwards over the lip of the plateau: after dropping very steeply downwards for perhaps 200yd, this reaches a wheatfield. Ahead and slightly to the left will be seen a steep-sided hill covered with scrub: this is the so-called 'conical hill' held by Conway's company. Cross the wheatfield and ascend the hill, at the summit of which the visitor will come to a roughly circular open space, it being here that Conway, Campeau and so many of their men were cut down. Just as was the case at the time of the battle, the ground will be observed to be both very hard and very stony, so much so, indeed, that it would have been very difficult for the volunteers to dig in even were they to have been provided with proper entrenching tools (the trenches and dug-outs that can be explored on the north-western face of the hill are relics not of the fighting of February 1937, but rather of the Nationalists' occupation of the area over the two years of war that were yet to come). At the same time, no more than 500yd to the north and on exactly the same level as the summit a prominent knoll will be seen standing forth from the slopes traversed by the Morata road: offering a perfect view, as it does, of the positions occupied by Conway's men, and, by extension, an excellent field of fire, it does not take much understanding to see why the Nationalists' placed a machine-gun company there. Beyond the road, meanwhile, will be observed the treeless plateau across which the Franco-Belges and the Dimitrovs attempted to advance, it being all too clear why they were driven back so quickly. Finally, due west of the summit of the conical hill, the broad swell of hillside covered with trees is Suicide Hill: although this is now devoid of any remains of the farmstead which crowned it at the time of the battle, this can be visited via a narrow path running westwards from the base of the conical hill.

Return to the sunken road and drive back to the M302. At the junction turn right and proceed along the road. Take the first turning to the right and follow it until a convenient parking area is encountered on the right-hand side of the track. Park here and continue along the track on foot to the monument at the summit. Erected in 2006 to mark the seventieth anniversary of the creation of the International Brigades, the entwined hands that form the basis of the 25ft-high structure are known as the 'Monumento a la Solidaridad' while on either side lies a stretch of preserved front-line trench: this last marks the position occupied by the British battalion at the end of the battle and occupied by it for several months thereafter.

Return to the M302 and turn right. At the road junction that follows almost immediately, turn right again onto the M311 following signs to Chinchón. After a short distance a small cluster of buildings will be encountered. Of these, the one set furthest back from the road and also the oldest is the so-called 'cookhouse' – actually an old inn dating from the sixteenth century – at which the British volunteers were fed prior to going into action (a sign beside the main entrance labels it as 'El Antiguo Parador de Frascuelo'). A private residence, it is, alas, closed to the public, but a track leading up into the hills from its northern face marks the route taken by Wintringham's men at the beginning of their advance.

Preserved trenches near the Monumento a la Solidaridad. Part of the new front line that emerged in the wake of the battle, they were the scene of great misery that inspired the famous line, 'There's a valley in Spain called Jarama'. (author's collection)

Return to the M311 and turn left in the direction of Morata. Heavily damaged in the Civil War, this is now a pleasant little town with plenty of places to eat. More importantly, it also houses a museum to the battle which contains a large collection of arms and other artefacts (Museo de la Batalla del Jarama, 28530 Morata de Tajuña). For travellers reliant on public transport, Morata is also the easiest base from which to access the battlefield (take the 336 or 337 bus from the Plaza del Conde de Casal and alight in the centre of Morata, from where the battlefield can be explored on foot: in so far as this last is concerned, there is a long-standing plan to set up a network of way-marked trails but this, alas, has yet come to fruition). Finally, every year the second weekend of March is marked by a festival organised by the town council and the Asociación de Tajar dedicated to the commemoration of the battle with concerts, lectures, film shows, guided walks and historical re-enactments. For full details, see <https://morataturismo.es/en/veryhacer/jornadas-de-la-batalla/>.

Chapter 4

The Battle of Brunete

The dawn was breaking in the mountains in the east. Tired and thirsty, we ended our twenty-mile march and flung ourselves down on the hillside. Down in the valley before us lay Villanueva de la Cañada. We were to rest here and watch it being captured: then our turn for action would come. A shattering roar, a long drawn-out whine overhead: our big guns … Now from our rear comes the thrumming of planes. They are over us, in front of us. Crash! Crash! Now Franco, you're getting what you are so used to giving us. Villanueva is wreathed in brown billows of smoke: good bombing that … There go the infantry … lines of specks snaking forward … Machine-guns and rifles are crackling; men are killing and being killed. It is unreal like something … on the screen in the cinema.[1]

With these words one anonymous British volunteer recorded his impressions of the opening moments of the Battle of Brunete. By far the biggest action of the conflict thus far, this affair took place on the rolling plains west of Madrid in the blazing heat of a Castilian summer. Its context was a war whose epicentre had switched from the Spanish capital to the narrow coastal strip encompassing the cities of Bilbao, Santander and Oviedo, which, though cut off from the rest of Republican Spain, had remained in the hands of the government. For the first six months of the war, this had very much been a secondary front: though fierce fighting had flared up from time to time, the bulk of the Nationalist energy had been expended on the attempt to take Madrid. Following the failure represented by the Battle of Jarama, Franco had made one more attempt to secure the objective to which obsession with personal prestige had kept him shackled for so long. Thus, at the beginning of March a large strike force consisting of the corps-sized contingent of Italian troops that Mussolini had sent to assist the Nationalist leader and a single Spanish division had struck south-westwards along the axis of the highway from Madrid to Zaragoza in a fresh attempt to cut the city's communications with the rest of Spain. Yet here too the result was frustration. Partly motorised, the Italians soon outstripped the Spanish troops fighting alongside them and drove a deep salient into the Republican positions. However, the further they advanced, the more their logistical situation deteriorated, the more their morale slumped in the face of the cold and rain in which the offensive was conducted, and, finally, the more they became vulnerable to counter-attacks. At length, the inevitable occurred: operating from improvised airfields north of the Guadarrama mountains, the Nationalist planes assigned to the offensive were effectively grounded, and this left the Republican Polikarpovs and Tupolevs, based as they were at the well-equipped civilian airport of Barajas, free to launch attack after attack on the Italian columns, while fresh troops closed in for the kill. As poorly armed as any Spaniard and, for that matter, International Brigader (not only did much of their artillery date from before the First World War, but their machine guns were dogged by numerous design faults), the Italians promptly fell back in disorder and within a few days had lost most of the territory they had captured.[2]

If not quite the overwhelming victory claimed by Republican propaganda, the Battle of Guadalajara was nonetheless a damaging blow to Franco's reputation, while it showed all too clearly that the Nationalists simply did not have the strength to take Madrid. What was needed, then, was a fresh front where victory would be within the insurgents' grasp. This being something for which the northern front seemed ideally suited, on 31 March the Nationalist forces in northern Spain launched an offensive on Bilbao. Faced by a situation in which, few Russian planes having been delivered to the northern zone, they were completely out-classed in the air, the defenders were steadily beaten back until, in the middle of June, they were forced to evacuate the Basque capital and fall back on Santander (it was, of course, this campaign that saw the Condor Legion obliterate the town of Guernica).[3]

From the beginning, the Republican high command had realised that Franco could not just be allowed to wipe out the northern zone, not least because its heavy industry and plentiful mineral resources could not but greatly strengthen the Nationalist war effort. In an attempt to slow down the attacking forces, then, diversionary offensives had been launched against the enemy bastions of Segovia and Huesca, but these had achieved very little. Too late to do anything, though it was, to help Bilbao, the imperative to attack remained unchanged, and, in an effort to delay the impending attack on Santander and Asturias, the Madrid front was chosen for a fresh effort that would dwarf its predecessors. In principle, the idea was simple enough. Thus, the Nationalist troops holding the trench lines that snaked from the Cerro de los Angeles through the Casa de Campo and University City, and then lined the highway to La Coruña as far as the village of Las Rozas, occupied the leading edge of an immense salient that was perhaps 10 miles deep and 20 miles wide. With Madrid no longer the chief target of Franco's attentions, the troops holding the Nationalist lines were stretched thin, and they therefore constituted an obvious target: pinch off the salient, indeed, and Franco would be forced to turn his attentions back to a battleground of the Republicans' choosing (and one, be it said, whose physical proximity to the capital meant that it fitted in very well with the determination of the Communists – always the leading backers of the scheme – to prioritise their political objectives at the expense of virtually every other consideration). In brief, then, what was supposed to happen was that the flanks of the salient would be hit simultaneously by troops driving south from the area of El Escorial and west from the southern reaches of the River Jarama.[4]

In the event, this plan was modified: rather than being launched simultaneously, the two thrusts would rather be delivered sequentially in that the troops mustered for the offensive west of Madrid would strike first, the operation in the southern outskirts of the capital being delayed until such time as the former had reached the important road junction of Navalcarnero (presumably, it was hoped that by the time that Navalcarnero had been taken, the Nationalists would be so preoccupied with the fighting that they would have little left to deal with anything else). Everything, then, depended on the western thrust. Heavily reinforced, this was to be delivered by two entire corps, namely V Corps and XVIII Corps, of which the former was headed by Juan Modesto and the latter by Enrique Jurado Barrío, an artillery officer who had stayed loyal despite strong *africanista* antecedents and played a major role in defeating the uprising in Madrid. Each of these corps, meanwhile, had three divisions, no fewer than four of which – 11 (Lister), 15 (Galiscz), 35 (Walter) and 46 (González) – were billed as shock troops (included in their order of battle was not just Lister's old I Mixed Brigade, but also XI, XIII and XV International Brigades).[5] Supporting the attack were no fewer than 250 guns and some 170 tanks and armoured cars (by far the largest force of armoured vehicles the Republicans had ever assembled), while the Madrid area was the base for about 200 planes, true though it was that few of them were bombers or ground-attack aircraft.[6]

Impressive as the force concerned was, meanwhile, it is worth pointing out that the terrain was very much in its favour. Thus, in the sector chosen for the attack, a broad space of open country immediately to the west of the north-to-south course of the River Guadarrama, the Republican front line ran along the crest of a low ridge that shielded low ground behind it from view, low ground, moreover, that was in large part covered with open woods of pine and ilex which made it easy to hide the thousands of troops moving into the area from probing enemy planes. Nor were these the only advantages offered by Modesto and Jurado's start line, for the same ridge completely dominated the rolling plains to its south and therefore offered excellent positions for the Republican artillery. As for the space in which the brunt of the battle would necessarily be waged, this

A Republican T26 tank. Armed with a 45mm gun, the T26 was by far the most modern armoured fighting vehicle to see service in the Spanish Civil War, but it was never used to its full effect, and proved a grave disappointment to the British battalion at both the Battle of Jarama and the Battle of Brunete. (Wikimedia Commons)

was devoid of good defensive positions other than the small town of Brunete, a crossroads settlement some 10 miles to the south of the Republican start line, and the villages of Villanueva de la Cañada, Villanueva del Pardillo and Quijorna. The only possible difficulty lay in the fact that, to east and west alike, the plains that surrounded these settlements were overlooked by low hills which would provide excellent positions for troops posted to ensure that the Republicans did not extend the ground which they had taken on either flank, the result being that the attackers risked ending up trapped in a salient which would be wide open to enemy counter-attack and open throughout to enemy artillery fire, a salient, moreover, whose only line of communication was the country road that ran north–south from El Escorial to Brunete.

What, though, of the British battalion? Kept in the front line for weeks after the Battle of Jarama finally drew to a close, it had, along with the rest of XV International Brigade, missed out on the Battle of Guadalajara and eventually

The low ridge that sheltered the Republican forces prior to the Battle of Brunete. (author's collection)

been withdrawn to a village a few miles east of Madrid called Mondéjar for a period of much-needed rest and re-organisation. Large numbers of fresh volunteers who had been training at Madrigueras were incorporated into the ranks, and the balance – even with the new arrivals, there were only around 500 Britons – made up from Spanish volunteers who were all placed in a separate company under the command of one Antonio Escuadero. Meanwhile, the old Colts and Chauchats were replaced with better Russian weapons in the form of the brand-new Degtyarev light machine gun and the older but still perfectly serviceable Maxim-Tokarev, a First-World-War conversion of the M1910 comparable with a very similar conversion of the German Maxim M1908 that featured among the weapons that Hitler had supplied to the Nationalists. That said, it is by no means clear that the Tokarevs and Degtyarevs were issued at the same rate as was the norm in other armies of the period. Equally, if hand grenades seem to have been reasonably plentiful, there were as yet neither mortars nor infantry guns – ultra-light artillery pieces such as the French 37mm Puteaux SA18 – much though these were weapons that the First World War had proved to be vital in infantry combat.

Also heartening was the formation, albeit at brigade level, of a British-crewed anti-tank battery armed with three highly effective Russian anti-tank guns.[7] Jock Cunningham having been wounded during the battalion's spell in the trenches, command was in the hands of the redoubtable Fred Copeman, and he, at least, was on fine form. As he later wrote of the battalion's transfer by lorry from its temporary quarters in Mondéjar to a holding area in the vicinity of the town of Torrelodones:

> The Fifteenth International Brigade was well known to the military commanders as the finest fighting unit in the peninsula, and our battalion had never been in better shape. The political commissars were now in the ranks [an apparent reference to suggestions that the so-called 'comic stars' had hitherto had a tendency to cluster in the rear] … Company commanders were all picked men with front-line experience and accepted by all as leaders of the highest calibre. Our journey to the front was one of the most pleasant of the entire campaign … The concerts, sing-songs and other entertainments at night proved the state of morale: many were the times when a

Members of the British-crewed XV Brigade anti-tank battery with one of its Russian 45mm guns. (Marx Memorial Library, London)

thousand men, including groups from a dozen nationalities, would sit round listening to the singing of a dozen Welsh miners. This action was to be a success – so we thought. We had tanks in numbers … never seen before … [and] guns bigger than any visualised … seemed to be plentiful, and the air force … flew over during the day, ensuring that no enemy spotter planes came within a hundred miles.[8]

Among the rank and file, meanwhile, there seems to have been a general mood of hope and expectation.[9] If the many new recruits were less than amenable to the parade-ground drill and other forms of generally rather unimpressive instruction to which they were subjected prior to joining the battalion, they were at the very least full of bravado, their thinking being exemplified by a new arrival from London named Fred Thomas. Thus: 'Our place was at the front with rifle in hand. Our self-discipline would show itself superior to the fear-inspired discipline of other armies, certainly to that of Franco. This was no time to be playing at soldiers.'[10] Here, too, we can cite a letter home that was hastily penned by a Welshman named Frank Owen, 'With a smashing victory to the Spanish Republic by the time you get this, you will have read of the big offensive. From now on it is to be war as it should be: Franco is not prepared for the reception that is being prepared for him, and … our side will leave very little quarter to the fascists.'[11] Equally excited was Ulsterman Sid Quinn, 'This was a different kettle of fish altogether: we had more troops than ever before … We thought this had to be the end of the bloody war.'[12] Finally, watching the Republican forces move off from the hospital to which she was attached at Torrelodones was 'Penny' (in reality Ada) Phelps, a slum-girl from Tottenham who had managed to secure training as a nurse, 'Troops moved up to the attack scheduled for the following day, tramping quietly past our building and singing while they marched … It was marvellous, the tramp-tramp and the sound of soft singing through the night … a deeply emotional experience'.[13]

Facing the imposing forces put together by the Republican high command, meanwhile, were no more than 3,000 men. Indeed, there was not even a front line properly speaking, but rather simply the loose chain of fortified strongpoints represented by Quijorna, Villanueva de la Cañada and Villanueva del Pardillo and a low hill by the name of Llanos, each of which was held only by two or three companies of infantry. Still worse, most of the defenders were Falangist militia, the only decent troops in the whole area being a single battalion of Tiradores de Ifni (Moorish infantrymen who prior to July 1936 had served as the garrison of the tiny Spanish enclave of Ifni in the south-west of present-day Morocco). When the attack went in at dawn on 6 July, it should therefore have been overwhelmingly successful, and at first all did, indeed, seem to go smoothly enough. Lacking in firepower, the Republican chief of staff, Vicente Rojo, had eschewed any form of preliminary bombardment – a decision that was to be a feature of all five of the great Republic offensives launched between July 1937 and January 1939 – and plumped instead for a silent approach that sought to outflank the scattered enemy positions and insert large forces of troops deep inside enemy territory under cover of darkness.[14] Attached to Galiscz's 15 Division, XV International Brigade was deployed on the left flank of the Republican array as part of Modesto's V Corps, though initially it was held back in reserve. In command, meanwhile, was the brigade's erstwhile political commissar, Vladimir Copic, a Croat veteran of the First World War who, like Stern and Galiscz, had been taken prisoner in Russia, turned Bolshevik and become a Red-Army general, though the fact that the brigade had increased from four to six battalions in the wake of Jarama meant that it had had to be split into two 'regiments' of which the one containing the British battalion had been given to a Jock Cunningham currently being lauded as the 'Spanish Chapayev' by the leadership of the Communist Party of Great Britain.[15]

Very quickly, however, the plan miscarried. By midday Lister had reached Brunete with his leading troops, but, closer to the old front line, real problems were developing in that the grievous faults in the People's Army's leadership and training were becoming cruelly apparent.[16] Coming under fire from the scattered Nationalist positions, many soldiers took cover and refused to advance any further, while their officers frequently showed a woeful lack of initiative and enterprise, the whole plan in consequence starting to stagnate. As cautious as ever, meanwhile, the tanks and armoured cars hung back, restricting themselves to firing at the enemy positions from long range. Watching the scene from the rear was Fred Thomas, who had eventually been posted to XV International Brigade's anti-tank battery:

> Seven a.m. On top of the world … Down in the plain are villages held by the fascists, and these our side has got to take. From just behind us, our artillery is blowing hell out of the villages: this is big stuff shaking the ground … Eight a.m.: moved up another half mile; from here we have an almost bird's-eye view. Immediately in front of our sector is a village … Villanueva de la Cañada, a mile or so away, which our troops are attacking … About twenty-five of our tanks are closing in … Our artillery has stopped. Troops can be seen behind the tanks … Horrible sight watching one … go up in flames: I hope the occupants were killed first. Nine a.m.: our artillery starting up again; tanks holding back a bit; can see smoke and hear firing from villages to right and left. Twelve noon: village not yet taken apparently … We are still waiting for orders.[17]

Given that Villanueva de la Cañada was held by nothing more than an incomplete battalion of Falangist militia, two anti-tank guns and two 75mm field guns, this performance was hardly inspiring. Afterwards Lister was particularly hard on the use made of the tanks. In his words:

> The manner in which the tanks and armoured cars was used could not have been more lamentable. For all its … strength and capacity for manoeuvre, the force which they represented … was employed in the most foolish of manners: there is no other word for it. They were just thrown straight at the guns, when beyond them stretched ground which offered the most wonderful opportunities to armoured forces.[18]

On one level, this is true enough, but the fact is that the bulk of the Republican infantry was so poor that, without armoured support, they could not be relied on to make head against determined opposition, this being a problem that was experienced by the British battalion just as much as it was by any of its fellow units. In the late morning, then, Copeman and his men were sent in to finish the job at Villanueva de la Cañada, their first objective being to take up a position blocking the road from Brunete. As Copeman remembered:

> We soon reached the flat cornfields. No English hedges here, no cover: a perfect carpet for military manoeuvres, but not good ground to attack on. Almost immediately three artillery shells landed: Alec Cummings' company had five killed and seven wounded … Heavy anti-tank and machine-gun fire was concentrated on us as we tore forward … Speed was the big thing here: once we reached the road, we should have the cover of dry ditches on either side … A burst from the Degtyarevs … and we were there.[19]

One man who had made the dash in safety was Walter Gregory:

> With the road cut, we began a cautious advance towards the village itself … As we drew closer we were subjected to a murderous hail of machine-gun fire … I threw myself into a road-side ditch and began to crawl on all fours towards the village … It was the very devil fighting in that heat with no protection from the sun's searing rays. Accurate shooting was impossible because everything was shimmering … All day we stayed in that ditch, ducking down

Republican infantry sprint for the shelter offered by a small Spanish village. (Wikimedia Commons)

low whenever a machine-gun swung in our direction and sprayed us with bullets, popping up as soon as it had traversed away and firing back with every weapon at our disposal. It was an awfully long day.[20]

If the ditches referred to by Copeman and Gregory certainly helped, they were scarcely the safest of refuges. Sid Quinn recalled:

The sun was beating down – God, it was warm! – [and] we were really thirsty. We had already taken a lot of casualties … My friend, Jones, from Belfast, was there: I saw him lying down, shot through the mouth, and could do nothing about it. He was quite phlegmatic about it – knew it was no good – so I just turned him over to make him more comfortable and he died.[21]

The unfortunate Jones was not alone. Having survived Jarama and temporarily been posted to the headquarters of the International Brigades at Albacete, James Prendergast passed through the area a day or two later in the company of Frank Ryan: 'Along the road from Villanueva to Brunete we came across rows and rows of bodies, many with their names pinned on slips of paper. Many of them were British lads. I remember one who had been a Labour councillor at home clutching, of all things, a dead rabbit.'[22]

If some of the volunteers beyond doubt showed great courage, this was no way to win a battle: apart from anything else, with the tank crews understandably extremely concerned by the Nationalist anti-tank guns, they could hardly be expected to move in to finish the job from close quarters.[23] As a result of such factors, although they were completely surrounded, the three villages were able to hold out for far longer than had been expected – Villanueva de la Cañada was taken some time before midnight on 7 July, but Quijorna continued to resist until 9 July and Villanueva del Pardillo for a day longer still[24] – while Republican attempts to expand the breakthrough were uniformly unsuccessful. Almost literally see Navalcarnero though they could, Lister and his men did not dare advance any further for fear that they would end up being cut off. Though the Communist commander is very obviously a partisan voice, his general conclusions cannot really be questioned:

> 11 Division occupied Brunete at six o'clock in the morning on 6 July. A single battalion continued on to Sevilla la Nueva and one company even got as far as the outskirts of Navalcarnero. The enemy front was broken, and our forces more than ten kilometres inside their lines. What would have been the right thing to do in this situation? Surround Villanueva de la Cañada with one brigade and Quijorna with another and send all the rest of the forces of V Corps through the gap opened by 11 Divison … What actually happened? For the whole day of 6 July, 34 Division did nothing but launch frontal attacks on Villanueva de la Cañada, losing many men and ten tanks in the process … Two desperate days passed by … I begged for reinforcements … until I was utterly frantic, but not a word did I get in response, and yet all that time … men and resources were being thrown away in stupid frontal attacks.[25]

Following the capture of Villanueva de la Cañada, meanwhile, the British had been ordered to push on to capture a ridge some distance to the south-east blocking the way to the same Boadilla del Monte where so many of Esmond Romilly's comrades had fallen in December, the route that had to be followed roughly paralleling the course of the River Aulencia, a tributary of the River Guadarrama that flowed into it a little north of the road from Brunete to Boadilla. Progress, however, was at best limited, not least because, thoroughly exhausted and denuded of some of its leading cadres – of the company commanders, Bob Meredith was dead and Alec Cummings badly wounded, another loss being company commissar George Brown – the battalion did not even get moving till the afternoon. Here, once again, is Fred Copeman:

> By now, our 600 had dwindled to about 350. Compared with Jarama the casualties were light: Joe Hinks assured me that quite a number of the missing were deserters, which later proved to be true; we must have lost about 100 men in this way. Our plan was to follow the course of a dry river bed with three sections deployed on either side of it. To get to the river, it would be necessary to cross some three miles of broken ground. The corn had been cut … and I prayed we'd pass this open ground before any bombing started.[26]

The track followed by the British battalion during its advance from Villanueva de la Cañada to the bridge over the River Guadarrama. (Antonio Requena)

The eastern part of the battlefield of Brunete viewed from the slopes crossed by the British battalion in the final stages of their advance; the ridge that marked the front line at the start of the battle is clearly visible. (Antonio Requena)

The slope up which the British battalion advanced after crossing the River Guadarrama during the Battle of Brunete; the volunteers advanced in the direction of the camera. (Antonio Requena)

In the event the battalion reached the vicinity of the ridge unscathed though not without a narrow escape when a flight of Nationalist bombers struck the newly formed George Washington battalion a few hundred yards ahead.[27] By the time that they got into position, it was late afternoon, but the weary men of the British battalion nevertheless made a serious effort to press on. Crossing the all but dried-up River Guadarrama just to the north of the road from Brunete to Boadilla, the volunteers advanced up the scrub-covered slopes beyond with the other two units of their 'regiment' – the American Abraham Lincoln and George Washington battalions – on their right on the other side of the highway. However, they were too late: whereas as late as the evening of 7 July the area had been all but undefended, it was now held by five companies of infantry – the VII Tabor de Regulares de Ceuta, a single company of the VII Tabor de Regulares de Tetuán and two companies of the Canarias infantry regiment; in support, meanwhile, were several 37mm anti-tank guns, a battery of 75mm field guns and three batteries of heavy artillery.[28] What happened next is recounted by Copeman:

The ridgeline which defied every effort of the British battalion during the Battle of Brunete.
(Antonio Requena)

Three tanks passed us. I thought, 'At least we've got ... support.'
I had spoken too soon. With a chug and a grunt, the leading one
stopped: it could not make the hill ... An enemy anti-tank battery
was covering the approaches. The rebels seemed to have got the
range and three-pounder shells were exploding dangerously close to
us ... There was an extra-sharp crack ... and I looked round to find
Charlie Goodfellow's brains spread over my shoulder: his head was
blown off less than three feet away from me; I hadn't a scratch ...
The opposition was getting tougher, and we made ground at a rate
of 100 yards an hour. Not so good: if we didn't reach the summit
by nightfall, the concentration of fire would be too heavy by the
morning ... Our position ... was terribly open. Casualties began to
mount. Sam Wild arrived with some ammunition: we were standing
talking with two or three others, when suddenly three of them
fell in a line; one bullet had passed through all of them ... A few
moments later ... Bob Elliott got one straight through the centre of
his forehead.[29]

The loss of Goodfellow and Elliott was particularly serious as the former was
Copeman's second-in-command and the latter a company commissar, another
loss among this last group being Alec McDade, a Scotsman who, somewhat
uncharacteristically for a Communist apparatchik, had a reputation for jovial
good humour. Casualties among the rank and file, meanwhile, included Albert
Charlesworth, who was caught in the face by shards of rock flung up by a bullet.[30]
As for the position of the British battalion, it was little short of desperate. 'The
shell fire at this point was very concentrated', remembered Hugh Sloan. 'There
was nothing but dead men and dead mules rotting in the sun. The smell of death
was unbearable. The decapitated body of a man lay with a board on his chest:
I looked around, but I couldn't find his head.'[31] Here and there were displays of
insouciance, indeed, even heroism – Sid Quinn, for example, noticed a notoriously
dapper fellow volunteer calmly shaving himself with the aid of a pocket mirror in
the midst of a series of explosions[32] – but progress was there none, and that despite
the fact that the official Nationalist history of the battle speaks of the ridgeline
being subjected to no fewer than five separate assaults.[33]

For the wounded, meanwhile, the situation was as bad as it had been at Jarama,
if not worse. In the words of Welshman Alun Williams:

There was no water at Brunete ... and no organization to bring up
water either. The only water we had was in our water bottles ...
The dressing station was ... at the bottom in a river bed. There 40–50

The remains of a complex of entrenchments beside the bridge that carried the road from Brunete to Villaviciosa de Odón across the River Guadarrama; it was here that volunteers who were wounded in the fighting on the slopes above were carried to await evacuation. (Antonio Requena)

fellows, badly wounded, were laid out. The cry was 'Water!' A lot died and there was nowhere ... and no-one to bury them.[34]

Yet, suffer though the wounded did, things were difficult for the whole battalion. One unidentified volunteer wrote:

Rations and water were a problem. Down from our positions into the valley and up the hillside behind us ran the line of communications. It was raked night and day by snipers and machine-guns, artillery and aviation. Yet the ration parties ran the gauntlet, using mules when they could be used, and, when these were killed, running, ducking, stumbling down the hillside, laden with sacks of grub ... The boys in the trenches could see them coming ... and laid bets on whether they would get through.[35]

To say that the fight was one-sided is an understatement. Deployed on the low rise overlooking the far bank of the Guadarrama, the three guns of the brigade anti-tank battery provided such support as they could, but they were subjected to such heavy shelling and machine-gun fire that they were repeatedly silenced and lost a third of their crew. To the south of the road, meanwhile, the two American battalions were pinned down in exactly the same fashion as their British comrades, the result being that their objective – a hill named Mosquito that constituted the highest point of the ridge – remained in the hands of the enemy. Finally, as for digging in, instead of proper trenches, all that could be managed were shallow ditches that gave little protection to the men even when they were lying flat. In brief, then, it was a second Suicide Hill. Unable to endure the unequal struggle any more, after two days a Copeman so traumatised and over-wrought that he was immediately evacuated to the rear therefore led the surviving volunteers back across the river. For this he was to pay deeply, the Communist leadership attempting to scapegoat him on the grounds of cowardice and lack of moral fibre. There was, however, nothing wrong with his assessment of the situation. Out of an initial 650 men, just 185 were left in the line, many even of these last casualties who had hastily been patched up and sent back to the battalion; the offensive was clearly at a standstill; and, to cap it all, as he later wrote, trying to keep the fight going on the basis of a single narrow country road was akin to 'holding a ton of coal by a thread of cotton – an impossible thing to do'.[36]

However, the battle was not just at a standstill but going into reverse. Much bolstered by the arrival of fresh troops from elsewhere, including the northern front, on 18 July, the Nationalist forces launched a powerful counter-attack.[37] In the face of this onslaught, the Republicans resisted with considerable determination, and the fighting was so intense that even on the Nationalist side of the lines the tension was stretched to breaking point.[38] Yet such was the superiority of the forces deployed against them that the Republicans were pushed back until all that was left in their hands was what little remained of Quijorna, Villanueva de la Canãda and Villanueva de Pardillo.[39]

Among the troops facing the Nationalist onslaught was the mere cadre to which the British battalion had now been reduced. Somewhat revived by four days' rest in the vicinity of Villanueva de la Cañada, the volunteers were now split into two ad hoc companies under Joe Hinks, who had begun the battle as commander of the machine-gun company, and the newly appointed and much liked political commissar, Walter Tapsell. Though wounded in the arm earlier in the battle, Walter Gregory had returned to the fighting line: 'The battalion received a terrible battering. The suffering from the heat and thirst was dreadful … Day after day the sun beat remorselessly down, the dust clutched at our throats, the flies drove us wild, and our losses crept inexorably upwards.'[40] What finally broke the battalion, however, was not so much the pounding it was receiving as the situation that developed on its flanks. Thus, on the evening of 23 July the unit next in line to the north – XIII International Brigade – broke and ran, while the next day saw repeated Nationalist attacks drive Lister from the ruins of Brunete, thereby exposing the British volunteers to attack from the rear and forcing Hinks and Tapsell to stage a fighting retreat up the valley of the River Aulencia in the direction of Villanueva de la Cañada.[41] Writing for the *Book of the XV Brigade*, Tapsell produced a long account of the withdrawal of which the following quote is but a highlight:

> We sent the wounded back and took what cover there was. The fascists rushed from the right to outflank us. The young Spaniards with me beat them off. They tried again: again we turned them back ... Our guns were red-hot with incessant fire. Yet it was only a question of time ... Our danger was that we would be outflanked as ... our force was too small to cover ... much territory ... There was only one thing to be done: to get up on the hills behind and establish contact with whatever troops had been on our flanks and get them to reform the line with us ... Luck came our way when we found two machine-gunners, one German and the other French. We put one on each flank. At 6 p.m. a company of Moors tried to cut us off on the right ... The German gunner mowed them down in heaps. We moved back to another hill. This time the attack was on the left and the French gunner did his bit ... It was perilous work steering our little band back, trying to ensure maximum cover, stopping every few yards to engage the enemy and keep his fire down, but we made it and eventually arrived at good cover behind a long hill-crest.[42]

Reduced to a mere handful – by the time it reached Villanueva, the battalion had just forty-two men left under arms – on 25 July the British were withdrawn from the battle, but even then their travails were not at an end, for, to the horror of all concerned, three days later orders arrived from Galiscz to the effect that they should resume their positions in the front line. There are, however, limits beyond which even the most fervent Communists cannot be pushed, the response of the exhausted and much tried survivors therefore being a unanimous refusal to move. What would have happened next is hard to say, but in the event the Nationalist assault that had precipitated the incident failed to materialise, a fact which enabled Galiscz to back down with reasonable grace.[43]

Thus ended the Battle of Brunete. By the time fighting came to an end on 25 July, over 20,000 Republican troops had been killed or wounded, while losses in terms of aircraft were probably about 50 (in this respect, the fact

A dead Republican machine-gunner. The Battle of Brunete dealt the British battalion a blow from which it never recovered. (Wikimedia Commons)

that the fighter pilots of the Condor Legion were now fully equipped with the Messerschmidt Me109 was decisive, the Nationalists, by contrast, losing just 17 aircraft). As for the British battalion, it had suffered about 400 casualties, including many of its most committed Party cadres, another British loss being the indomitable and ever immaculately uniformed George Nathan, the some-time Scots Guard having been felled by a fragment from a Nationalist bomb while serving on the staff of XIV International Brigade. The British battalion would never be the same again, while, for the Republican cause as a whole, the whole affair had turned into a disaster of the first magnitude: setting aside the fact that the offensive had not succeeded in delaying Nationalist operations in the north for more than a couple of weeks, losses of the sort incurred by the troops that had fought at Brunete simply could not be sustained. As for the performance of the Republic's soldiers, Spanish and foreign alike, it had been uniformly dismal, while the British battalion had done no better than anyone else, its failure to rush the weakly defended village of Villanueva de la Cañada when it had got into a position where it could attack the garrison from the rear constituting an episode that was particularly damning. Committed Communists could whistle all they liked, then, but it would now ever be a case of whistling in the dark. For a particularly damning verdict, we have only to turn to George Hills. Thus, 'The Battle of Brunete was over ... The Nationalists had brought into the battle eighty-seven battalions, the Republicans 119; the Nationalists ... 170 guns against 217; [the Nationalists] some sixty armoured vehicles against 100; and [the Nationalists again] 120 aircraft against 200'.[44]

The Battlefield Today

The battlefield of Brunete is one that is at one and the same time both bitterly disappointing and deeply rewarding. On the one hand the key settlements, including most importantly Villanueva de la Cañada, are completely unrecognisable from the isolated Castilian *pueblos* of 1937, having been not just rebuilt, but transformed into prosperous commuter communities, but, on the other, the basic configuration of the area's geography is not much altered: in 2020 as in 1937 the visitor is confronted by immense vistas in which seeming endless expanses of wheat are interspersed with large patches of scrubby Spanish woodland. That said, the eastern fringes of the battlefield in particular have been heavily infringed upon by new up-market housing estates.

In so far as the experiences of the British battalion are concerned, these are best followed in chronological fashion, the first point to head for being the ridge over which the Republican forces advanced at the beginning of the battle. Assuming that the visitor is in the centre of Madrid, this is best reached by taking the M503 from its start on the M500 south-west of the city centre and from there heading west in the direction of Valdemorillo. At Junction 24, fork right onto the M853 (signposted Urbanización Puente la Sierra) and at a staggered crossroads turn right onto an unnumbered road and head northwards until a bridge is reached crossing the River Aulencia at the El Molino hiking area. At the T-junction beyond the bridge, turn right and follow the road until it makes a sharp turn to the left: XV Brigade assembled for battle along the continuation of the same road as it climbs out of the valley from said turn.

Starting from this point, the visitor can now trace the first part of the British battalion's advance by returning to the junction with the M853. In 1937 the volunteers would have followed the continuation of the same track in the direction of Villanueva, but the construction of various new roads has closed off this route, and so it is best to follow the M853 back to the M503 at Junction 24. At said junction turn south (signposted Villanueva) and follow the road to the roundabout. At the roundabout take the second exit and head straight on. After a short distance, a second roundabout will be encountered at which point take the second exit and join the M600 (signposted Villanueva), this being the old road northwards and therefore the route that would have been followed by the British battalion.

At the roundabout at the northern edge of the built-up area go straight on and head for the town centre along the Calle Real. After perhaps a mile the Plaza de España marks what was in 1937 the centre of the village and with it the much-reconstructed parish church and town hall, both of which look much the same as they would have done at the time of the battle. Unfortunately, the massive growth in the size of Villanueva means that the open ground over which the Republicans had to attack is now completely lost, but some sense of it may be obtained in the course of the next leg of the tour. Thus, continue south through the village until the M600 is reached once more (it was approximately at this spot that the British battalion was pinned down during its attack on the village). At the roundabout turn left onto the Avenida de la Dehesa and circle back to the north until a large roundabout is reached in the centre of which, somewhat bizarrely, is the village cemetery, this being a spot that saw fierce fighting during the course of the battle.

Though rather tortuous, the route that follows is that followed by the British battalion on its advance on the River Guadarrama. At the roundabout turn right onto the Avenida de Madrid (after a short distance this becomes the Camino de las Carretas). Continue for some miles first eastwards and then more and more southwards through a stretch of ilex woodland identical to the terrain of 1937 until the road reaches a T-junction. At this spot turn left. Very soon there is a second T-junction. Turn right and continue southwards for a short distance and take the first turning on the left. Very soon this road turns south and runs beside the River Guadarrama. Keep going southwards ignoring all turn-offs until a fourth T-junction is reached, this time with the M513 (the high ground on the right marks the position occupied by the anti-tank battery: this may be reached by taking the first track on the right and heading uphill away from the river). Turn left, cross the river and very shortly afterwards turn left onto an unnumbered road and then immediately right onto a second such road which climbs up out of the valley, this road marking the general line of the British battalion's advance towards the crest of the ridge. After a mile or more a large wheatfield will be observed on the right: the position where the British battalion was checked followed the latter's edge and then curved back to the left shortly before the route which the visitor is following reaches a T-junction with another un-numbered road. At the T-junction turn left and follow the road north and then west until it reaches a second T-junction: the area to the right saw the other half of XV Brigade make an equally fruitless advance on the hill to the north-east. At the T-junction turn left and return to the M503 at the same point at which it was left.

To complete the tour, turn right onto the M513. After some miles the road reaches the outskirts of Brunete. At the junction with the M600, drive on into the town centre and park on one of the streets lining the municipal park. A few yards to the north will be found the Plaza Mayor, a classic example of post-Civil-War neo-'imperial' architecture (so named because it was modelled on that of the 'Golden Age' of the sixteenth century) adorned with both numerous symbols of the Franco regime and plaques commemorating the Nationalist victory. Just beyond the Plaza Mayor, meanwhile, is the parish church: rebuilt after the war, this is nonetheless still heavily pockmarked with the impacts of rifle and machine-gun bullets.

From Brunete drive northwards up the M600 to the roundabout with the M503. Some distance north of the village, the visitor will encounter a number of concrete bunkers: like all the other pill boxes and other fortifications that can be seen on the battlefield, these date from after the battle, but they are nonetheless worth pausing at as they mark the furthest point reached by the Nationalist counter-offensive.

Given that the battlefield is so extensive, it is one that is hard to explore for those dependent on public transport. However, Brunete is served by frequent buses from Madrid's Moncloa bus station and these follow the M513, thereby giving the visitor direct access to the Mosquito area.

Chapter 5

The Battle of Belchite

There can be no doubt that Brunete marks a pivotal moment in the history of the International Brigades. In the first place, the heavy losses suffered in the offensive coincided with a crisis in the recruitment situation. As news spread of the brutal reality of the Civil War and the ranks of the most determined, brave and politically militant were drained, so the flow of recruits steadily declined. Exactly what the impact of this development on the quality of the International Brigades was is hard to assess – on the one hand, a continued willingness to come forward could be assumed to reflect a particularly high level of commitment, but, on the other, it seems clear that, desperate to get any men they could, Communist-Party recruiters increasingly turned a blind eye to physical defects, while at the same time asking fewer questions in respect of the political reliability of the men who came before them and leaning ever harder on Party militants to sign up – but on the whole the effects were probably negative. All too typical was a group of men who arrived in Catalonia in December 1937, including, not least, the noted writer Laurie Lee. In charge was a veteran of the Irish Republican Army named Bob Doyle. As the latter reported:

> I will say of the whole group, only about six of them may be loyal; the rest I class as [being] opportunists and adventurers. They may [turn out] alright, but they need a lot of lecturing, particularly on morale (they don't know what it means). This is the best report I can give: in plain words … the group is a disgrace.[1]

Meanwhile, if three friends from St Helens who reached Spain in the course of the autumn were all workers committed to the fight against Franco, one of them, a certain Jim Johnson, had immediately to be sent home when it was discovered that a serious heart ailment had been missed (or, possibly, simply ignored) in the course of his enlistment.[2] Finally, even before Brunete, the battalion had been burdened with a man named Sam Parkes whom a fellow combatant remembered as a simpleton – 'one of many who should not have been allowed to go to

Spain' – who openly admitted that 'he had been out of work a long time before volunteering ... [and] that he had no idea what it was about'.[3] Accept such men as Johnson, Parkes or, for that matter, Laurie Lee (an epileptic) though the Party did, however, nothing could be done in respect of the shortage of numbers, the ranks of all the battalions in the XV Brigade, and, indeed, all the other foreign battalions as well, having henceforth to be made up with ever larger numbers of Spaniards, and a complete Spanish battalion added to its order of battle, dressed up though this was with a small cadre of Latin-American volunteers, most of them Cuban.[4]

According to Communist stalwarts, the incorporation of large numbers of Spaniards into the International Brigades was a great success. Bill Alexander, some-time commander of the British battalion, wrote:

> As was well known, the International Brigades had been involved in nearly all the bloodiest fighting. However, the first drafts of Spaniards to join them were all volunteers from other units of the Republican army. This demonstrated not only the courage and conviction of the Spanish volunteers themselves, but also the affection and respect which the Internationals had already gained among most of the Spanish people ... After August 1937 the Spanish brothers-in-arms who fought shoulder-to-shoulder with the British ... formed the majority of the battalion's effectives. Without their courage, high morale and combative qualities, the British battalion would have been able to achieve little.[5]

This, however, is little short of nonsense, not the least of the problems being that the supply of volunteers was soon exhausted. Thus, assigned to train some of the Spanish recruits, Walter Gregory paints a very different picture; as he says, indeed, 'The Spanish lads were simple peasants. Few of them had been to school or ... seen, let alone held, a rifle.'[6] To quote Aberdonian John Londragon, meanwhile, 'They were very child-like. I don't use the word in an insulting way ... They had never been involved in war before and had known nothing about it at all.'[7] In short, very soon, all that the battalion was getting was raw conscripts, and not just that but men who were not always friendly to the Communist line. As Edinburgh volunteer John Dunlop complained:

> Initially the Spaniards who were attached to the battalion didn't come from an Anarchist background. However, we did now get groups of Anarchists because Anarchist battalions were being broken up because of their unsatisfactory record ... They were not prepared to accept discipline ... and it was quite a problem to make them understand

why … in military matters anyway, orders had to be obeyed. The other point they jibbed about was singing *The Internationale*. They said, 'Why do we have to sing *The Internationale*? After all, *The Internationale* is not a Spanish song. It is not the Anarchist song. It is the … Communist song. Why should we have to sing it?'[8]

If the men coming out from Britain were few in numbers and less and less suitable for the demands of combat and the Spaniards in reality little more than unwilling make-weights, the battalion whose ranks they joined was a force whose morale had fallen to zero. Ever since the Battle of Jarama, the rank and file had been seething with an undercurrent of disaffection fuelled by a number of factors including the poor food, the many weeks the battalion had endured in the trenches in the wake of the repulse of the Nationalist offensive, the lack of leave and the realisation that, once a man was in Spain, he was there for good, and that despite the promises many volunteers claimed to have received to the effect that they would be repatriated after six or nine months' service.[9] Added to these grumbles was the discontent stoked up even among loyal Party members by the Communists' management of the International Brigades. For example, the South-African sculptor Jason Gurney (admittedly, a non-Communist) was convalescing from a wound he had received on the Jarama front in April at the International Brigades' base at Albacete when he found himself being addressed by Harry Pollitt, the Secretary-General of the Communist Party of Great Britain:

> I had never seen Pollitt at close quarters before. He was a smallish, balding individual with small dark eyes that looked as though he had never smiled in his life … We had been warned that he was coming to see us and everybody was full of the expectation that he would bring a message of encouragement and joy. On the contrary: he had evidently come down with the express purpose of bawling us out. The general line of the argument was that we needn't think that, just because we had served in the battalion and been wounded, anybody owed us anything. Quite the reverse, we had been given this opportunity to serve in this glorious cause and that should be enough for anyone … Let us not think that we were in the vanguard of the revolutionary struggle. Far from it: we were merely the raw material, while the real revolutionary workers slaved night and day in the Party offices to bring about the millenium.[10]

If he was unimpressed by Pollitt, Gurney positively despised the Comintern functionaries who staffed the base at Albacete, an operation that was at this moment absorbing the attentions of no fewer than 3,657 of the 10,015 foreigners who were all that was left to the Brigades.[11] As he complained, 'Albacete, at this time, was full of party bureaucrats of all shapes and sizes. They were immediately recognisable by their black leather jackets, Sam-Browne belts with large automatic pistols and huge black berets.'[12] One man who was particularly hated, meanwhile, was the supreme head of the International Brigades' *apparat*, André Marty, a ruthless individual who boasted that he had as many as 500 volunteers executed for desertion and other crimes. A particularly obstreperous human being, Fred Copeman eventually broke all ties with the Communist Party, but there is no reason to doubt his assessment of Marty. Thus, 'Marty ... was a bloody madman if ever there was one. He just got an idea and carried it out and dabbled in everything. His idea of discipline was to court-martial and shoot you.'[13]

Only slightly less unpopular than the Party apparatchiks who thronged Albacete, meanwhile, were the political commissars, of which there was one to each company, battalion and brigade, staunch Communists whose task it was to preach the party line, watch out for treason and, at least in theory, attend to the welfare of the men.[14] As the Scottish volunteer John Dunlop remembered:

> Commissars were probably about the most highly-paid people in the battalion. Once they became commissars, they all seemed to go and get themselves those high-legged boots which nobody else seemed to wear ... There was quite a feeling among certain of the rank and file against commissars. In fact, the boots they wore seemed to excite either the anger or the envy of a lot of people, considering that most of us had to wear just any kind of footwear we could get hold of.[15]

As to whether such men had any positive effect, loyal Communists, of course, were unstinting in their praise, and, to the extent that the commissars were able and willing to procure better supplies of food and cigarettes, take complaints up the chain of command and offer a listening ear to men who were homesick and miserable, they may have done some good. Equally, if some of their counterparts in other battalions were as bloodthirsty in their methods as André Marty, from Aitken onwards no British commissar was prepared to tolerate execution except in the most extreme of circumstances, the general line that they followed rather being to seek to persuade offenders of the errors of their ways; more than that, indeed, at least some of them were genuinely personable individuals who took the 'welfare' side of their appointments very seriously. However, even the most decent of them were fixated on correct political education, the constant lecturing and discussion sessions that resulted being something that was widely loathed even by men who were loyal Party members, one volunteer later stating that it was his firm belief that all [the commissars] achieved was 'to get our backs up'.[16]

Thus far, we have looked at the numerous structural problems that plagued the British battalion. However, the summer of 1937 found them affected by a number of issues that are better described as being situational. In the wake of Brunete, morale among the British volunteers was at a low ebb. According to Walter Gregory, there were just 42 men left of the 300 who had set out for the battle and, of these, only 24 were fit for service.[17] Typical enough was the fate that had befallen four close friends – John Roberts from Abertridw, Richard Bird from Hammersmith, Leo Price from Abertillery and Frank Owen from Mardy: by the end of the first day of the battle, Bird and Owen were dead and Price badly wounded, the only one of the four to come though the ordeal unscathed being Roberts.[18] As can be imagined, then, the general mood was anything but good. 'On our return to Mondejar', wrote Walter Gregory, 'a number of meetings,

A typical group of British volunteers; the figure dressed in a beret and leather jacket in the centre of photograph is Sam Wild, the erstwhile boatswain's mate in the Royal Navy who became the last commander of the British battalion. (Department of Special Collections, University of Swansea)

organised by the battalion's political commissar [i.e. Walter Tapsell], were held at which we tried to assess the events … of our offensive at Brunete … We blamed Hitler, we blamed Mussolini, we blamed the non-intervention committee and we blamed ourselves for making mistakes.'[19] This account, however, is beyond doubt extremely sugar-coated, the real state of affairs being suggested by a searing row that had broken out among the leadership. On the one side were those whose faith in the Party's omnisicience had been sufficiently shaken by the defeat to lay the blame on the high command, Tapsell, for example, claiming of the long struggle on the high ground above the Guadarrama that 'only stupidity or a deliberate disregard for life would keep men in such an exposed position' and, further, that Galiscz was unfit 'to command a troop of Brownies, let alone a people's army'.[20] Ranged alongside Tapsell were Cunningham, the acting battalion commander, Joe Hinks, and the ever pugnacious Copeman, while on the other side were, predictably enough, Galiscz and a variety of officials with posts at brigade headquarters or elsewhere in the Communist *apparat*, including, not least George Aitken, the line taken by these worthies being that blame for the defeat lay further down the chain of command and that Tapsell and his fellows were both mentally over-wrought and suffering from 'rank-and-file tendencies'. So ferocious was the dispute that the leading protagonists were called back to England for a meeting of the CPGB's politbureau which saw Pollitt attempt to come up with a compromise solution whereby Cunningham and Aitken were dismissed from their positions and barred from returning to Spain, Copeman and Tapsell confirmed in their posts and XV International Brigade transferred from Galiscz's 45 Division to 35 Division, a formation commanded by Karol Swierczewski, aka Walter, yet another Habsburg turned Bolshevik.[21]

In fairness to Pollitt, there was some sense in his decisions respecting his warring subordinates in that Cunningham had shown himself to be out of his depth as anything higher than a battalion commander – according to David Hooper, for example, 'We soon found out Cunningham was no soldier. He was also full of bull-shit … [and] tried everything to get his Scottish pals into key positions as officers … Aitken took the can … time after time for his mistakes.'[22] – while the initially well-liked Aitken had of late made himself very unpopular by affecting a variety of unbecoming airs and graces – but they yet pleased no one. Thus while, some of the volunteers regarded Copeman as dangerously unstable and Tapsell as a defeatist and therefore remained bitterly opposed to their reinstatement, others liked Cunningham tremendously and believed he had been treated as a scapegoat.[23] For those inclined to side with Tapsell and Cunningham, meanwhile, there came a further blow in that, alarmed at the large numbers of valuable cadres that they were losing in Spain, the Communist hierarchy made use of the turmoil to shift a number of trusties from front-line positions to ones that were less dangerous.[24]

At all events, the mood of the battalion did not improve: at least one-third of the men who had survived the battle deserted over the course of the summer, while even staunch Communists found themselves questioning the value of fighting on. Here, for example, is Sydney Quinn, a long-standing Scottish militant who had been involved in the 'hunger-march' movement:

> It was after Brunete that I decided the war was hopeless. I was asked if I would like to go on leave and do some propaganda work at home and I decided I'd go. There were hardly any of us left from that original party which fought at Lopera. It was very disconcerting when people kept saying to me, 'My God, are you still alive?' I didn't think my luck would hold out.[25]

In ordinary circumstances, a unit that had gone through experiences as traumatic as those experienced by the British battalion would have required many months of rest, recuperation and re-organisation before it was deemed capable of going back into action. However, in the Republican Spain of the summer of 1937, the circumstances were anything but ordinary. Far from being given the rest they needed, the men who had fought at Brunete found themselves getting fresh arms and equipment, while their ranks were replenished with men who had been recovering from wounds, together with such few new recruits as happened to be available at Albacete. Indeed, in less than one month, now headed, in the absence of Fred Copeman, who had not yet returned from London, by Peter Daly, an unskilled labourer who had fought in the Irish Civil War on the side of the anti-treaty forces and later fled to England where, unable to find any other way of keeping body and soul together, he had enlisted in the British army, the battalion was heading for a fresh bloodletting.[26] That Daly was a brave man there was no doubt – the Civil War had already cost him two wounds – while he was noted for his charm and general friendliness, but, for all that, there were serious doubts about his fitness for command. To quote one volunteer, 'I would suspect that his knowledge of … strategy and tactics was no greater than that of our previous commanders'.[27]

Usually known as the Battle of Belchite, like Brunete before it, the new struggle was essentially intended as a diversionary operation that would, or so it was hoped, force Franco to call a temporary halt to the offensive in the north (having quickly over-run weakly manned Santander, this was now threatening the iconic Republican bastion of Asturias). This time, however, the venue was the long-quiet Aragón front, a choice that, not least because it was very weakly held, made good strategic sense, but also served a major political end in that the troops who would have to be transferred there from the Madrid front could also be used to put paid to the domination of the region by the Anarchists and, above all, reverse the collectivisation of agriculture that the latter had embarked on in the course of the revolution, this being something that the Communists regarded as a serious affront. Setting the politics aside, a new force known as the Army of Manoeuvre – in essence, the troops dispatched from Madrid – and the existing Army of the East were to launch a converging assault on the city of Zaragoza from both sides of the River Ebro, the first step in this operation being the capture of the string of fortified settlements which was all the Nationalist front line consisted of. In the southern sector (the one that we shall be concerned with in this chapter given that this was the one allocated to the Army of Manoeuvre), the key points being the towns of Belchite, Fuentes de Ebro, Quinto de Ebro and Mediana, it was against these that the international volunteers were to go into action, a decision that reflected neither their fighting spirit nor level of training and armament, but rather the Communist Party's constant desire to see them used a shock troops and thereby to keep them in the headlines.

Of the fighting that followed the launch of the offensive in the small hours of 24 August 1937, by far the most well-known is that which took place at Belchite, but we will here rather concentrate on the action that took place further to the east at Quinto de Ebro, a small town of about 2,000 souls nestling on the very edge of the green expanse of the Ebro valley on the one hand and the empty steppes that are so characteristic of southern Aragón on the other: while the main streets were on the flat ground at the foot of the bluffs which form the edge of the valley, the poorer districts clustered on the steep slopes leading up to the steppes above, and, with them, a prominent knoll crowned by the parish church known as El Piquete. Several hundred yards further out again could be found the village cemetery, but, beyond its walls, empty space stretched away to the horizon. Leaving the town to the south the main road along which it was built split, with one branch curving round to the left to follow the Ebro valley in the direction of Caspe, Gandesa and, ultimately at least, Tortosa, and the other winding its way up to the steppes in the direction of the village of Azaila via a re-entrant overlooked on its left by a particularly massive bluff known as the Cerro del Purburrel. From the town, then, the impression is of a site almost entirely overshadowed by steep hills, but, from the perspective of someone approaching it from the west or south – precisely the direction from which the Republicans advanced on the town – the view was very different, namely a level plain whose only distinguishing landmark was the parish church.

This is not quite the end of the story, however. Though more-or-less the same height as the rest of the upland, the Cerro de Purburrel was almost completely cut off from the ground to the east and south by deep ravines that ran down to the roads on each side, thereby making it extremely difficult to access, and all the more

The main street of the village of Quinto; much of the town was destroyed in the fighting of 25–8 August 1937. (author's collection)

The parish church of Quinto; the village is out of sight in the dead ground beyond.
(author's collection)

so as the summit is ringed by an artificial step in the slope cut out by long years of quarrying that, while never more than 5 or 6ft high, nevertheless presented a serious obstacle to attacking infantry. Further protected by a network of trenches on the table-like summit, Purburrel was to be a mainstay of the defence, though other positions had been prepared around the cemetery, the railway station (a halt on the main line from Zaragoza to Barcelona) and the cement factory that stood beside it, and, finally, a bluff not dissimilar from the Cerro de Purburrel on the western side of the Azaila road. As for the garrison, this consisted of half the second battalion of Infantry Regiment No. 17, the María-de-Molina Carlist battalion, 3 companies of the fifth battalion of the Falange of Aragón, a detachment of Civil Guards, 1 battery of 105mm guns and 1 battery of 75mm guns, all this making a total of some 1,200 men and 8 pieces of artillery.[28]

Heading for these troops was 35 Division and, more particularly, XV International Brigade. Still commanded by the Croat Copic, this had now been reduced to four infantry battalions – the British, the Lincoln-Washington (American and Canadian), the Dimitrov (Slavic) and the so-called 'Español' –

The cement factory that served as one of the chief Nationalist strongpoints at Quinto. (author's collection)

The cemetery at Quinto. Note the damage to the brickwork; meanwhile the tower of the church can just be seen protruding above the wall. (author's collection)

the British-manned anti-tank guns and the 'John Brown Battery', an American artillery unit armed with three 75mm field guns. In support, meanwhile, was a company of Russian T26 tanks and the Ana Pauker artillery battalion, a formation consisting of three batteries each of three Skoda 75mm guns. Aside from Daly, the battalion commanders were the American Hans Amlie, a Hungarian named Szalway and Alfredo Balsa, a Galician from Lugo who had spent his early years in Cuba and Argentina and fought in the Moroccan Wars. Finally, the chief of staff was the first commander of the Lincoln battalion and sometime college professor Robert Merriman, and the brigade commissar first-generation Croat immigrant Stjepan Mesaros, better known by his adopted name of Steve Nelson, who had joined the Communist Party in 1925 and since then operated as a Labour organiser in Chicago.[29]

Fighting began at dawn on 24 August with the largely Yugoslav Dimitrov battalion driving straight along the Azaila road in what appears to have been an attempt to rush the defences of the village and secure it by a *coup de main*. However, no sooner had the attackers started to descend the re-entrant that

Nationalist trenches on the summit of the Cerro de Purburrel. (author's collection)

The empty plain from which the Abraham Lincoln battalion approached Quinto. (author's collection)

led to the town than it discovered that their way was blocked by a deep cut in the road that made all further progress impossible. By now under heavy fire from both sides, the battalion hastily withdrew and took post in rear of the Lincoln battalion, which was now circling round to the western side of the town. Under fire from the Nationalist positions west of the Azaila road, the Americans took up positions opposite the cemetery, but at first they made no move to attack, perhaps because they were waiting for the Dimitrov battalion to complete an enveloping movement that was seeing them pass behind the Lincoln battalion and head around the northern side of the town so as to cut the road to Zaragoza. Although a dozen Republican bombers made a pass across the defenders' positions at about midday, not until late in the afternoon did the attack get moving. Eight T26 tanks having come up in support of the Americans, the latter now finally made their move, storming the cemetery and rushing the first buildings of the town. If we are to believe Arthur H. Landis, a volunteer from Alabama who was to go on to become a noted author of fantasy fiction, the advance was stirring stuff:

What happened … was right out of the manual. Despite the fact that they … were receiving heavy mortar and machine-gun fire, plus bursts of overhead shrapnel, battalion troops moved into the attack without a hitch. Where the tanks crushed the barbed wire, the Americans poured through … grenading and shooting their way into the trenches, while the remnants of the enemy fled down into the streets of the village … Rebel losses were heavy: their trenches were full of dead and wounded. There were fewer than ten American casualties, proof positive of what could be done with even a modicum of well co-ordinated support.[30]

Yet all was not well. Landis places the greatest weight on the actions of the American infantry, but in fact it was the tanks that produced the breakthrough, and all the more so as they appear to have been used far more aggressively than had generally been the case in the Jarama and Brunete battles. Herewith the account of another eyewitness, 'The tanks came on, blasting the fascist fortifications. Over the top we went … The fascists ran back to the town, and we followed closely on their heels … The tanks pursued the fleeing enemy right into Quinto, firing at fortified houses and destroying the machine-gun nests.'[31] Still worse, the operation was well behind schedule. For the offensive to succeed, Quinto and its fellows had to be over-run immediately, but by the end of the day little had been achieved other than the capture of a few outlying positions, true though it is that a night-time foray headed by two American lieutenants succeeded in cutting the pipeline that was the garrison of Purburrel's only source of water. Fighting resumed the next day with the Dimitrov battalion pushing into the town from the north and the Lincoln battalion doing the same thing from the west, but there was much confusion and several instances of friendly fire, while the thick mediaeval walls of many of the houses made winkling out the defenders a difficult task. One officer wrote:

The town simply swarmed with snipers, who, aided by machine-guns in the church and other key positions, kept up a deadly fire on our advancing parties. When our section reached the first street we split up in groups. Our group took a street that … led past the church one block to the right of it … We checked every house carefully, banging on the door and yelling to see if anybody was within. If there was no reply, we broke the door open and threw a couple of hand grenades inside just to make sure … One of our comrades was hit by a sniper in the leg. He fell to the ground and made feeble efforts to drag himself to safety while bullets from the church and surrounding

The bullet-scarred interior of the parish church at Quinto. (author's collection)

houses were crackling all around him. William Frame, first-aid man, saw his plight. He and two [other] volunteers ran to his assistance immediately, and, disregarding the snipers, carried him to safety.[32]

For the capture of a particularly prominent building that stood near the church, we can turn to the account of Carl Bradley, a captain who was at that time serving on the brigade staff. Thus:

> We waited until our anti-tanks began to pound the building to keep the snipers away from the windows. Then we went armed with bottles of nitro-glycerine to about eight yards from it. Two men were wounded on the way to the building [and] three had to carry them back. This left only five of us to carry on. But five was enough! We each picked a window, and, bang, every bottle went home, exploding with tremendous flames … Next we rolled a drum of gasoline inside with a fuse attached to it. This finished the job: the building burned all night.[33]

In this fashion most of the town was gradually occupied, and, with it, the railway station and the cement factory. Not least because many of the volunteers took the opportunity to ransack shops and private houses alike, perched on the bluff high above, however, the church continued to hold out. Crammed with a mixture of defenders who had taken refuge in the building after being driven from the cemetery and other positions and terrified civilians, this now became the focus of the battle. Yet the attackers, a mixture of Americans and Slavs, seem to have been unwilling to press home their attack, it undoubtedly being this problem that accounts for the sudden appearance in the thick of the fighting of a suspiciously large number of officers from brigade headquarters including Merriman, Nelson, Bradley and the Englishmen Tom Wintringham and Malcolm Dunbar. Under their leadership, small parties of volunteers managed to reach the walls and thereby lob grenades through the windows, but the defenders continued to hold firm, and that despite the fact that they were being subjected to concentrated artillery fire. Also supporting the attack on the church was the Brigade's three-gun anti-tank battery. One of the gunners was a Labour-Party activist from a Welsh mining village who had secured a scholarship to Ruskin College named Jim Brewer:

> We were blazing away when suddenly, the Number One on my anti-tank gun, Chris Smith, fell over … Blood was seeping around the bottom of his abdomen … We had no bandages, but I noticed that over to our left on the road was an ambulance … I didn't know where

the bullet had come from … but I picked him up and shielded him with my body and walked across to the ambulance … When I got back … Wintringham, [Hugh] Slater and Dunbar were standing there discussing what they had to do when suddenly Wintringham was hit in the shoulder … Dunbar said, 'There is a sniper on the church tower', so we turned our gun on it, and first of all we … got a shot plum on [the bell], an armour-piercing shot. We thought that the sniper would be coming down from the … tower, so we put another high-explosive shell through the door of the church, followed by a high explosive one. I didn't like it – I knew the building was sacred to other people, and I didn't like the idea of stooping to the level of the enemy in regarding it as a fortified place – but, of course, that was a bit too chivalrous.[34]

Curiously enough, we have a detailed account of the shelling of the church tower from one of the defenders, namely a youth of right-wing sympathies named Pascual Porroche who had grown up in the town and come forward to offer his services: seemingly, two men were killed, both of them grandfathers. Porroche himself, meanwhile, had been posted at a hole that had been blown in the wall in the main part of the church, but he, too, was in much danger: a soldier fighting beside him suffered a terrible face wound, while a sergeant of the Civil Guard had his hand blown off by a hand grenade in the very act of upbraiding the man with the face wound for making such a fuss.[35] With the situation ever more desperate – the soldiers and civilians trapped in the church had run out of water by the end of the first 24 hours – a few men slipped out during the night of 25 July and managed to reach a hiding place in the town below, while still others made a break for it in the course of the next day, only to be rounded up the moment they stumbled out of the building.[36]

While street fighting raged from one end of the town to the other, another sector of the front was erupting. Having initially been in reserve, the British battalion was ordered to defeat the troops who, having been completely isolated by the loss of the town, were still clinging to Purburrel. Realising, perhaps, that even a handful of machine guns would be enough to mow his men down by the score if he took the obvious route across the plateau, Daly elected to launch his attack from the re-entrant followed by the Azaila road in the apparent hope that he would thereby enjoy the protection of dead ground. Herewith an anonymous account that was later printed in *The Book of the XV Brigade*, a propaganda work put together by the Commissariat of XV Brigade in 1938:

The three companies descended into the gully, [two] along … old fascist communication trenches, the third along the ground between.

There was a little artillery preparation commensurate with the report that Purburrel was not strongly held. The companies deployed and climbed the slopes … Then hell was let loose. The fascist trenches near the summit became one line of continuous crackling machine-gun fire. Not an inch could we advance in the face of such a rain of steel.[37]

Supported though they were by the Republican artillery, progress was minimal, and that despite the fact that, with their trenches set well back from the lip of the plateau, the defenders could not fire at them without considerable risk to life and limb. Among the attackers was Walter Gregory:

As the fascists were in possession, they had made good use of this advantage to prepare well-designed fortifications surrounded by barbed wire, a multitude of slit trenches and gun emplacements. Care had also been taken to camouflage many of their positions so they could not be readily spotted from the air … Expecting little

The precipitous slope which faced the British battalion in its attempt to take the Cerro de Purburrel. (author's collection)

resistance, the British battalion began its ascent of the steep hillside, only to be met by a murderous machine-gun fire. We sought what natural cover there was: every undulation in the rocky ground, no matter how insignificant it appeared at a first, casual glance, housed one or more men trying to bury themselves in the unyielding earth to avoid the bullets which flew ceaselessly overhead. Rifles and hand-grenades were useless against the armaments massed on the higher ground above us. Our commander, Peter Daly, was wounded in the opening moments of our initial attack … Those of us fortunate enough to have survived the first onslaught sought what protection we could as, throughout a long, hot, bloody day, we waited for the sun to go down and the arrival of darkness to shield our retreat from those bullet-swept slopes. Many died before nightfall gave us the protection we so desperately needed to fall back and regroup.[38]

The unfortunate Daly succumbed to his wounds a few days later. Meanwhile, it cannot but be felt that there is something awry in the accounts we have just cited. Far from 'many' volunteers losing their lives in the attack, the actual number of those killed seems to have been just three, namely Daly, a Cockney sergeant named Guerin and Alcide Brigas, a stray French-Canadian, though to these should be added a number of wounded, one of them the new Battalion Commissar, Jack Roberts, hit in the shoulder while attempting to hasten the advance of the badly lagging machine-gun company.[39] Yet, even with the addition of Roberts and his fellows, what emerges is a scene that does not add much to the battalion's reputation: conscious that their men were low in morale, Daly and Roberts had clearly sought to lead from the front, only for the men following them to go to ground the moment they had been shot down. To make matters worse, not even the accidental bombing of the defenders by a flight of Italian aircraft was enough to get the volunteers on their feet, and that despite the fact that the enemy bombing run seemingly persuaded a number of men to raise the white flag: suppressed though the mutiny quickly was, it should have been clear that a determined effort would probably have secured a rapid victory.[40] Yet determined efforts were a thing of the past. To quote Bolton volunteer, Joe Norman, 'Discipline [had begun] to slip a bit … The symptoms … were disinterest [sic] and no enthusiasm to fight. [The men] never refused an order, but they didn't fight with enthusiasm like they did in the early days.'[41]

Thanks to the failings of the British and American volunteers alike, the battle dragged on into a third day. With the defenders not only low on ammunition but suffering agonies from thirst, they were on their last legs, but, even so, it was not until late afternoon that the parish church and Purburrel fell into the hands of the XV Brigade, while it took a concentrated barrage of anti-tank shells to persuade the British that it was safe to advance on the latter. In the words of the battalion adjutant, Arthur Ollerenshaw, 'The anti-tank battery did marvellous work. [The guns] sent over salvos without a pause, raking the fascist trenches [and] searching out the machine-gun nests and destroying them one-by-one … Cheered by the visible damage our guns were doing, we began the advance down the slope again … and across the road.'[42] Yet, even then, fire from a particularly stubborn machine-gun post pinned down the advance and the new commander of the battalion, another Irishman named Paddy O'Daire, had to call down an artillery barrage from the Anna Pauker battalion before the advance could resume.[43] Last to give up in both places were the surviving officers, in several instances the men concerned shooting themselves rather than let themselves be taken alive, those who did not then being summarily executed anyway. As Miles Tomalin of the anti-tank battery wrote in his diary, 'Officers are shot. What else can you do? Every convinced fascist alive adds to the danger in which their kind have placed the world.'[44]

Setting aside the qualms that cannot but be called forth by these actions, Quinto was very much a hollow triumph. In the first place, there was the fact that the town was little more than a ruin, in which respect we can cite the account of Lluis Puig Casas, a devout Catholic from Terrassa who had been conscripted in the summer of 1937 and was now serving in the signals section of an infantry battalion in CXLIII Brigade, 44 Division:

> Quinto came into view … We shuddered as we saw innumerable corpses, semi-decomposed and abandoned, which gave off an unbearably putrid stench … No more than a few dozen houses could still be of any use … We could hear the pitiful howling of dogs calling their masters … We went into the houses … and saw … trunks, chests of drawers and shelves all turned upside down … You cannot imagine how terrible a war is until you have seen what I saw with my own eyes.[45]

Meanwhile, as if this was not enough, the capture of Quinto in itself meant nothing: north of the Ebro, other Republican troops were pushing south-west towards Zaragoza, while the path of 35 Division and its fellows was still blocked by the strongholds of Belchite, Mediana and Fuentes de Ebro. Operations continued, then, but, so far as the British were concerned, the story was not a pretty one. Sent to attack Mediana, the battalion, which, astonishingly enough, was now down to the last 100 of the 400 effectives with which it had started, ran into a column of Nationalist reinforcements just south of the village and came to a grinding halt.[46] In confirmation of the parlous state of the men's morale, there followed an incident which makes for embarrassing reading. In brief, no sooner had the volunteers disembarked from the trucks that had carried them from Quinto than a serious mutiny broke out on the pretext that the Spanish troops in the vicinity were showing no signs of giving the British any support. In the event, frantic efforts on the part of a number of Communist militants got the men on the move, but there was no assault on the village, O'Daire contenting himself with occupying the ridge that overlooked it from the south and taking up defensive positions.[47]

Other than for the anti-tank battery, which seems to have fought well enough throughout, not just in the action at Quinto, but also the nine days of street fighting that it took to capture Belchite, so far as the British were concerned the battles of the last days of August constituted a singularly inglorious affair, Quinto and Mediana – the only places where the British battalion came under fire – having both suggested that it was no longer remotely capable of offensive action.[48] Staunch Communist as he was, Walter Gregory later did his level best to keep the red flag flying. Thus: 'Looking back on the Aragón campaign, I feel that the British battalion … fought remarkably well. We scored a number of victories against a well-prepared and resolute enemy, and our morale was never dampened by the setbacks we encountered, the inhospitable terrain and the vagaries of the weather.'[49] As witness a valedictory circular letter written by fellow Communist stalwart Will Paynter on his return home to stand for election to the executive of the South-Wales Miners' Federation after a six-month stint at Albacete, this was so much nonsense. As he expostulated:

> The People's Army must be disciplined and efficient. Commands, no matter how difficult it may be at times to carry them out, must be promptly obeyed and without question. Discipline must be strengthened and there must be a political understanding of the reasons why absolute obedience to the commanders is a vital necessity for victory … Even closer relationships must be developed between the British in the battalion and the Spanish comrades. In training, in reserve, in rest, in battle, there must be no separation by nationalities … Without this close cohesion of all sections and companies, the battalion cannot be an effective fighting unit. We have therefore to remove bad habits of the past and attain a more intimate relationship with our Spanish comrades.[50]

Setting aside the issue of the Spanish troops being denigrated and looked down upon by the volunteers, much though it might be added that, like the rest of his ilk, Paynter was ducking the Party's share of the responsibility of a policy that had become a murderous fiasco, what we have here is a damning indictment of the British battalion's fighting power. Coded though the language might be, the message was all too clear: the troops had failed to show sufficient spirit and all too often been sluggish, if not downright disobedient, in their response to orders. Still worse, on show was also a tendency to take refuge in excuses that were patently untrue. Here, for example, is the same anonymous account that we had occasion to quote from on a previous page, 'Inspecting the fort we had captured, we felt proud of ourselves ... Revolving gun-turrets with over-head cover commanded the country for miles around ... To us it was an object lesson in fortifications.'[51] Such rodomontade, however, was of no use in military terms – the Nationalist fortifications on Purburrel were far more rudimentary than is claimed here, the only concrete fortification being a single machine-gun nest[52] – and served only to mask the cruel reality. Meanwhile, the Lincoln battalion had done little better, its advance on the cemetery having clearly been pinned down for hours. In short, if Brunete had been highly suggestive of the fact that the International Brigades were little more enthusiastic than the rest of the People's Army and suffered from precisely the same tactical defects, Belchite put the issue beyond doubt, and it is therefore no surprise to find that on 23 September 1937 the Republican government issued a decree abolishing the administrative autonomy that the International Brigades had hitherto enjoyed throughout and subjected them to the authority of the Ministry of War.[53]

As for the Battle of Belchite as a whole, this produced results that were no more cheerful: it could be said, indeed, that the Republic's hopes were quite literally in ruins, the only gains that could be boasted of being the shattered wreckage of two small towns of no strategic importance whatsoever. By 6 September, the battle was over. In the front line, the men who had bypassed Belchite had managed to beat off repeated enemy counter-attacks, but this was at best an empty achievement. At about 10,000 men, Republican casualties were once again very heavy, while even less had been achieved than at Brunete in that 1 September had seen the troops that had just over-run Santander go into action against Oviedo: some planes had temporarily been transferred to the Aragón front, but that was all.

The Battlefield Today

As a place to visit, Quinto is one of the most rewarding battlefields of the Spanish Civil War: not only has the town experienced only limited modern development, but the area of the fighting is small enough to be walked over in the course of a single day, while the town is easily accessible from Zaragoza by both bus and rail.

Our tour begins at the railway station, a building that remains much as it would have looked in 1937; across the tracks, meanwhile, the open fields across which the Dimitrov battalion circled the town to take the defenders in the rear are equally evocative. Walking along the station approach – the Camino de la Estación – the visitor will almost immediately come to the cement factory: just as unchanged as the station, this was, as has been noted, a major bastion of the defenders.

At the main road, turn right and walk in the direction of the town centre. After perhaps 300yd cross the road and fork left onto the Calle San Roque: in 1937, this was the route followed by the highway. Pass through the medieval gateway – the Portal San Roque – and continue straight on to the Plaza Vieja: as witness the many post-Civil-War buildings, this area of the town was particularly badly damaged in the fighting.

At the Plaza Vieja turn left into the Calle de la Herrería (the road down which the Lincoln battalion fought its way into the town) and climb the hill to the T-junction, at which point turn right into the Calle Isabel II. After a few yards turn left and take the flight of steep stairs ascending the hill: at the top will be found the old parish church (the church in the town centre is a replacement built in the Franquist era). Dedicated to the Assumption of Our Lady, the church is a solidly built medieval building dating in its earliest parts from the fourteenth century and as such was a natural fortress, and all the more so as the outer faces of the knoll on which it stood had at some point been scarped and given a stone facing that rendered it all but inaccessible; as can be appreciated, it also completely dominated the western approaches to the town. Abandoned after the war, it is now a museum dedicated to a cache of extraordinary mummies that were discovered beneath the paving of the church during restoration work in 2011 (something that makes Quinto worth a visit even for those with no interest in the Civil War), but in its basic structure has been little altered: the walls are pitted with the impacts of rifle and machine guns while the roof remains holed in various places; it is, then, very easy to visualise the trauma experienced by Pascual Parroche and his fellow defenders.

Descend the stairs from the esplanade, cross the street below and head away from the church up the Calle Albar. After a short distance this swings sharply to the left and takes the visitor directly to the main gate of the walled cemetery that checked the initial advance of the Lincoln battalion: although this was extended after the war, by walking around its wall to the right, a good view can be obtained of the empty plain from which the chief assault on the village was launched, this being defended by an outer ring of trenches, some traces of which are visible in the empty space between the farm buildings on the other side of the motorcycle racetrack immediately adjacent to the cemetery.

Returning to the cemetery gate, go past it and carry straight on. At the junction with the Calle Corna go straight across and take the Calle Doña Urraca. At the far corner of the Piquete Knoll bear left and take the Calle Ramón y Cajal. Follow this down hill until it reaches the Calle San Roque. At this point turn right and return to the main road. Straight ahead is a prominent bluff: this is the Cerro de Pingarrón.

Walk on down the main road (the N232). At the road junction bear round to the right and head uphill. To the left beside the road is the Barranco del Magarro (the ravine crossed by the British battalion in the course of its attack on Pingarrón) and beyond it the slopes where it was checked by enemy fire. In theory, it is possible to scale the hill from many points along the road, but the gradient is extremely steep and the going very difficult, and so the ascent is not for anyone but the fittest and most intrepid. Far better, then, to carry on up the N232 to the summit, passing the spot where the defenders blocked all passage along it by excavating a deep cut from one side to the other (this was probably somewhere in the vicinity of the junction with a service road coming down from the right about halfway up). Just beyond where the highway emerges on to the plateau beyond the bluffs, take a track that leads away from it to the left at right angles and follow this as it curves back around towards Pingarrón; meanwhile, the line of distant hills on the southern horizon marks the positions from which the Republican artillery bombarded the Nationalists.

After perhaps 1 mile the track reaches the narrow nek of land which connected the summit of Pingarrón to the main body of the plateau: the ravines on either side constitute massive obstacles which would have had to be negotiated under heavy close-range fire after crossing hundreds of yards of open steppe that was not just flat as a pancake but bereft of any cover, the result being that it is easy to see why the British battalion chose the approach that it did.

Continue along the track. After several hundred yards it will be found that this crosses over the Nationalist front line, this last being marked by a well-defined trench that extends for some distance to both right and left (visitors with cars should be able to reach this point without trouble: unmade though it is, the track is easy going). At the far end of the summit will be found a stone commemorating two Nationalist officers who were either killed in the fighting or, more likely, executed in cold blood.

To return to Quinto, while it is possible to scramble down the northern slope of the massif, it is safer either to retrace the same route or to take the well-made track that branches off to the left near the nek and, after many twists and turns, reaches a metalled road (the A221). At the junction turn left and return to Quinto, bearing right at the junction with the N232.

Chapter 6

The Battle of Teruel

What remained of the year 1937 in the wake of the Battle of Belchite was a period of relative quiet in the history of the International Brigades, the only action in which any of them were involved being an abortive assault on the village of Fuentes de Ebro just a few miles further along the road to Zaragoza from Quinto on 13 October. That this was the case was probably just as well, for, if this attack is anything to go by, the only result would have been still more casualties. Entrusted to the XV Brigade and a newly arrived battalion of fifty Russian BT5 tanks, it was put together at the last moment and almost immediately foundered for want of adequate planning and reconnaissance alike. Thus, there was no artillery support; co-operation between the tanks and the infantry was non-existent; the armour became trapped in a killing ground in which all further progress was blocked by a low cliff; the soldiers, all of them members of the Spanish battalion, who suddenly found themselves being piled on to the BT5s, Russian-style, as 'tank-riders' either fell off as their rides lurched across the uneven terrain or were eliminated by enemy machine-gun fire; and the supporting infantry battalions – the British, the Lincoln-Washington and the newly arrived Canadian Mackenzie-Papineau[1] – went to ground rather than brave the fire of the defenders.[2]

Morale in the battalion had not been wonderful even before this unfortunate affair. Thus, there were grumbles about the manner in which the XV Brigade had become dominated by Americans, Nelson and Merriman having been kept on as chief-of-staff and political commissar, and the consolidated training camp for new recruits that had been established at Tarrazona de la Mancha – the very village where all the American volunteers who had arrived at Albacete hitherto had been put through their paces – placed in the hands of Bostonian Allan Johnson, 'The Americans … wanted to run the show', complained one volunteer. 'They did everything in this big, brash American way.'[3] Another gripe was centred on the decree of 26 September 1937: in the words of David Hooper, 'Aitken [*sic*: by the time the decree concerned had been issued, Aitken had long since left for England] … told us that the International Brigade [*sic*] was to be disbanded … This upset us and we told him that we were volunteers and would not join the

Spanish army.'[4] And, last but not least, the failure of the Republican offensive had not been without its effects, even a Communist as staunch and hard-core as Bill Alexander having to admit that, post-Belchite, 'we were in a state of complete exhaustion and [gripped by] a certain sense of defeat'.[5]

With matters in this state, the repulse at Fuentes de Ebro was witnessed with rage and incredulity. To quote Hugh Sloane, 'To me, the tank attack was a disaster that should never have happened. In my opinion, [it] was poorly conceived. There was no preparatory bombardment … Nothing like that happened. Instead, there was that ridiculous charge: [it was] like the charge of the Light Brigade – a gallant effort, but a stupid effort.'[6] On their return from Spain, then, Copeman and Tapsell faced a difficult task. However, bolstered by the simultaneous arrival of a few new recruits, the two of them flung themselves into rebuilding the British battalion as a fighting force. In the words of Bill Alexander:

> There was regular training of all kinds, with a young … Soviet instructor attached for a time: special emphasis was laid on digging in, mobility and the use of ground cover. Morale and physical health were improved by the provision of regular meals, washing facilities and sufficient sleep, together with concerts, sports and short leaves to Madrid. By 15 November 1937, with the return of wounded men from hospital, the British numbers had been built up to 150 out of the battalion strength of 600.[7]

In all this Copeman and Tapsell were assisted by a substantial political offensive. Christmas was celebrated at the battalion's new base at the village of Mas de las

One of the BT5 tanks employed by the Republicans at Fuentes de Ebro. (Wikimedia Commons)

Matas in the presence of Harry Pollitt, while other visitors included the editor of the *Daily Worker*, William Rust, and the Labour dignitaries, Clement Attlee and Ellen Wilkinson (to commemorate the appearance of Attlee and Wilkinson, No. 1 Company was given the name of the future Labour leader). Yet how far the men were really cheered by all this it is hard to say: relations between the British and Spanish contingents ranged from the indifferent to the frankly hostile; apathy and general sloppiness were widespread, and many of the old tensions and jealousies continued to bubble away beneath the surface.[8]

In short, the British battalion was far from being in good shape, yet looming on the horizon was an ordeal just as gruelling as anything that its members had experienced hitherto (in the circumstances, then, it was probably just as well that Copeman was rushed into hospital with appendicitis two days after Christmas and the command taken over by the widely respected and very competent Bill Alexander). Thus, driven by a variety of military and political considerations, the Republican government had been planning a new offensive. This time the target was the Nationalist bastion of Teruel, a provincial capital perhaps 100 miles due east of Madrid, which was almost surrounded – it was situated at a spot where, having run more-or-less due south all the way from the Pyrenees, the front doubled back on itself in a tight hairpin bend before curving away westwards to run along the summit of the Guadarrama mountains north of Madrid – lightly garrisoned, and difficult to defend. Entrusted to a specially created force – the Army of the Levante – from which all formations, and, indeed, military commanders, associated with the Communists were excluded, under the non-Communist Republican Juan Hernández Saravia, the assault began on 15 December without, as at Brunete and Belchite, any aerial and artillery bombardment. Aided by the fact that the Nationalist air force was grounded by inclement weather, 100,000 Republican troops surrounded the Nationalist garrison and occupied a large expanse of territory to the north and north-west.[9]

There remained, however, the city of Teruel. Trapped inside the Republican ring were 2,000 troops under the governor, Colonel Rey d'Harcourt, and another 2,000 civilians. For a little while the defending troops made an attempt to hang on to a hill called La Muela that overlooked the city, but very soon it became clear that the only hope was to withdraw inside the built-up area and await relief. Here, however, there was an ideal refuge. Perched on the very edge of the bluff on which the city was built were two close-set clusters of substantial buildings of which the first was centred on the diocesan seminary, the convent of Santa Clara and the church of Santiago, and the second on the Bank of Spain, the offices of the civil government, the casino, the medieval hospital of the Asunción and the church of San Juan, and Rey d'Harcourt and his men duly barricaded themselves inside together with many civilians, including the city's bishop, Ramón Polanco. All of

Republican infantry on the advance in the Battle of Teruel. (Wikimedia Commons)

a sudden, then, the Republicans' triumphal advance came to an end. Having got into the web of streets surrounding the enemy strongpoints, the attackers found themselves completely pinned down. Indeed, far from having administered such a shock to Franco that he would be forced to accept a compromise peace – the sub-text of the whole operation – the Army of the Levante found itself facing the full wrath of an angry generalissimo, and, what is worse, having to do so relying on supply lines consisting of little more than narrow mountain roads. Though taken by surprise – he had actually been massing his forces for a fresh offensive against Madrid via the old battlefield of Guadalajara – Franco quickly launched a massive counter-offensive, this being something in which he was much assisted by the fact that his forces were had recently been organised into proper First-World-War-style army corps, each of them composed of several divisions.[10] Hampered by a prolonged blizzard, the relief forces did not reach the city in time – after a Stalingrad-like struggle, the garrison surrendered on 8 January[11] – but, no sooner had the snow abated than the Nationalist advance continued, the increasingly exhausted Republicans being driven back ever closer to their original positions.[12]

Hitherto kept back for political reasons, XI and XV International Brigades were now sent into the line in the empty steppes north-east of Teruel. After a brief spell in the line in the desolate de Sierra Palomera, they were both pulled in nearer to the heart of the action. Closest to the city itself and in positions which blocked the chief Nationalist axis of advance, namely the main road from Zaragoza, was XV Brigade, the British being stationed on the right flank along a steep escarpment overlooking the valley of the River Alfambra, a tributary of the River Turia which joined it from the east. As for XI Brigade, this was posted a little further north on a bare ridge called El Muletón. With the countryside still shrouded in deep snow, it was bitterly cold. Among the British volunteers was

The seminary taken over by the defenders of Teruel. (author's collection)

A good example of the shell damage that still pocks the walls of many houses in the older parts of Teruel. (author's collection)

Jack Edwards, a lorry driver employed in XV Brigade's transport column. As he recalled long afterwards, 'At Teruel ... I know it was bloody cold because we had some bloody oranges and they got bloody frozen. That's how bloody cold it was.'[13] Yet the men's clothing was at best inadequate, and they had no option but to improvise. 'A useful device for protection of the body was to cut a slit in a blanket which could then be slipped over the head to act as a poncho', remembered Bill Alexander. 'It broke the snow-filled winds, but allowed freedom of movement.'[14]

To extreme cold was soon added extreme danger, for, on 17 January, the Nationalists launched a ferocious assault on the defenders spearheaded by the fire of some 500 guns.[15] Initially, the brunt of the attack was borne by the more outlying XI Brigade, but, even so, Alexander's men were subjected to heavy bombardment. Among the volunteers crouching in the trenches was anti-tank gunner Fred Thomas. To quote the entry in his diary for 17 January:

> At the moment I am watching ... the biggest artillery barrage and longest air-raid I have seen so far in this war. It began about seven o'clock this morning when their heavy guns opened up.

El Muletón, the commanding ridge lost by XI International Brigade on 17 January 1938. (author's collection)

After shelling more or less indiscriminately for an hour or so, they concentrated everything on a small crest to our right. At the same time, judging by the sound of rifle and machine-gun fire, their troops began a fierce attack in that area which is still going on at 3 p.m. A thick pall of black smoke hangs over the surrounding crests. They probably have more artillery here than at Brunete, and that beat all records for this war. Twenty-odd of their bombers and twice as many chasers [i.e. fighters] are giving us some unpleasant moments … The whole damned ground is shaking: ever since they have first come over, they have been circling round and round, bombing, bombing, bombing.[16]

The accounts of International Brigades are inclined to be replete with stories of skies filled with enemy aircraft, but in this instance Thomas was not exaggerating, the Nationalists having finally won complete control of the skies in part because the fighter squadrons of the Condor Legion had now been completely re-equipped with the Me109, a plane that was infinitely superior to the Russian Polikarpovs that were all that the Republicans could put up to oppose them, and, in part, too, because of the elimination of the northern front.[17] 'For the whole day nobody could move an inch', wrote a Republican artillery officer stationed in the rear of El Muletón. 'From the earliest hours of the morning, bombs never ceased to fall on our positions … I would not have liked to be in the shoes of my comrades posted a little further south, for down there it was an absolute slaughter-house.'[18] To their credit, however, the British battalion did not just remain inert. Bob Clark was a casual labourer from Liverpool who had arrived in Spain to fight with the British battalion in the autumn of 1937 and was now undergoing his baptism of fire with the machine-gun company:

The fascist artillery opened up … The whole trench trembled and showers of earth poured from the parapet above. This shelling continued for about half an hour. After our first fright we began to feel fairly safe: the shells were continually dropping about fifty to one hundred yards in the rear of our trench and a surprising number of them were duds … Suddenly what looked like black ants came crawling up the valley evidently intent on occupying the forward positions … We sprang to life … and in a few seconds had a perfect bead on the advancing enemy … We kept on firing for quite a long time. How exhilarating it all was: I felt almost ashamed of myself when I remembered afterwards how full of joy I felt.[19]

Posted as they were, Thomas, Clark and the rest were relatively safe, but, with resistance on El Muletón rapidly crumbling to pieces, Brigade Headquarters sent out fresh orders. Covered by the Maxims of the machine-gun company, on 18 January the three rifle companies were directed to leave their trenches, cross the River Alfambra and advance into the open plain beyond. For a reasonably unvarnished account of what happened next, we can turn to Bill Alexander:

> The brigade now ordered the three … rifle companies to move down … to the valley below across the Alfambra … The river was fast flowing, but … only fifteen feet wide and two feet deep, and … therefore no obstacle to infantry movement … The move, in full view of the enemy … came under heavy fire as the men scrambled down the cliff-face. One of the casualties was Francisco Zamorra, a Spanish-speaking Welshman from Abercrave in West Wales, the battalion interpreter …The battalion hastily dug in, forming a 5–600-yard arc with its back to the Alfambra … The command post was on a fortified hillock … by the gulley which ran due north to Concud. The night was spent digging and … checking weapons and ammunition since everyone knew what the dawn would bring. Next morning the fascist artillery plastered the whole battalion front, an extra share falling on No. 1 Company.[20]

Watching the last stand from the escarpment above the river was another man fresh from home, namely Glasgow blacksmith's assistant, Garry Macartney:

> The fascists pin-pointed the position where our comrades had gone. They landed shells marking out a square of quite large dimensions and then not only saturated that square with shell fire and machine-gun fire, but [also] sent their aircraft to bomb it … There were tremendous casualties, not only down in the valley: the shelling was most accurate and caused havoc … It was quite a remarkable day from very early in the morning till late at night.[21]

Very soon, however, it transpired that the situation in which the British battalion now found itself was untenable. Alexander's three companies had dug themselves in along a low ridge running more-or-less due north, and this meant that they were exposed to enfilade fire from the Nationalist forces who had just occupied El Muletón. As John Dunlop later recalled, 'The Major-Attlee Company [i.e. No. 1 Company] … discovered they were being fired on from both front and flank: there was enemy machine-gun fire going right down along the trench, and quite a

Above: *The empty plain north of Teruel that the British battalion was sent out to defend on 17 January.* (author's collection)

Right: *Republican soldiers fighting in the ruins of Teruel, December 1937.* (Wikimedia Commons)

number of lads were either killed or wounded.'[22] Despite this problem, Alexander held his ground for the whole of 18 January, but the next day he found himself under infantry attack as well. The result was inevitable. To quote the battalion commander once again:

> In this situation the three companies were compelled to retreat and again dig in on a narrow arc only 100 yards around the command post: the machine-guns on the cliffs kept up a nearly continuous …

fire, enabling the retreat to take place in an orderly way. The next day the fascists made a concentrated attack … but the battalion stood its ground and [they] were beaten back.[23]

If anything marked the finest hour of the British battalion, it was this desperate battle on the plain north of Teruel. Certainly, the losses had been far higher than at either Quinto or Fuentes de Ebro. As Bill Feeley – like Bob Clark, a new recruit who had just reached the battalion from Britain and been assigned to a Maxim crew – later noted, 'The machine-gun company occupied a deep … trench which successfully withstood the full power of Franco's artillery. We were luckier than the rifle companies who were caught in the open … and severely mauled. The Major-Attlee Company lost thirteen killed, including my former tent-mates, Bill Donaldson and Joe Fillingham, [while] eight more battalion soldiers died in the same battle.'[24] Meanwhile, whether or not it was due to the efforts of Alexander and his men, the direct attack on the city was not pressed home any further, Franco instead opting to embark on a dramatic envelopment of the defenders from the north that was to become known as the Battle of the River Alfambra (Teruel was not, in fact, to fall until 21 February).[25] Nonetheless, the pressure was utterly relentless with day after day of shelling and bombing. An entry in Thomas' diary scrawled on 22 January reads as follows:

> Well, we have just had a very nasty half hour. About 4.30 we sent over twenty shells … and of course enjoyed it. However, then their '75's', a much bigger gun, had us bang in sight, and, oh boy, the bloody things came one-two-three-four, one-two-three-four, for half an hour, hitting everywhere except the actual gun. By a sheer stroke of luck there were no casualties, but you feel like a wet rag after that sort of experience. If we had tried to keep firing, we would have had no gun crew left. Everything is covered now by a foot or so of earth and debris (as we were also at times), and has to be dug out.[26]

Only on 24 January was the British battalion pulled back from the positions it had clung on to on the right bank of the Alfambra and sent to the rear along with the rest of XV Brigade. Like all their fellows, Alexander's men were utterly spent. In all, twenty-one British volunteers had been killed, while a number of others had been wounded or fallen prey to sickness or shell shock. Spanish casualties are unknown, but losses in the 600-strong battalion came to one-third of its strength, so we may assume that at least 150 of the Spaniards had been killed or wounded.[27] As well, they might, the survivors felt utterly bereft. 'It was a very trying time', remarked a British doctor who had treated some of the wounded. 'The situation was very unpredictable and so cold and so miserable.'[28]

Confronted by all this, there was little for the volunteers to do, but to clutch at straws. In fairness, there was no repeat of the near mutiny that had broken out in the closing stages of the Battle of Brunete: following its evacuation from Teruel, XV International Brigade was not given any proper chance of recovery, but rather dispatched to the further side of the huge salient created by the Battle of the River Alhambra to take part in a diversionary offensive launched from the town of Segura de los Baños, Alexander and his men seemingly taking part in this without a murmur.[29] And, in fairness, too, the British battalion had performed better than it had at either Brunete or Quinto. Yet, in truth, all this was but cold comfort: the British part in the offensive at Segura de los Baños was limited to one minor skirmish in which casualties came to just two dead and a handful of wounded, the fact that one of these last was Bill Alexander suggesting all too clearly that the only way of getting the men moving was for prominent figures such as him to expose themselves to enemy fire. Equally, if the volunteers had done well at Teruel, it has to be pointed out that they were not trying to attack – holding trenches, even in the face of sustained artillery and aerial bombardment was one thing, but going over the top quite another – and were also facing troops who were exhausted after up to three weeks' battling in the bitter cold. Meanwhile, even the most staunch of optimists could not pretend that the battle as a whole had been anything other than a disaster: at some 54,000, Republican casualties had over-topped those of their opponents by at least 10,000 men; many near irreplaceable arms had fallen into the hands of the victors including 3,080 rifles, 104 light machine guns, 123 machine guns,

A Republican T26 tank in the snows of Teruel. (Wikimedia Commons)

Bill Alexander (left) and Sam Wild. Alexander commanded the British battalion at Teruel while Wild was his replacement. (Marx Memorial Library)

9 mortars, 7 artillery pieces and 22 tanks; and, thanks to the Battle of the River Alhambra, far more territory had been taken by Franco's forces than the Army of the Levante had occupied in the course of its own advance.[30] As befits the greatest writer to see service with the International Brigades, let us leave the last word to Laurie Lee. As he lamented in his memoir, *A Moment of War*, 'The gift of Teruel … had become no more than a poisoned toy: it was meant to be the victory that would change the war; it was, indeed, the seal of defeat'.[31]

The Battlefield Today

Any visit to the battlefield of Teruel should begin with a tour of the old city and, more especially, the two enclaves held with such tenacity by Rey d'Harcourt and his men, both of which were completely rebuilt after the war. Of these, the one at the southern end of the old town is, it has to be said, somewhat disappointing, though this is the best place from which to begin any Civil-War itinerary. The square that was its nucleus – the Plaza de San Juan – is still there, but is much more spacious than it was in 1937, the church of San Juan that then filled the whole of the southern part of the current area having been so badly damaged that it was judged to be not worth reconstructing and razed to the ground. Also gone for good is the Hospital de la Asunción, the result being that only some of the buildings – most notably the Banco de España and the Teatro Marín (in 1937 the town's gentleman's club) – bear much relation to those that were there in 1936. That said, by passing through the gap in the southern face constituted by the Calle Portal de Valencia to the Ronda de Ambeles, it is easy to see just how effectively the Nationalist redoubt dominated the southern approaches to the city, and, still more so, the imposing bridge that spanned the deep ravine that surrounds so much of the old town.

Having viewed the bridge and the view beyond follow the Ronda de Ambeles around the edge of the old town in a clockwise direction along the edge of the ravine until it reaches the Calle Nueva. On the way those feeling energetic may care to descend the so-called Escalinata, a monumental stairway leading down to the railway station in the ravine below, from which point an excellent impression may be obtained of the second Nationalist redoubt, this having been centred on the range of buildings on the lip of the ravine to the north of the station. At the Calle Nueva, meanwhile, turn back into the old town and follow the street until it reaches the emblematic Plaza del Torico, a spot which both the Republicans and the Nationalists chose to make extensive use of in photographic celebrations of the capture of the city on the one hand, and its recapture on the other: judging by the many results, its aspect is but little changed.

Situated in the Plaza de San Juan, the Teruel branch of the Banco de España was an important Nationalist bastion in the siege of December 1936–January 1937. (author's collection)

From the Plaza del Torico carry straight on and then take the first left into the Calle Mariano Múñoz Nogales: from there the route runs parallel to the inner front of the second Nationalist redoubt, this last being just two blocks to the south, and was in consequence much used by the Republicans as a species of 'covered way'. After a short distance the Plaza de la Catedral opens out on the left. Walk past the cathedral into the square beyond: directly in front, the further entrance to the square leads into the area held by the Nationalists, the result being that the whole area is spattered with bullet holes.

Half-way across the Plaza de la Catedral, turn right into the Calle de los Amantes and proceed to the far end at which point the visitor will come to the Torre de San y Martín, a Mudejar-style tower dating from 1316 above one of the city's surviving medieval gates which was held by the Republicans throughout the siege and is again much marked by the fighting.

At the tower turn left into the Plaza del Pérez Prado (at the time of the Civil War the Plaza del Seminario). Straight in front will be found the building that in 1937 housed the diocesan seminary and, adjoining it to its left, first, the Convento de Santa Clara and then the church of Santiago: very heavily damaged during the siege, the complex formed the northernmost part of the second Nationalist redoubt and stands right on the edge of the ravine followed by the River Turia: as a glance over the parapet to the right will reveal, this last both gave it a very dominant position and rendered it inaccessible to infantry attack (that said, the fact that it overhung the cliff made it highly vulnerable to mining operations, 27–8 December seeing the destruction of a large part of the seminary and convent alike by these means). Some idea of the devastation is provided by Nationalist officer Eduardo Fuembuena. Thus:

> The area of Teruel known as the Cuatro Esquinas had been destroyed in so barbaric a fashion that every road through it was blocked, the piles of rubble being so great that they reached a height of two or three metres. As for the zone constituted by the cathedral, the Convento de Santa Clara and the seminary, it had the appearance of a single rocky mountain, the only thing that protruded from it, by some miracle of balance being the Torre de San Martín, though it has to be said that, shot to pieces by shellfire, it presented the most desolate of spectacles.[32]

From the Plaza de Seminario walk along the Calle Yagüe de Salas in the process passing to the left of the church of Santiago, in which building the defenders made their last stand, having been driven from the northern end of the complex (see below) and forced to evacuate both the seminary and the convent due to the damage they had suffered in the explosions mentioned above. Beyond the church will be found the Plaza de Cristo Rey. Directly opposite stands the old post office, a building held as an advanced post by the Republicans throughout the siege, and to the right the Convento de Santa Teresa, which was stormed by the Republicans on 28 December.

From the Plaza del Cristo Rey carry straight along the Calle de Santa Teresa de Jesus and the Calle Santiago to the Calle del Salvador, at which point turn left and go up the street to the Plaza del Torico. In the Plaza turn right, cross the Calle Nueva and turn right again into the Calle Ramón y Cajal to return to the starting point in the Plaza de San Juan.

To visit the areas which saw direct British involvement, the visitor will either need access to a car or negotiate with the generally friendly and obliging local taxi drivers. First stop should be the cemetery, this being perched on a hill on what was in 1937 the northern edge of the city. This offers an excellent panorama of the Muela de Teruel (the hill across the River Turia to the west); the valley of the River Alhambra and the empty plains and hills beyond it which formed the battlefield of 17–21 January; and, finally, to the east, the Cerro de Santa Barbara. During the last stages of the battle, the cemetery was an important Republican defensive position until it was finally overrun on 20 February. However, the structure that is visible has been much enlarged: in 1937 the only part that existed was the southernmost quarter of the complex: this is the section immediately on the right of the driveway as the visitor ascends from the direction of the town.

The rest of the area where Alexander and his men fought is further out again. To reach the site of the three rifle companies' action, it is best to begin some 2 miles to the north-west of Teruel city at the junction of the N420 with the TE-V-1001. Taking the latter road (direction Celadas), head northwards and after a short distance fork right onto the Camino Bajo de Concud. Go under the railway and continue through the belt of trees on the far side. Just after the sharp bend by the cluster of buildings (an institute of agronomy called the Centro de Mejora Agro-Pecaria 'El Chantre'), turn left and proceed to the far side of the complex. Just beyond will be seen a low hill. Ascend this hill on foot by means of the rough track opposite, and remains of trenches will soon be found ringing the summit, together with a further trench heading to left and right a few yards to the north-west. This was the position that was initially occupied by the rifle companies, it being very easy to appreciate why they were so vulnerable to enfilade fire.

Having retraced one's steps to the road, turn left and pass beneath the main road: the line to which the rifle companies fell back runs either beneath or just to the south of the embankment; sadly, not a trace of it remains. On the other side of the N420 turn left onto the first track: this will shortly curve sharply to the right in the direction of Teruel and at the next junction turn right. After a short distance a small house will be observed in the low ground to the left: this was Alexander's headquarters. Just beyond, the wooded area in the valley marks the line of the River Alfambra: the machine-gun company was dug in on the top of the escarpment on the far side.

Finally, return to the TE-V-1001 and turn right at the junction after the railway line. Follow the road northwards across the plain. The hills that come into view after passing beneath the motorway mark the area from which the XI International Brigade was driven on 17 January, the nearest ridge being El Muletón. Drive on until the road winds up into the high ground. An easy climb upwards and to the left will then take the visitor to a viewpoint marked by traces of what appear to be improvised defensive positions from which an excellent panorama may be obtained of the whole sector defended by XV International Brigade as well as an appreciation of the importance of El Muletón to both sides. Meanwhile, the entire area is littered with the detritus of war: rifle bullets, machine-gun bullets, shell fragments and rusty tin cans.

Chapter 7

From Belchite to Corbera

Defeat at Teruel was but the beginning of a period of absolute disaster for the Republic. In brief, for the first time in the war, Franco resolved to embark on one of the bold strategic strokes that were constantly being urged on him by the representatives of Germany and Italy. Rapidly re-deploying his troops (a task in which he was much aided by the large numbers of trucks which the Nationalist cause had been able to acquire from the decidedly friendly American automobile industry), he arrayed four Spanish army corps and the Italian CTV along the length of the front stretching from Teruel to Huesca, and by the first week of March he had 150,000 men ready to go into action backed by 700 guns and 200 tanks. In the trenches facing them were just two Corps – XII and XXI – most of whose men were nothing but raw conscripts, many of them not even fully armed. At dawn on 9 March the offensive began with a thunderous artillery bombardment and numerous air attacks on Republican airfields that destroyed many planes on the ground (so thinly spread were the defenders that it was deemed to be wasteful to use airpower against them until such time as knots of resistance had been identified).[1]

In the face of such an onslaught, there was little that the Republicans could do and within three days all the gains that they had made in the Battle of Belchite, including, not least, the much battered town itself, had been lost to the enemy. A week later the Nationalists were threatening Caspe, an advance that had not been equalled since the days of the march on Madrid. Resistance, meanwhile, was almost non-existent, many units marching for days on end without having to fire a single shot. Behind the Republican lines, meanwhile, all was confusion. Among the forces caught up in the nightmare were the XI, XII, XIII, XIV and XV International Brigades (though initially only the first and the last were near the front line, the XII and XIII Brigades being rushed up from reserve after some days and the XIV Brigade sent round from the Madrid front). Inevitably, it is the travails of the XV Brigade which are best covered in the literature, this being just as well, for it is precisely this unit that most concerns us here: with regard to the other four, all that need be said is that

their experiences were not dissimilar and that by the end of the campaign they
had all been reduced to mere shadows of their former selves, if not destroyed
altogether.[2] At rest in the area south of Belchite when the attack began, on
10 March the four battalions of which it consisted – the British (commanded
in the absence of the wounded Bill Alexander by former company commander
Sam Wild), the American Lincoln-Washington, the Canadian Mackenzie-
Papineau and the Spanish Fifty-Ninth – were ordered into the line. Scattered
over far too wide a front in the empty countryside to the north of the town,
they had little chance and were overwhelmed by a hail of fire that cut them
to pieces in a matter of hours. Among the approximately 200-strong British
contingent was Irish Communist Bob Doyle, who had, as we have seen, arrived
in Spain in December 1937, but had thus far seen no action, having been kept
back at the training camp at Tarazona as an instructor:

> We soon came under fire. We were walking along a road beside an
> olive grove when Italian fighters came low, strafing us and throwing
> small bombs or grenades … We quickly scattered into the grove
> and, when the plane had passed, I remember Paddy Tighe got out
> in the road and did an Irish jig. We marched on in the direction of
> Belchite, where we became involved in the second battle for the
> town's church … My [Degtyarev] machine-gun developed a fault
> and stopped working. I threw it from me, throwing away the lock
> separately so it could not be used. Fletcher, the commander of my …
> unit, got a bullet through the hand, so I took his rifle. We were about
> fifty yards in front of the church, and the enemy's bullets were hitting
> the church wall behind us … The fascist troops and tanks were getting
> nearer. We were likely to be cut off and surrounded … I was firing
> between trees … at the enemy … on the hill in front. You could see
> the fascists moving, so I kept firing … until the rifle got too hot …
> I thought this was going to be the end: the bloke beside me was killed
> and he was lying there; a bullet hit the wall behind me … It was a
> miracle I wasn't touched.[3]

Also fighting with the rifle companies was newly promoted company commissar
Bob Cooney:

> Belchite was really something … We lay there firing on top of a
> little low house and behind us we could see the bullets bouncing
> off the stones. I finally ended up behind a low stone wall thanks to
> Sam [Wild] and three other lads who were covering for me. It got

The church defended by the British battalion at Belchite at the start of the Nationalist offensive of March 1938. (author's collection)

so muddled that it was hard to hit the fascists and not our lads …
I remember George Fletcher turning to me and saying, 'God, this is
pretty hot.' He had been wounded for the fourth time.[4]

Supporting the battalion were the three 45mm guns of the XV Brigade's British-
manned anti-tank battery. With them was battery paymaster Hugh Sloan, who had
just got back from a two-day trip to brigade headquarters at Hijar to collect a large
sum of back pay owing to the gunners:

> After travelling all night … I found that the anti-tank battery had
> located itself three kilometres outside Belchite … by the side of a
> road … About eleven o'clock in the morning, an American came
> running by and told us we had better get off the mark quick as the
> enemy had broken through. We just had time to load our trucks with
> our guns and go the three kilometres back to Belchite. [There was]
> intense artillery fire … Somebody – Bill Cranston I think it was –
> remarked, 'Jesus Christ, they're firing anti-aircraft guns at us.' A shell
> would explode in the air and you would see shrapnel splashing off
> the buildings all round about us … On the other side of the town, we
> decided that a number of us would wait back on the ground … from
> which we had originally taken Belchite and on which fortifications
> remained. [I] left the guns then … [and] was attached to a group that
> Major Merriman had rallied … about himself on the south side of
> [the town].[5]

Another witness to the fighting was the Liverpool volunteer Bob Clark. In
hospital with dysentery for the past week, he returned in the very midst of the
Nationalist attack to find the Brigade caught up in a desperate battle in which
he could play no part (like most men sent to the rear, he had been stripped of his
rifle on departure):

> The military situation was bad: there was no doubt about that …
> Runners were dashing along the communication trenches with
> messages … It was all very bewildering. The crump of shells
> was … very close. The enemy had obviously got the range on
> brigade headquarters: a large lorry with an anti-tank gun on it
> had sunk its front wheels into one of the communication trenches,
> offering a beautiful target … Shellfire became heavier and
> continuous and the sharp rat-tat-tat of machine-guns could be
> heard very close.[6]

Ruined houses on the outskirts of Belchite. (author's collection)

Few heavy weapons were available to support the defenders, but, hampered though it was by a lack of orders, the anti-tank battery did what it could. Welshman Jim Brewer recalled:

> We had a tremendous field of fire … but we got no instructions and were just there waiting for the enemy. These light Italian tanks came over the hill and I told the Number One, Jimmy Sullivan, 'Hold your fire' …but he fired an armour-piercing round that missed by about twenty yards. Those damned tanks turned around going back over the hill: they weren't going to risk coming forward and risk coming on to our guns.[7]

Very soon the defence was falling apart. 'We discovered that the enemy had occupied the town lying below us 200 or 300 metres away and … installed a machine-gun in the church tower … and also that [they were] firing anti-tank guns on the left of us,' recalled Hugh Sloan. As the same observer continued, 'One of our tanks had been set on fire and was blazing away. They … had us practically surrounded.'[8] Thanks to the leadership of Robert Merriman and a number of other officers, the XV Brigade was kept from breaking and running altogether, but the hours of darkness inevitably found it trudging towards the rear with the rest of the Republican forces. Many men, however, were left behind or became separated from the rest of their units. Typical of the experience of the men was that of George Dreever, a poverty-stricken working-class boy from Leith who had nevertheless – and most extraordinarily – secured both a BA and a PhD from the University of Edinburgh. As he later recalled:

> We sat …or lay there with our rifles, saw men in the distance, fired at them and so on. And then tanks were coming and I think we were told to retreat, but I didn't: the tanks were more-or-less on top of us … There were three fellows with me and I said, 'Right-o … Just lie down in this ditch and let the tanks pass over.' [However], then there were infantry … We were … cut off.[9]

At first, Dreever and his companions managed to elude the victorious Nationalists, but, after three days on the run, they were captured by a cavalry patrol. Much luckier was Hugh Sloan, who, having successfully escaped the clutches of Franco's forces at Belchite, trekked through the night with a small group of men, and by sheer chance the next day came across what was left of the anti-tank battery trying to drag the single 45mm gun that was all that remained to it to safety. Meanwhile, desperate rearguard actions at Lécera and Hijar notwithstanding, the dwindling ranks of the brigade had no option but to keep going. 'The scene beggared description', wrote Cooney. 'As the long black column climbed wearily up the steep rocky hillsides, enemy planes came swooping down and machine-gunned their helpless victims … I did not see a single Republican plane for the whole of that dreadful week.'[10] Constantly attacked from the air, after three days the volunteers reached Caspe in a state of considerable disorder. Back as an acting lieutenant from his spell at Tarazona, Walter Gregory recalled the retreat as an experience that was nightmarish beyond belief:

> This march proved to be one of the worst I … ever experienced. The heat was intense, there was no water [and] we had little to eat and were fast approaching exhaustion even before we set out. To add to our misery, we were strafed by low-flying aircraft for mile after agonising mile which threw the … column into constant turmoil and tried our patience to breaking point … News that we were again surrounded … constantly [presented] us with the problem of finding the weakest link in the encircling forces, breaking through at that

point with all speed before reinforcements could be pitted against us and then continuing to fall back until such time as the entire process began again ... As we slumped to the ground in the olive groves outside Caspe it was difficult to think of ourselves as a fighting force ... It had been at least three days since any of us ... had slept for even a few minutes. The almost total absence of food and water, the energy-sapping marches across rough country under a ferocious sun and the constant harassment by the enemy ... meant that we were completely drained, physically and mentally. Five hundred men had marched through Belchite, but I doubt if more than 150 reached Caspe, and not one of us could have offered even token resistance had we been attacked at that moment.[11]

Behind them, meanwhile, the road was strewn with the detritus of a beaten army:

The evidence of an army in retreat was everywhere. Here a large lorry loaded with hundreds of picks and spades lay with its back axle in a ditch, the driver's heavy coat lying discarded on the roadside. Further along, another lorry had run into a clump of trees ... A dead Spaniard lying with a bullet hole neatly drilled through his head and a number of bullet holes in the lorry's mudguard testified to enemy aircraft strafing. Everywhere lay empty and full ammunition boxes, odd rifles, bayonets, gas-mask containers, discarded greatcoats. A donkey with a raw bleeding wound hobbled pitifully alongside the road.[12]

It was not, of course, just Republican troops who were on the move. On the contrary, the area was teeming with hundreds of refugees desperate to escape the brutality, rapine and political reprisals for which Franco's forces were well known. 'We had the humiliating experience ... of watching the flight of hundreds of people who had lived for centuries in their own little provincial set-up,' remembered Hugh Sloan, 'possibly they had never moved out of their villages in their lives ... The road was filled with them ... carrying their bedding, with old grey-haired women on ... *burros* or maybe donkey-carts and things like that'.[13]

Weary and demoralised, the men who reached Caspe nonetheless made a brave effort to defend the town along with the rest of the brigade when the Nationalists attacked on 16 March: after so exhausting an experience, the men who had come through were in the nature of things the toughest and most committed. Typical enough was Walter Gregory, who was not only a hard-line Communist, but also, as one of the few men still with the battalion who had served in the Battle of Jarama, as much of a veteran as the British battalion possessed:

When we were called upon … to fill our ammunition pouches and move through Caspe to take the heights which the fascists held to the west of the town, we did so with something resembling our old resolve. Again we were battered from the air and by artillery assaults before becoming partially encircled by a sustained fascist infantry attack. Now events became very confused and hand-to-hand fighting … the order of the day. I abandoned any attempt to give orders to what remained of my company: it was simply a case of every man for himself. At one point Sam Wild was actually captured along with a small group of comrades, all of whom managed to escape after an old-fashioned free-for-all with their guards. Somehow, and I do not know how even to this day, those of us who were still able to stand and fight formed a defensive cordon on the east side of Caspe to hold the advanced enemy patrols which were working their way forward through the shattered buildings. By nightfall, the fascists had brought tanks into [the town] itself, and we were forced to retreat under intense close-range rifle and machine-gun fire … across country towards Maella.[14]

With no more than 700 men able to fight, XV Brigade was lucky to have achieved even so much as a momentary check on the progress of the enemy. Meanwhile, with casualties very heavy – the 150 men of the British battalion alone had lost nearly 40 killed and wounded, including 3 officers and the acting battalion commissar, Tom Oldershaw[15] – the only option was to continue the retreat, first to Batea and finally to Gandesa, an important road junction that would soon feature prominently in the Battle of the Ebro, while its ranks were filled up by a mixture of raw recruits (almost all of them Spanish) and men who had for one reason or another missed the first part of the campaign, most of them convalescents who had been enjoying a period of extended convalescence at the pleasant coastal town of Benicasim. New weapons were handed out – having lost his old one at Belchite, Doyle got a fresh Degtyarev[16] – while the British battalion obtained a new commander in the person of erstwhile long-serving regular soldier George Fletcher, who had hitherto been serving as second-in-command, Sam Wild having succumbed to exhaustion and been sent on leave across the Ebro, and was somewhat cheered by the return of the mostly very popular Walter Tapsell from a period of sick leave.[17]

Dug in on the hills that overlooked Gandesa from the north, the Internationals might have achieved something, but they were instead ordered to advance on the enemy and pushed north and west into open country. There was, however, little knowledge of the exact positions of the enemy, and the result was a disaster,

31 March seeing the British battalion suffer terrible casualties when they were taken by surprise by a motorised Italian force consisting of tanks, lorried infantry and motorcyclists while they marching westwards along a narrow road flanked by high ground on its left and terraced slopes covered with vines and olive trees dropping down to the right just after they had left the small town of Calaceite. Unlike the actions at Belchite and Caspe, this affair is very well documented. For a succinct account, we can do no better than turn to Walter Gregory. Thus:

> As we turned a bend in the road, we ran foul of a column of enemy light tanks ... Another group of tanks broke cover from a wood on our flank, and Italian infantry in large numbers entered the fray in support of their armour ... We broke into ones and twos and sought cover wherever we could find it. Fortunately our machine-gun company, which had been at the rear of the battalion, was able to secure some high ground and bring its guns quickly into action, thus affording crucial covering fire while those of us on the road sought to ... make good our escape.[18]

Among these last was Bob Doyle. As he later wrote:

> We heard a terrific roar of engines ... like a motorised column getting nearer to us. A patrol of two was sent out to investigate, but never came back. Frank [Bright] suggested that me and Johnny Lemon take my machine-gun ... to the bend a couple of yards up the road to provide cover. I went forwards and the rest of the unit went past me and left me there. Then, out of the bushes, came a Spanish ... patrol. Suddenly we were surrounded at close quarters ... by Franco's soldiers. [They were] shouting, 'Manos arriba!' Coming up the middle of the road ... led by a tank were motor-cycles with machine-guns mounted on the handle-bars ... They opened fire over our heads, shouting 'Abajo!' to us as they fired, effectively cutting us off from the rest of the battalion ... There was a smell of cordite, the noise of men shouting and bullets flying overhead. Wally Tapsell was at the side of the road and he shouted to the fascist officer standing up in the tank turret, 'You bloody fool! Do you want to kill your own men?' Wally thought they were our tanks: we all [believed] that the Lister Division were up ahead of us and hadn't realised that the front had broken. The officer ... opened fire with a revolver and shot him dead. It all happened so quickly: he wasn't carrying a weapon when he was shot.[19]

The spot just west of Calaceite where the British battalion came face-to-face with an Italian column; most of the survivors escaped by scrambling up the hill to the right. (Alan Warren)

Taken completely by surprise, the rifle companies disintegrated almost at once. Bob Cooney recalled:

> George Fletcher told us to take to the high ground and get by as best we could', said Bob Cooney. 'There were hordes of yelling Italians and some of our lads got held down. Jack Coward … said to me, 'Let's get the hell out of this lot!' It was every man for himself and we got out as best we could. I remember … [crawling up] and down the hillside terraces, hoping we'd get to the top of the hill and … into cover.[20]

Although many men were shot down, rounded up as prisoners or forced to take to their heels to save themselves, some of the volunteers were not dealt with so easily. As Gregory says, because the machine-gunners were at the rear of the column, they were able to put up more of a fight. With the rest of his crew, Welsh volunteer Morien Morgan, for example, was among a number who sought shelter in the cultivated area on the right-hand side of the road:

> When the firing started, we got down into the terraces and set up [our] machine-guns. Normally, the practice … was to have Molotov

cocktails ... to burn the tanks and lorries, but this [clash] was much too sudden for anything to be prepared for that sort of attack: all we could do was to use the machine-guns ... We were lucky enough to hit [i.e. disable] a tank somehow ... but inevitably their men got up on the hillside and shot down at us with heavier fire than we had. In the end there were very few of us left. One chap was badly wounded in his arm and knee and ... for safety's sake, we put him in a culvert ... His name was Morgan Havard. We kept them back for some hours, [but] then we felt that it was hopeless, so ... we decided to retreat, taking Morgan Havard with us on a stretcher.[21]

On the road itself, meanwhile, was Bill Feeley from Manchester:

We were marching along a road with the machine-gun company in the rear. The men in front had passed round a bend ... where they were out of our sight. Then there was a hold-up. We had no idea what was happening until we heard a loud roar of engines and the crackle of machine-gun fire. Next an Italian whippet [i.e. light] tank came round the corner firing at us. The battalion had walked straight into an enemy armoured column, and it had taken some minutes to realise that they were not with friends. We hastily set up the machine-guns at the roadside and opened fire ... As we were moving to a better vantage point, one of the other crews got in a lucky shot and the tank burst into flames. Two men jumped out, but died instantly in a hail of bullets. The road was now blocked by the burning tank, but a second one kept nosing into sight round the bend. Each time I sprayed it with bullets, [whereupon] the driver, fearing to share the fate of his comrades, backed off. Once we saw a group of foot-soldiers ... but they evidently lacked enthusiasm and dived back to cover.[22]

The other crew to which Feeley refers to was that of Glaswegian David Stirrat. As he remembered in old age:

The first thing I knew, we were getting machine-gunned from a tank that was sitting in the middle of the road ... There was a general *mêlée*. I set up my gun ... on the right-hand side of the road and another gun was set up on the left-hand side ... We started firing at the tank ... but it kept coming down the road. We didn't have any anti-tank ammunition or anything, just an ordinary belt of ammunition, but the tank went on fire anyway ... The crew jumped out ... and ran up the road. I don't think they survived the journey. By this time some of our fellows had been getting wounded: we were getting attacked from the right flank. When I looked round, the other machine-gun had completely disappeared ... Another tank appeared on the road: we fired at [it] and it retreated; I don't know whether it was damaged or not, but it seemed to pull in to the side of the road ... The next thing that happened was that an aircraft appeared and started to strafe us. We pulled away ... towards our right flank ... This, of course, cleared the road, and the tanks poured through in a column ... There were maybe about thirty of us left by this time [with] no officers or [anybody] in command ... The situation was hopeless so we discussed what to do ... I decided that the only possibility of anybody getting out was to split up and let every man attend to himself.[23]

Like a number of other fugitives, Stirrat and and his companions eventually escaped to the safety of the left bank of the River Ebro. To put it mildly, however, Calaceite was a disaster. Also killed beside Tapsell was George Fletcher, while total losses in terms of dead, wounded and missing came to 290 of the 650 men who had set out from Gandesa, including some 140 unwounded prisoners.[24] Already badly battered, the British battalion now ceased to exist as an organised

The site of the Calaceite disaster looking west. (Alan Warren)

fighting force: while some of the men who had managed to avoid being taken prisoner dispersed into the hills overlooking the road they were advancing along and eventually made their way to the main coastal highway, thereafter getting across the Ebro via the bridge at Tortosa, others fell back on Gandesa, where they joined a small force of Spaniards in defending a position a mile or so along the road to Tortosa where the latter plunged into a line of hills rising steeply from the coastal plain for a day or more, the survivors retiring in good order to the river. Among the men who held the defile concerned was Walter Gregory:

> In the early afternoon the inevitable fascist assault began, but it lost much of the effect that it might otherwise have had because low cloud precluded air-strikes against our position and because the speed of the enemy advance had not permitted him the time to bring his heavy artillery up to the front line. We successfully repulsed the Nationalists' leading cavalry patrols with little difficulty, and an infantry attack

The defile just east of Gandesa where a handful of stragglers from the British battalion and other units held up the Nationalists for a day in the wake of the Calaceite disaster. Hill 481, the site of the battalion's chief engagement in the Battle of the Ebro, lies a few hundred yards off camera to the left. (author's collection)

that took place … was a rather half-hearted affair and posed no real
threat … Despite the constant harassment we endured, our casualties
were few because of the protection given by the terrain.[25]

The bravery shown by such men as Morgan, Feeley, Stirrat and Gregory was
without doubt a source of consolation to many of the volunteers who in the end
came through the 'Great Retreat', much the same being true of the gallant efforts
that were made to hold Belchite and Caspe. At the same time, it would be unfair to
be too critical, for the British battalion and its fellows had been especially badly
out-gunned in the fighting of March 1938, while the Nationalist break-through
had given rise to a situation which even highly trained veterans would have found
hard to cope with. As such, it is scarcely fair to use the actions at Belchite, Caspe
and Calaceite as guides to the competence and military importance of any of the
foreign volunteers. The same, alas, cannot be said of their sequel, namely the
titanic Battle of the Ebro, the fact being that, as we shall see, many of the self-
same problems surfaced as had been visible at Brunete and Quinto. Before we
move on to this next clash of arms, however, we must first say a little about the
background.

   In the circumstances, in which the Republic was placed in the spring of 1938, a
defensive strategy might have seemed the obvious choice: following the disasters
in Aragón, the Nationalist forces had pushed ever further south-eastwards until
they reached the sea, thereby cutting its territory in two; notwithstanding a
temporary windfall that stemmed from a sudden decision on the part of the French
government to re-open the border, Russian aid was fast drying up on account of
the Nationalists' naval superiority and the plentiful efforts of the Italian fleet; and
the population was close to starvation. However, the prime minister, Negrín, and
those around him saw clearly that such a policy equated to doing little more than
exposing the Republic's collective neck and waiting for the axe to fall. That being
the case, it was therefore decided that the substantial forces in Catalonia should
rather seek to launch a great offensive that, much as had been attempted at Teruel,
would bludgeon the Nationalists into coming to terms, and in the process might
even re-open communications with the central zone. With this end in mind, then, a
new Army of the Ebro was established under the command of the erstwhile sergeant
Juan Modesto, this eventually consisting of three corps (the V Corps of Enrique
Lister, the XII Corps of Etelvino Vega and the XV Corps of Manuel Tagüeña,
each of which had three divisions); four companies of tanks; three companies of
armoured cars; two brigades of heavy artillery; two anti-aircraft brigades, each
consisting of three batteries of Russian 76.2mm M31s, two batteries of 40mm
Bofors guns, eight batteries of 20mm Oerlikon guns and a single company of
quadruple Maxim machine guns; a brigade of cavalry; a heavy machine-gun

battalion; a signals battalion; and a specially formed bridging battalion.[26] As for the target of this array, the greatest in the history of the Republican war effort, there was but one possibility, namely the area in which the Ebro forces its way through the chain of mountains that all round the periphery of Spain marks the frontier between the *meseta* of the interior and the coastal plain by means of a great bend that in effect traces three sides of a square: not only was the river much narrower here than was usually the case, but the defenders – a single division of the Army Corps of Morocco – were vulnerable to being surrounded and wiped out.

So far so good, but from the beginning the plan was flawed by the simple fact that the materiel acquired thanks to the opening of the French frontier had not been nearly enough to make up the devastating losses suffered in the course of 1937 and the first months of 1938. As had been the case in every preceding battle, artillery was in disproportionately short supply, while there were not enough shells for the guns and howitzers the Republic did possess, many of which were in any case either damaged or worn out.[27] Nor was this the limit of the trouble, for the infantry, too, were at best ill-armed. Let us take, for example, V Corps' Thirty-Fifth Division. Composed of the XI, XIII and XV International Brigades, this could expect to have got the cream of what was available, and yet the 9,600 men in its front-line infantry units had only some 5,400 rifles, 143 light

Bob Cooney and George Fletcher; both men were to play prominent roles in the last months of the existence of the British battalion. (Marx Memorial Library)

machine guns, 23 heavy machine guns, 18 mortars and 4 anti-tank guns (one thing that is indicative of the state into which XV Brigade, in particular, had fallen is that it had too few machine guns for each of its battalions to have a machine-gun company of their own, all the weapons concerned having rather been massed in a single company at the disposal of brigade headquarters).[28] Finally, as if all this was not enough, in the air the Republicans were now both badly outnumbered and badly out classed: at most they could put 250 planes into the sky as opposed to the Nationalists' 408, while their Russian fighters had little chance against the Condor Legion's Messerschmidt Me109s, yet another problem being that most of their flyers were far less well-trained than those of their opponents.[29]

If the situation with regard to armaments was bad, the question of manpower was just as worrying. Never anything like as enthusiastic to take up arms to defend the Republic as is often claimed, the civilian population was deeply war-weary and violently opposed to the extension of conscription which was the Republican government's most practical response to the disaster in Aragón, such men as were produced by the new levies therefore being not only poorly trained but unlikely to show much vigour on the battlefield: on his way to the front prior to the battle, Bill Feeley saw one young conscript literally thrown into convulsions at the thought of going into battle, while he later observed that two of the three Spaniards assigned to his machine-gun team were 'newly conscripted from the depleted manpower of the Republic's shrunken territory' and 'had little heart for soldiering'.[30] As for the International Brigades, their battalions were now mere skeletons: if the British unit was brought back to a strength of at least 500 men and possibly even more (Alexander claims the total was rather 650), the arrival of one last group of new recruits from home could not raise the proportion of Britons to anything in excess of one-third, while the Spaniards were to a man raw conscripts without the least military knowledge. There was time, true, for a period of intensive training and of still more intensive propaganda work, while the battalion was quartered well behind the lines in a pleasant valley where it was able to take its ease, enjoy a range of sporting activities and engage in a variety of attempts to fraternise with the local population.[31] According to many accounts, when the time came to go into action morale was as high as it had ever been: Londoner George Wheeler recalled that the news that battle was imminent 'provoked tremendous enthusiasm and excitement', while hardened veteran Walter Gregory was more effusive still:

> The Republicans were going on the offensive … Once this dawned
> on us, our morale rose and our confidence grew. The long retreat
> from Belchite became a thing of the past: once again we were going
> to show our enemy and the world at large that the Republic was not

prepared to submit meekly to a defeat … We knew that it would be our own effort that would determine whether or not the plan would work and were prepared to give of our all.[32]

Well, perhaps, but it is difficult not to suspect that such sentiments were expressed as much with a view to the historical record as they were with a view to the truth. In view of the horrors of the Aragón campaign, it cannot but be felt that there were plenty of volunteers who were full of foreboding. At best, then, the general mood was probably that expressed by the future trade-union leader Jack Jones. Thus:

> We were fighting quite strong forces with not the strongest resources in our case, so it was against the odds, but it was for the right cause, the Republican cause … Besides I was a single individual and wasn't afraid of the consequences whatever they were … The generals may have planned recklessly and in desperation, but the men were not aware of the considerations which influenced decisions at the top and we were glad to advance.[33]

The parlous situation of the Army of the Ebro counted for little, however. The situation brooking no delay whatsoever, on the night of 24–5 July 80,000 Republican troops therefore began to cross the River Ebro between Cherta and Mequinenza, the operation showing a degree of sophistication that the People's Army had never yet demonstrated. Simply getting across the river required the construction of several pontoon bridges and the use of large numbers of assault boats, while, as at Brunete and Belchite, the Republicans foreswore

Republican forces crossing the River Ebro by means of a pontoon bridge. (Wikimedia Commons)

any form of preliminary bombardment. Thus began the most terrible battle of the war. Rapidly overwhelming the thin defending forces, the Republicans had soon occupied a major bridgehead. That said, from the very beginning, the outnumbered Nationalists made lavish use of airpower to slow down the Republican advance. Among the thousands of men trudging along the narrow mountain roads was Fred Thomas of the XV Brigade's anti-tank battery (not that this had been restored to anything like its previous condition, consisting as it now did of a mere eight men armed with what appears to have been a Russian 37mm infantry gun of First-World-War vintage):

> Christ! That last hour had the worst bit of bombing I have ever experienced. At about five p.m. we got orders to move down … an old dusty track leading to the pontoon bridge our men have put across. About half an hour after we arrived over came fifteen or so bombers, and, blimey, I never want bombs closer. Lousy to be once again at the old game of burying your nose in the ground.[34]

Another volunteer who was awed by the Nationalist air attacks was George Wheeler. As he later wrote:

> Looking up, I could see the planes, big Italian bombers. I counted six of them gleaming in the early morning twilight, and, as I watched, I could see bombs hurtling earthwards. They appeared to be coming straight towards me, and, on hearing an awful, screaming swishing sound, I hugged the ground which shook as I imagined an earthquake would. Once, twice, three times they flew back. Each time was a nightmare as they dropped their hellish cargo, but worse was to follow as they flew low and opened up with machine-guns: I heard bullets … crashing into the earth just a few yards away.[35]

Commanded, as before, by Sam Wild and possessed of a new battalion commissar in the person of Bob Cooney, the battalion made for the small town of Corbera. Reaching this last in the late afternoon, it found itself confronted by a determined enemy rearguard. For George Wheeler, as for many of his comrades, it was his baptism of fire:

> Immediately in front of us was a small bridge over a dried up river. We filed down to the river-bank, our movements concealed from the fascists by foliage and undulations in the ground. We were to

use the riverbed as cover while we worked our way to the rear of their strongpoint. There was a gap in the protective screen of trees and bushes, and, as we dashed across, enemy machine-guns opened up … We now had to work our way upwards, and, putting our … training into effect, we began to move in formation, gradually getting nearer to the enemy in order to engage him … Progress was rather slow and protracted: it was late evening before we really got to grips with the fascists and dawn was breaking before we finally winkled them out.[36]

From Wheeler's account, it is clear that there had at least been some improvement in the standard of instruction. As so often before, however, initial success was followed by stalemate, this time at the town of Gandesa. Faced by determined resistance – typically enough, Franco had rushed reinforcements to the sector from far and wide – the Republicans suffered heavy casualties and were brought to a halt. As ever, Walter Gregory was fighting with the British battalion, the objective of this unit being a steep-sided knoll just to the south-east of Gandesa, officially known as Hill 481 but more commonly termed 'the Pimple', that overlooked the defile held by Gregory and his fellows in the wake of the Calaceite disaster. Approaching this position along the crest of a long ridge that stretched south-westwards from the vicinity of Corbera to that of Gandesa known as the Sierra de Laval de la Torre, Wild and his men found themselves confronted by a steep scrub-covered drop followed by an equally steep and equally scrub-covered ascent.[37] Nothing daunted, however, the battalion pressed on. Among the first to go forward was George Wheeler:

We formed up into our squads, platoons and sections … and waited for the order to attack. At last the order came: 'Over you go, lads!' Bending almost double, we plunged over the crest … It was hard going down the steep and wooded slope, and I soon went sprawling and lost my rifle. The air was dense with bullets that whizzed and ricocheted off rocks and trees. Hastily retrieving my rifle, I safely reached the bottom of the hill where we were to assemble before pressing on. After a brief rest, we began the climb up to the fascist positions until we were 100 metres from them. From here onwards, there was practically no cover, and it was obvious that a final assault would have been fatal. We opened up a steady … fire, which they answered with a terrific bombardment, and it was all we could do to retreat to safer positions and hang on. Thus the first attack on Hill 481 ended in failure.[38]

The summit of Hill 481 viewed from the north-east. The British battalion attacked from the low ground to the left. Meanwhile, the jagged massif on the skyline is the Sierra de Pàndols. (author's collection)

So near yet so far – the summit of Hill 481 as seen by the leading elements of the British battalion. (author's collection)

The date of this attack was 27 July. Over the next three days there followed a further series of attacks, but these, too, were beaten off without difficulty. Fighting with one of the rifle companies of the British battalion was Liverpudlian Bob Clark:

> The whole crest of the hill was a death trap ... By some piece of sheer luck, I found that I had reached a position from where I could see the enemy machine-guns ... Peering cautiously around, I noticed a dip in the hillside which would give a measure of protection. Slowly crawling along on my belly ... I suddenly felt as if I had been hit in the face with a sledge-hammer. Jumping about five feet in the air, I felt a terrible emotion of seeing a searing wall of flame followed immediately by a dreadful darkness.[39]

Badly wounded, Clark had to be evacuated to the rear. Rather more lucky was Steven Fullarton, a volunteer from the Glasgow area, a machine-gunner attached to No. 1 Company:

> We were put in a forward position at Hill 481 which was within sight of Gandesa ...They had their machine-guns fortified up there ... Seven tanks appeared from well over on our right. They ... stopped and fired some shells, and then they just withdrew ... After some long time – we were supposed to wait for this artillery bombardment which never materialised ... off we went to make a frontal attack. Having run as hard as we could to get as near as

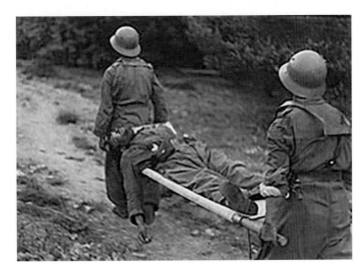

A wounded Republican soldier being carried to the rear during the Battle of the Ebro. The stretcher bearers are wearing Czech steel helmets, a common sight in the Republican armies in 1938. (Wikimedia Commons)

possible to the fascists and then found it was practically a sheer rise in front of us, our attack came to a halt … I ran out of ammunition for the Degtyarev, firing up at those machine-gun posts … They had us in a very sticky situation … All around, anybody that I could see or hear was either dead or wounded … I realised there was not much more I could do … so I started to attend to the people who had been wounded round about me. One in particular that I can name is Kelly from, I think, Dunbarton … While I was attending to Kelly – he was … lying feet downhill on his back, and I was feet uphill, lying head to head with him, a shell exploded just about his feet. Of course, I got a shower of grit, but that's all I got, no shrapnel.[40]

With casualties mounting rapidly, on 30 July yet another attack was made on the Nationalist positions. In charge of the assault was Walter Gregory:

Just before dawn we started our … ascent, crawling from rock to rock, keeping as low as possible and trying to leave the loose shale undisturbed … We had moved but a short distance beyond our own front line when we were greeted by a fusillade of rifle and machine-gun fire and any semblance of an orderly advance disappeared as each man sought cover for himself … It was now simply a matter of returning fire whenever each man thought that it was safe enough for him to expose himself for as long as it took to discharge a few rounds of ammunition at the heights above.[41]

Wounded that same day by a bullet in the neck, Gregory was sent to the rear. For three days the attacks continued, but, with paralysis spreading all along the line, the Republicans were at length forced to suspend the offensive. Since crossing the river, the troops had suffered heavy losses – at least 12,000 men according to Martínez Bande[42] – while the shortage of motorised transport, the wretched condition of the roads in a mountainous district almost totally devoid of centres of population and the sheer distance of the new front line from the Ebro meant that keeping the assault going was never really a serious possibility. On the slopes below Hill 481, certainly, the British had shot their bolt. Not the least of the problems was the heavy losses that had been suffered among the leadership cadres. Gregory, as we have seen, had been wounded on 30 July, but also down was his predecessor as the commander of No. 2 Company, John Argus, and his successor, Lewis Clive, a graduate of the University of Oxford and Rowing Blue who had won a gold medal for Britain in the 1932 Olympics and obtained a commission

The rugged terrain between the battlefront and the River Ebro which confronted the medical orderlies tasked with evacuating the British volunteers wounded at Gandesa. (author's collection)

in the Grenadier Guards, only almost immediately to resign and instead become a Labour councillor in London. A witness to his passing was George Wheeler:

> Lewis Clive excelled himself as company commander. He was everywhere, directing, organising, encouraging. One morning he selected three of us to take up vantage points on a ridge facing the fascists. We were instructed to keep up a constant rifle fire on their position. I was in a rather exposed spot, my only cover a gorse bush, [but] concentrated my aim on a movement I detected at the base of an enemy pill-box and fired round after round until my rifle bolt became almost too hot to handle. Lewis ... reappeared and asked about the activity in the fascist lines ... At that moment I felt splashes on my forearm and, glancing down, was astonished to see they were splashes of blood. Turning I saw Lewis reel and fall ... The top of his head was severed completely and, as he lay there, the brain was spilling from its case.[43]

Given the expectation that in combat they would do all they could to animate the men in their charge, commissars also suffered heavier losses than the men. In this category, three of the five who served at company level were dead, namely Harry Dobson, Morris Miller and Mike Economides, and another, Jack Jones, badly wounded, while, like Jones, Cooney's deputy, Alan Gilchrist, was out of the fight after being hit. Finally, though the man concerned was possessed of no rank, another important loss was that of David Guest, a gifted scientist from Southampton who, like many others, had become a Communist while studying at the University of Cambridge and might well have gone on to important things (at Cambridge, he had been the controller of the Communist cell belonged to by the notorious foursome of Blunt, Philby, Burgess and Maclean). Such losses would have been hard enough to endure at the best of times, but the situation the battalion was in anything but merited such a description. Erstwhile battalion commander Bill Alexander, who had recovered from his wounds and come back to Spain to take up a post in the supply echelon, recalled:

> Conditions in the battalion area were almost beyond description. The heat was intense, the bare rocks were shell-shattered, the debris of war was everywhere and the stench of blood and bodies nauseating. The boots of those fortunate [enough] to have them were cut to pieces by the rock splinters, while … rope-soled *alpagartas* gave no protection. The men were emaciated and exhausted from the heat … inadequate food and … lack of … sleep. All supplies – ammunition, food and liquid – had to be … brought by reluctant mules over the rocks … Collection of the wounded was difficult, slow and painful for the [former] and physically and emotionally exhausting for those who carried them.[44]

Given the appalling heat, meanwhile, water was particularly difficult. As one volunteer remembered:

> It was a hell of a job… Away up on those mountain tops, there was no water at all: it had all to be carted up from down below. [Once] we sent one or two comrades down with sixteen water-bottles … [but] but shells … killed them and peppered every one of the … bottles so that they wouldn't hold water … There was one fellow … who was from Glasgow: his tongue swelled up … his lips were swollen, and it was making him cry almost.[45]

Digging in, the Republicans were now subjected to a ferocious counter-offensive designed, first, to restore Franco's prestige, and, second, to wreck the forces defending Catalonia beyond repair. Much criticised as it has been by those who say that the Nationalist commander should have simply contained the Republican incursion while launching a massive offensive north of the Ebro that would supposedly have carried all before it and led to the fall of Barcelona, there was some logic to Franco's decision: as at Brunete, Belchite and Teruel, the engagement and destruction of the main enemy fighting force could be argued to trump even the most important of geographical objectives. At the Ebro, however, there was a crucial difference in that almost all the ground occupied by the Republicans was a tangle of jagged *sierras* that offered far better defensive positions than the plains of Brunete or the steppes of Teruel, the result being that progress was very slow and casualties enormous. That said, the experience of the defenders was still gruelling to say the least. Pulled out of the line on 3 August for a short time, within a few days the battalion was back in action, this time in the massif south of Gandesa known as the Sierra de Pàndols. Morale, however, was none too high, much discontent having been aroused by the fact that the Communist leadership had once again intervened in the affairs of the battalion by evacuating a number of Party stalwarts who either already occupied useful positions back in Britain or were earmarked for such roles in the future. As Hugh Sloan remembered, 'Lying around in the sun ... among the olive trees, we ruminated a lot ... and began to show signs of wanting to go home. I think it was because we had reached the point where a certain tiredness had crept into us. There was also a realisation that ... some [comrades] were being sent home.'[46] Coupled with jealousy of men who were being favoured for political reasons alone, and had on occasion proved less than first-class soldiers, was a grim realism that eclipsed the enthusiasm with which the battalion had gone into action on 25 July (if, indeed, such was the case). As a Walter Gregory returned to the battalion after recovering from the wound he had suffered on 30 July admitted, 'We knew what we were in for and there was little joy in our ranks.'[47]

Such forebodings were all too acute. Edwin Greening, for example, was a volunteer from Wales:

> We were all filthy, unshaven. Everywhere was the smell of urine, excreta, dead men and dead mules. It was hell on earth ... We had another terrific barrage. And I heard a shout, 'Come quick, Taff!' Tom Howell Jones had been hit, so I crawled down ... to where Tom and his friends were ... They'd had a direct hit and [been] killed. I just held [Tom] in my arms ... You can imagine how I felt. The next day we got them out and buried them ... by covering them with stones: there was no earth there.[48]

A company commissar from Scotland newly arrived in Spain, Tom Murray had a similar experience:

> Of course, we had no backing: we had no reserves ... and no equipment to make up for losses ... We had our machine-guns established at the top of the hill, and on one occasion there were three of my Scots comrades killed by an anti-tank gun that had been firing from the valley below ... I was down the hill a little bit when Paddy Duff, an Irishman, who was the adjutant of our company, came running down ... There was a great big chunk of flesh out of his arm just as though a dog had bitten it. Paddy said, 'Christ almighty, you'd better go ... to the top of the hill. There's some dead.' I tore off his shirt and made a kind of tourniquet for his arm ... and [then] up ... I went ... There were shells bursting and all sorts of things: it was a nasty situation ... I found George Jackson lying stretched out ... Charlie McLeod of Aberdeen lying with his head on [George's] chest, and Malcolm Smith of Dundee ... lying about a yard or so away.[49]

Still another new arrival, albeit one who was far less enthusiastic, was Cambridge graduate John Bassett:

> I had come too late: all the romance had gone. It might have been different had there been a prospect of victory ... There was little comradeship: hope and certainty had gone [and] everybody seemed tired, tense and intent only on survival ... I never saw a map and nothing was ever explained to me ... During those weeks at the front, the accuracy of the shelling turned my stomach to water. As the guns modified their range, the warning rush of air became short and shorter, [and] the bursts closer and closer until dirt and stones poured into the trench and rattled on the shovel which I was holding over my head and neck ... I had been allotted the end of the line, adjoining a narrow macadam road along which I expected to see enemy vehicles at any minute. All day long men would crawl over me and relieve themselves at the end of the trench: I ceased to brush the flies off my face ... and I could not help wishing I had never come. During the nights, our sleep was fitful. We took turns to prowl in no-man's-land, alert for every sound, among the shattered trees. Almost every night somebody would take fright, and, for five or ten minutes, whole hillsides would be lit up to a cacophony of rifle fire and bursting grenades.[50]

Despite the facts, first, that the summit which the British battalion was particularly charged with defending – the ominously numbered Hill 666 – possessed no other fortifications than low rock walls that sent jagged splinters flying in all directions every time they were struck by a bullet, and, second, that Sam Wild had to be replaced after being hit by a shell fragment, the volunteers and their Spanish comrades held out for a full eleven days before they were at long last relieved and filed back to the rear, only to be flung into action almost immediately as part of a counter-attack near Corbera designed to regain control of yet another nameless eminence, this one denominated Hill 356 (in the literature this action is always stated as having taken place near a village called 'Sandesco', but no such settlement can be located on any map: however, it is known that the period 5–7 September saw 35 Division – XV International Brigade's parent formation – take part in a series of counter-attacks aimed at re-taking the key village of Corbera, this last having just fallen to the Nationalists). So far as can be judged from the rather vague accounts in the literature of the relatively brief stint in the line that followed, however, the British part in this fighting was very limited, not to say anti-climactic. Having just returned from a spell in hospital for treatment for an infected boil on his arm, George Wheeler was now a section commander. He wrote:

> Joining up with another section we approached the ridge the fascists were thought to have captured. On the way up, I had a problem with one of my men. A Spaniard, he was … reluctant to move. 'Adelante!' ('Forward!'), I yelled, and prodded him from behind with my bayonet … We reached the top … with great apprehension, expecting to be met by a withering fire … [but] to our relief and astonishment, we found the ridge was unoccupied. There had been considerable shelling, and we had sustained casualties, but no fascists were to be seen.[51]

What is clear, however, is that the battalion was subjected to heavy aerial and artillery bombardment. In the words of Walter Gregory:

> We had no trenches, no protection: we just lay flat on the ground with our arms covering our heads. The bombs burst all about us. The impact was terrific: the ground trembled and heaved, and clouds of swirling dust reduced visibility to a few inches … I do not think I recovered from that bombing for a long time: had I been in the British forces I am sure that I could not only have legitimately gone sick with shock, but that I would have been made to do so …

If the bombing was horrendous, the constant barrages of artillery fire were little better: probably the cumulative effect of them was every bit a detrimental as [that of] the more sporadic heavy bombing … How we came to hate planes and cannon![52]

As witness the following account from George Wheeler, such experiences were clearly terrifying:

The *avión* whistle sounded, and I dashed for a trench. I lay flat on my back looking up at the clear blue sky … Suddenly I felt intense heat and saw a wall of flame shoot across the confined space of the trench, The walls … seemed to close together above me, and for a brief moment I had the feeling that I was about to be buried. Just as suddenly, [they] sprang back to their original positions … After the planes passed, I scrambled out, unscathed … Only a few yards away, I saw a large bomb crater and marvelled at my lucky escape.[53]

Pulled out of the line once more, the remnants of the battalion now enjoyed a few days' rest, and even received a draft of reinforcements. Yet, even to the most committed Communists, it was clear that the situation was desperate. Herewith Gregory once again:

We continued to have casualties from artillery fire and aerial bombing for rest areas were no longer safe areas, just patches of calm in a landscape of noise, chaos, danger and death … Of the 150 men of my company who had crossed the Ebro on the night of 25 July, I had just under two dozen still with me: the rest were either dead, wounded or missing … Our numbers had been supplemented by the addition of some 130 Spanish lads, but they were raw recruits, novices to the savagery of war, and my heart went out to them as they took in the scenes of devastation through frightened eyes.[54]

Bleak as the possibilities were of using such tattered forces with any success, the night of 21 September saw the battalion being rushed back into the line once more, this time to a position on the road that led from Gandesa to the Ebrine town of Asco, below a windmill called the Molina de Farriols; to the right, meanwhile, was the Lincoln battalion and to the left the Canadian Mackenzie-Papineau, while a limited amount of fire support was available in the form of a new brigade anti-tank battery, crewed though this was almost entirely by Spaniards.[55] Other than a heavy air-raid in the afternoon, the next day was quiet, and, some 377 men-strong, of whom 106 were British, the battalion was able to dig in, albeit with some difficulty. 'The trenches were dug in hard rocky soil and in places were less than a metre deep', recalled George Wheeler. 'I was compelled to lie flat as … the fascists began sniping at us … Lying full length in a crowded trench wielding a pick is tiring work. Wielding one on rocky soil is more tiring still, and, when one has had no sleep for days, the task is enervating.'[56]

Positioned in rolling, scrub-covered open country, the XV Brigade did not even possess the advantage of the rocky, precipitous slopes that had been of such value to them at Hill 666. When the Nationalists attacked first thing in the morning of 23 September, the British, Americans and Canadians and their Spanish auxiliaries therefore had little chance. Advancing under cover of a massive artillery bombardment, the assault troops over-ran some troops, including George Wheeler and his section, and took them prisoner before they had the chance to fire a single shot. The reason, as erstwhile anti-tank gunner John Dunlop later inferred, was in part the dust and smoke caused by the bombardment and, in part, the fact that the defences had been poorly positioned. Thus:

> We were strung round this hill in trenches … only two or three feet deep … [and] had very little cover, indeed. It was only myself and another man on the right that managed to get away. Johnny Power [the commander of No. 1 Company] and one or two others got away on the left flank … We were attacked by airplanes, by bombing … and, with the smoke of the bombs, and the dust and grit that was flying around, our visibility was very seriously impaired … It was only when it had cleared that we discovered that the enemy were advancing … They had advanced round to our right in between us and the nearest company of the battalion … and they were just moving down on the backs of these poor chaps who were … in a sort-of half moon … position on a lower slope of the hill … There was nothing we could do about it. The grit from the atmosphere had filled up the locks of our rifles and I got away three shots before my rifle jammed … Even hitting the bolt with a stone, I couldn't open it … for re-firing.[57]

Dunlop eventually escaped to the comparative safety of brigade headquarters without a scratch, and that despite the fact that a grenade flung at him by an enemy soldier actually bounced off his shoulder before exploding a few feet away.

Another man who made it, meanwhile, was Bill Feeley who was stationed with the brigade's newly acquired machine-gun company:

> Out front, everything was shrouded in smoke and dirt ... [but] we spotted some vague figures moving on the crest of another ridge. I called over Jack Nalty, the Irish company commander, and asked if they were enemy troops. He shouted, 'Yes, that's them', and we opened fire. The figures kept disappearing, but we kept firing bursts at the position. I occasionally caught glimpses of Nalty passing the back of our emplacement, going from one gun to another. As we were firing blind, I decided to ask for his advice. On emerging from the redoubt, I saw below us and to our right a stream of Republican soldiers retreating at the double across a dip and up the opposite slope, with machine-gun bullets kicking up the soil around them ... I warned Syd [i.e. Syd Booth, the only other British volunteer in Feeley's crew] and in a few minutes Nalty came running with the order for us to get out. We stripped the gun and Syd began lifting the carriage onto his shoulders ... The Spanish lads seemed to have disappeared, so I grabbed the gun and we ran down the slope ... Something hit my temple and, when I put my hand to it, it came away bloody [so] I dived behind a scraggy olive tree ... I had lost Syd, and unrecognisable men were still dashing madly through a hail of lead ... I was preparing myself for a dash, when ... a jagged hole appeared in the top of my left trouser leg ... Fearing to draw fire on the other wounded men lying around, I played dead until [the] ... machine-gunners raised their sights and began firing ... at some target further back.[58]

Still able to walk despite the wound to his leg, Feeley made it to safety, but both Nalty – one of the very few men left of the company that had fought at Lopera – and Booth were killed. Other men who fell, meanwhile, included Dubliner Liam McGregor, George Green from Stockport, whose wife, Nan, was a nurse in a Republican hospital, and Ivor Hickman from Southampton. If any men got away from the first-line positions at all, meanwhile, it was in part the work of Walter Gregory, who led the survivors of his company in putting up a fierce fight before being taken in the rear and forced to surrender.[59] At the end of the day, the fighting petered out with the Republican line still more-or-less intact, but once again the battalion was reduced to a mere shell: of the 377 men in the ranks when it went back into the line, only 173 were left including 58 British.[60] Such losses were truly tragic, for barely 2 days before, the Republican government had signed an agreement whereby it promised to send home all the surviving Internationals in exchange for the repatriation of 10,000 Italians by the Nationalists.[61] It was the end of the road for the British volunteers, but their story and those of all the rest was only just beginning, a story whose tone was set by the impassioned speech delivered by the prominent Communist parliamentary deputy Dolores Ibárruri at the farewell parade that was organised for the survivors of the International Brigades in Barcelona prior to their evacuation. Thus, 'Comrades of the International Brigades ... You can go proudly: you are history; you are legend!'[62]

What, though, of the military performance of the British battalion during the Nationalist conquest of Aragón and the Battle of the Ebro? Clearly, this had been none too good, but, before going any further, it is but fair to point out that the Nationalists had enjoyed complete air superiority in a manner that had not been the case for most of the campaigns of 1937, let alone those of 1936. Meanwhile, much though it might be pointed out that a good part of the aid that Franco received from Germany and Italy in terms of tanks and artillery was no better than, and sometimes inferior to, that received from Russia, by 1938 the organisational superiority of the Nationalist forces was starting to have its full effect, the result being that Franco's generals were able to call down artillery bombardments of unprecedented magnitude, bombardments, moreover, that improved training and communications had rendered far more accurate than ever before. As had not been nearly so much the case in the battles of 1937, the repeated claims on the part of International-Brigade veterans that their repeated failures were the fruit of the Nationalists' overwhelming material superiority therefore have much validity. At the same time, too, if, contrary to myth, most volunteers had adequate rifles in the form of Russian Moisin-Nagants or, at the Battle of the Ebro, more up-to-date Czech or Polish Mausers, clothing was at best inadequate, steel helmets anything but universal, personal equipment scanty, creature comforts such as chocolate, good-quality cigarettes and mail from home very scarce, and food universally monotonous, inadequate and of poor quality. In the words of Bob Doyle, then, the International Brigades were 'a decrepit, dirty, unshaven and disorganised lot'.[63]

With matters in this state, and the British battles conducted in the midst, successively, of bitter cold, pouring rain and blazing heat, it seems entirely permissible to express a considerable degree of wonder that any of the volunteers stuck to their guns at all. Yet, beneath the surface lurked a picture that was much murkier. In the first place, to the extent that it had existed at all, the elan of the early days was a thing of the past. In the eyes of many of the volunteers and their apologists, the chief problem here was the constant dilution of the battalion with ever greater numbers of unwilling Spanish conscripts. To the extent that a growing body of revisionist literature has suggested that, irrespective of whether the Republic was fighting a revolutionary war or not, enthusiasm for the war against Franco was far more limited than the traditional view would have it, there is an element of truth to this assertion.[64] Yet, the volunteers' views of their Spanish comrades being all too often shaped by cultural prejudice, namely the ingrained belief that Spain was hopelessly backward and the Spanish people, at best, ignorant and lackadaisical and, at worst, incompetent and cowardly, this is simply not sufficient as an answer.[65] On the contrary, what we have is rather a convenient smoke-screen. Thus, as the war went on, so fewer and fewer of the Britons who travelled out to Spain to join the International Brigades were starry-eyed idealists avid to defend the cause of democracy against fascism. Even as early as the winter of 1936 officials of Communist branches were having actively to solicit recruits to fill up the ranks – committed a combatant as he became, Walter Gregory did not come forward until he was invited to do by so by the Party organiser in charge of his home county[66] – and, in addition, to have recourse, whether in good faith or bad, to the blatant untruth that men would only have to serve for a limited period that might, perhaps, be as short as six months. Also quick to fall by the wayside were initial attempts to ensure the suitability of recruits, whether this was measured in terms of political reliability, fitness for combat or home situation (above all, the existence of dependents who could potentially become both a political liability and a charge on the Party's limited financial resources). The result of all this, of course, was a great deal of sickness, combat fatigue or downright shirking of one form or another, while the stress that the Communists placed on 'political work' – in essence, the propagation and enforcement of the Party line – meant that an inordinately large number of men were able to find safe employment well behind the lines. With the manpower shortage ever more acute, there was little option but to 'comb out' the *retaguardia* so as to gather in as much of the resultant missing manpower as possible, the result being the British battalion of February 1938, let alone July 1938, was not the British battalion of February 1937: in brief, men plucked from hiding, punishment stockades or cushy billets were anything but enthusiastic about risking their lives in action for a cause which many were inclined to see as utterly hopeless. To make matters worse, meanwhile, the shrinking cadre of veterans who should have been the glue that held the battalion together was exhausted and demoralised: suffering terribly from boils, for example, Manchester volunteer Albert Charlesworth deserted rather than take part in the initial advance across the Ebro.[67]

By 1938, then, the British battalion was a slender reed and, indeed, one that got still slimmer as month succeeded month. To expect too much from it was therefore foolhardy, but there was yet another problem. Thus, from the beginning the culture that reigned among the volunteers was profoundly unmilitary. Discipline was patchy; respect for rank was conditional at best; there was much resentment of the manner in which officers enjoyed better conditions than the rank and file; and there was much resistance to, much less understanding of, the norms of army life. Nor did it help that too many men were imbued with notions that correct political thinking was enough to make any man a soldier. With training never much more than inadequate and officers who were all too often devoid of any military experience other than at the lowest level, the result was that few volunteers were prepared for the realities of combat when they went into action, nor, still less, ready to withstand its rigours for any length of time.[68] It was not just heavy fire that had checked the attack on Hill 481, then, while both the actions of 31 March and 23 September were marked by a failure to implement even the most basic security precautions. Taken by surprise on both occasions, the battalion was completely broken, while, in the case of the latter, it did not even put up much of a fight. To quote Fred Thomas, 'The story of the 23rd … was, I'm afraid, a somewhat inglorious one'.[69]

The Battlefields Today

The battlefields of March–September 1938 make for an interesting tour of an area whose scenery is often highly dramatic. Let us begin with Belchite. Famously left in ruins after the war not so much as a monument to the horrors of war as a reminder to the Spanish people of their likely fate should they take it into their heads to challenge the established order for a second time, the remains of the town fought over in 1936 can be visited by means of guided tours run by the local council. However, well worth it though these are, for the purposes of looking at the action of March 1938, it is better to view the ruins from without. From the entrance to the *plaza* in front of the main gate into the old town, then, head east along the A220 until it reaches the A222. At this point, turn south and follow the highway until a service road is encountered on the right. Take this turning and at the bend turn right onto the unmetalled track. Following this all the way around to the right will take the visitor back to the starting point of the walk at the main entrance to the old town, while the route offers good views of both the ruins and the heights south of the town where Merriman rallied the remnants of the brigade. In addition, a number of tracks lead up into the hills that offer more adventurous routes, one such beginning back at the service road mentioned above. Thus, instead of turning right along the unmetalled track follow the service road around the bend towards the highway. Immediately before this last is reached take the track angling off to the right and walk up the hill. Take the second turning right and follow this new track in a generally westerly direction along the edge of a belt of scrub and olive groves to a T-junction. At said T-junction turn right and proceed downhill into the valley beneath the town: once on the low ground, the periphery track that formed the basis for the first route will be picked up almost immediately.

From Belchite, the route of XV Brigade's retreat to Caspe can be followed by taking the A222 to Lécera and there turning left onto A223 to Albalate de Arzobispo, at which place the A223 leads after a short distance to Hijar. From Hijar take the A224 northeastwards to Escatrón via Samper de Colanda, Jatiel and Castelnou. Finally, at Escatrón turn right onto the A221 and follow it eastwards to Caspe. The drive is a long one and, until the Ebro valley is reached in the last stretch, much of the countryside barren and desolate: if the British volunteers were exhausted when they arrived at their destination, then, it is hardly surprising. In the action at Caspe, meanwhile, the survivors of the British battalion were deployed on the southern outskirts of the town along with what was left of the XII and XIV International Brigades. Unfortunately, it is not possible to establish the exact positions defended by Gregory and his fellows, but, starting with its right flank resting on the River Ebro, the Republican defensive line curled around the western sides of the town before running roughly south-eastwards parallel to the road to Gandesa (i.e. the A221), and from Gregory's account it seems likely that they were stationed somewhere near the turn-off that leads from the A221 to the neighbouring industrial estate just before the road enters the town. Meanwhile, the low ridge occupied by said industrial estate marks the area where the survivors were when the fighting drew to a close.

Having crossed the River Guadolope and ascended the slopes on the far side continue along the A221 to Maella, Batea and, finally, Gandesa. Immediately before the last town is reached, the highway – now the C221 – passes through an area of high ground. This is the Sierra de Fatarella and was the scene of bitter fighting in the first phase of the Nationalist attempt to oust the Republicans from the ground they had seized at the start of the Battle of the Ebro.

Gandesa is an excellent centre for an exploration of the battlefield, in that it possesses a modern museum dedicated to the subject and numerous monuments to the fallen, while at the same time literally being situated on the front line: in brief, this ran in a north-south arc around the eastern edge of the town (situated just to the north on the by-road to Fayón, the municipal cemetery marks the furthest point of the Republican advance). Today part of the scene of the fighting is buried beneath industrial estates and new housing, but in the vicinity of the bus station the perimeter of the built-up area is much the same as it was in 1938, while an unnamed road leading out into the plain beside the Hotel Pliqué gives the visitor access to a part of the battlefield that remains little changed (for a quick tour, walk north-eastwards along this track until it reaches a T-junction; at the T-junction turn right and head in the direction of the industrial estate until the track reaches a roundabout; at the roundabout turn right and take the road heading back into town). To reach Hill 481, meanwhile, take the C43 (signposted Xerta) and head south-eastwards out of town: Hill 481 is the prominent tooth-like summit on the skyline of the wooded ridge ahead and to the left, said wooded ridge being the Serra Laval de la Torre. Very shortly the road bends round to the right and starts to climb into the hills, it being more-or-less this spot which marked the rearguard action in which Walter Gregory fought in the wake of the action of Calaceite. Just past the 'Construccions Grar' site, take the unmetalled track on the left and follow this up hill, taking care to ignore the turning off to the left that will be encountered some 400yd along the way. Eventually, the track crosses over a crest and drops down to a concrete construction that is probably a cistern: from here it is possible both to ascend the slope to the left and thereby reach the summit of Hill 481 or to descend into the declivity beneath it and thereby reach the area where the successive attacks of the British battalion came to grief. Finally, for an alternative route back to Gandesa, having crossed back over the crest on the same track as before, take the turning that was ignored on the way up: this drops straight down into the valley below and leads directly to the same roundabout encountered before.

The next spot associated with the British battalion – Hill 666 – is situated on the other side of the C43 a short distance away from Hill 481 in the Serra de Pàndols. To reach it continue along the road until it reaches a picnic area and car park, Hill 666 being the massif that overhangs the C43 directly ahead and to the right. To reach it take the way-marked path that ascends from the other side of the main road: this is part of a circular route that eventually leads back to the C43 a little distance further east. Be warned, however: the track is often extremely steep. For a map, see <https://www.wikiloc.com/hiking-trails/serres-de-pandols-i-cavalls-9506383>.

There remains the site of the last action of the British battalion. This may be found by following the N420 northwards from Gandesa to Corbere d'Ebre. Like Gandesa, this has a museum dedicated to the battle, but the town one sees today is not the one that existed in 1938, the original having been so badly damaged that it was completely reconstructed on the more convenient site afforded by the valley bottom: the ruins of the old village may be found on the hillside to the north (look for the Carrer del Poble Vell).

For the site of the action of 23 September, carry on along the N420. A mile beyond the outskirts of the town, the road crosses a small stream running down to the nearby river by means of a modern embankment. Just before said embankment turn left onto the service road to the left. The 1938 highway, this crosses the stream a few yards to the north of its modern replacement, the spot where it does so marking the epicentre of the fighting. The area bearing little relation to either such descriptions of the terrain we have or the sketch map provided by Bill Alexander in *British Volunteers for Liberty*, it is difficult to be certain exactly where the volunteers took up position, but a few yards back along N420 in the direction of Corbera, a steep scrub-covered slope overhangs the road and it is likely that immediately beneath it was the advanced post where George Wheeler was taken prisoner. Again, it is not possible to be certain, but the main line of defence was probably sited on the eastern bank of the ravine, what appears to be a line of trenches running south-eastwards from the main road along the edge of the line of trees that marks its course.

Conclusion

As might be expected, for those bound up in the official line that to this day pervades the historiography of the International Brigades, there has never been the slightest willingness to back away from their stated convictions, whether genuine or otherwise: in so far as they are concerned, the British volunteers never either wavered in their enthusiasm or failed to make a significant contribution to the defence of the Republic in the battles in which they took part. In the words of Bill Alexander, for example, 'the British volunteers … fought as bravely and as skilfully' in their last action at Corbera 'as they had in their first action … at Jarama'.[1] However, such comments are difficult to sustain. Indeed, one might even turn Alexander's claim back on itself, for, if very harsh, it would be just as valid to say that the performance of the volunteers in the summer of 1938 was characterised by the same lack of resolution and proficiency as their performance in February 1937. Let us first begin with the issue of courage. While the men of the British battalion were generally capable of putting up a reasonable fight when they were on the defensive, getting them to advance in the face of even the most minimal fire was very difficult: hence the terrible losses incurred among the battalion and company commanders and political commissars; equally, if there were some men who showed real heroism on the battlefield or, at the very least, proved unwavering in their commitment and dedication, there were plenty of others who ran away, deserted or simply cracked under the strain. As for military proficiency, the picture was even bleaker, for, so far as can be judged, neither tactics nor weapon handling nor standards of discipline made much progress. There is, then, little more that needs to be said: while it may have been somewhat better than many other units of the Republican army – an achievement which, it has to be said, was far from difficult – *a corps d'élite* the British battalion was not. As for the contribution that it made to the Republican cause, the fact was that the 1,800 casualties it lost on the battlefields of the Civil War counted for nothing. As we have seen, in his recent military history of the conflict Edward Hooton has painted a picture of the International Brigaders as innocents sacrificed on the altar of Communist policy, men, indeed, whose lives were cast away in a struggle to which they could make little contribution. This judgement has been fiercely contested by Alexander Clifford in a study published too late for it to be made full use of in the preparation of this work, but his claims ring hollow, and all the more so as the best he can do to substantiate them is to cite a quote from the leading specialist on the Republican army, Michael Alpert, to the effect that their achievement was no greater than that of the best of the latter's Spanish units. To be blunt, then, the current author remains deeply unpersuaded by Clifford's efforts.[2]

Nor is the question of military competence the only manner in which the heroic image of the International Brigades can be challenged. In this work we have concentrated on the battles and skirmishes which cost so many of the British volunteers so heavily (a fact that nobody is seeking to deny even if it is in part one more factor that calls into question their prowess on the battlefield and general worth as a fighting unit), but there is also another area that is ripe for discussion. We come here to the question of the political impulse that gave rise to the International Brigades. In the first instance, of course, it was maintained that this was entirely spontaneous, a matter, indeed, of workers by hand and by brain rushing forward of their own volition to defend the cause of peace and democracy against the threat of fascism. So ludicrous was this version of events that it failed to stand the test of time for more than a matter of months, if that, and so a rather different version of events was soon being put about to the effect that, while there had indeed been a spontaneous flood of volunteers, the task of getting them to Spain and providing them with leadership and organisation had been taken on by a Communist movement selflessly committed to the idea of the 'popular front', the idea, to reiterate, that all good men and true – indeed, all good parties and true – should come together to oppose Hitler and Mussolini and their many admirers.

Broadly speaking, this is the line that has continued to prevail among those who admire the International Brigades right down to the current day, but at its heart there remains a further obfuscation, namely the idea that the volunteers represented a broad range of political opinion: if their ranks included many Communists, there were also plenty of men who had remained loyal to the original socialist movements (in the British case, the Labour Party and the Independent Labour Party), not to mention a sprinkling of bourgeois liberals; it was, then, no coincidence that much stress was laid on the presence of poets, writers and university graduates and, for that matter, Winston Churchill's nephew Esmond Romilly. Exactly as with the issue of a widespread desire to uphold the Second Republic against Franco and his fellow generals, as witness the appearance of not just Romilly but also Laurie Lee and the sculptor Jason Gurney, the fact that recruitment to the International Brigades extended beyond the Communist movement is not in itself to be gainsaid, but here, too, there is a deeper reality. Thus, both in Britain and elsewhere, from the very beginning the vast majority of the volunteers – as many as 80 per cent, indeed – were either Communist militants or men who had been involved in one or other of their numerous front organisations, while the appearance of a broad class base was belied by the fact that the bourgeois intellectuals involved – John Cornford is one example, David Guest another – were all too often themselves Communists.

The International Brigades, then, were from the very beginning a Communist 'show' and, till the very end, that is exactly what they remained, their subservience to the Comintern being reinforced by the fact that officers and political commissars alike were almost to a man loyal – and, not just loyal, but also dependable – members of the Party and the men appointed to the command of each individual brigade officers of the Red Army or even NKVD. If this was the case, it follows that there are other questions that must also be asked. Over and over again, we are told that the volunteers were defending democracy and that their political masters had no interest in building anything other than a common front against fascism. In the short term, this was indeed the case: Stalin and, with him, the Comintern, were horrified by the outbreak of revolution in Spain and threw themselves into the task of restoring order, not least by a policy of militarisation of which the International Brigades were living exponents, it being in part this that gave rise to the legend that it was the volunteers that saved Madrid in November 1936. Yet, Communist policy in Spain was not just motivated by the need for Soviet Russia to forge an alliance with Britain and France in what was always the diplomatic sub-text to the policy of 'popular front'. Clearly, images of 'red' revolution in Madrid and Barcelona were not likely go down well in London and Paris – still worse, indeed, it was Stalin and his minions who were certain to be blamed. Building the International Brigades, then, also stood for something else, namely the desire of the Communist movement to build a strong base in Spain – a base, be it said, that, given the Partido Comunista de España's exiguous representation among the Spanish working classes, could only be found among the middle classes – and destroy, discredit or, at the very least, destabilise their rivals, namely the Socialists, the Anarchists and the dissident Communist group known as the Partido Obrero de Unificación Marxista. Does all this mean that the intention from the beginning was to build a 'people's democracy' in Spain *avant la lettre*? In and of itself, the answer must be 'no', for Stalin was ever an opportunist whose views were based on a response to whatever situation he faced at any given moment, but the fact is that the aim, and one that was to a very considerable extent achieved, was to turn the Second Republic into a creature of Soviet Russia that could be used, abused or downright discarded in accordance with the behests of Moscow.

To return to the volunteers, none of this is to suggest that even the most hard-line Communists among them were necessarily aware of the reality of the policy whose military arm they represented: ignorant as they invariably were of the complex reality of the politics of the Second Republic, there is no reason to doubt that they sincerely believed they were fighting for democracy and, by extension, against fascism. Meanwhile, credit is beyond doubt due to them for their willingness, in the words (slightly modified) of one poem of the period, 'to wrap their colours round their breasts on the blood-red field of Spain' and for the courage that they in many instances showed on the battlefields of the River Jarama and the rest. Yet, the stories to the effect that the Russians and their agents had to keep them in line by means of terror having to a very large extent been discredited, it follows that they were staunchly loyal to the Party: hence the all too evident absence of any revulsion at the destruction of the POUM and the Council of Aragón in the summer of 1937 (if the scene in the Ken Loach film *Land and Freedom* in which a unit of International-Brigaders is sent to disarm a militia column by force of arms is based on invention alone, the idea does not require much of a leap of imagination). If the men who went to fight in Spain set out as 'volunteers for liberty', one cannot but doubt whether they would have continued to merit that description, something that cannot be denied being the fact that many of the leaders of the states of the Warsaw Pact were either veterans of the conflict of 1936–9 or, at the very least, apparatchiks who had been heavily involved in channelling the flow of recruits to Spain in one country or another. To conclude, then, not only did the International Brigades in general, and the British battalion thereof in particular, make less of a military contribution than the legend suggests, but, other than in the most vestigial sense, the men concerned were not even fighting for the cause in which they believed they had enlisted: a happy story it is not, but to tell it otherwise than in the current fashion is to risk charges of dishonesty.

Notes

Preface

1. See I. MacDougall (ed.), *Voices from the Spanish Civil War: Personal Recollections of Scottish Volunteers in Spain, 1936–1939* (Edinburgh, 1986), p. vi.
2. For example, R. Baxell, *Unlikely Warriors: the British in the Spanish Civil War and the Struggle against Fascism* (London, 2012), p. 345.
3. For a full exposition of the thinking behind this claim, see C.J. Esdaile, *The Spanish Civil War: a Military History* (Abingdon, 2019), pp. 351–4.
4. The fundamental English-language text for an understanding of the nature of the Republican army is M. Alpert, *The Republican Army in the Spanish Civil War* (Cambridge, 2013).

Chapter 1

1. A concept inherited from the Moroccan conflict of 1909–26, the mixed brigade was envisaged as a self-contained force capable of operating independently in a war of manoeuvre. Consisting, in theory at least, of three battalions of infantry, a battery of artillery and a variety of support units, the units concerned were little different from the ad hoc columns made use of by the Nationalists in the first months of the war, but, once the conflict had become a positional struggle akin to that of 1914–18, their many infelicities, including, not least, the fact that artillery was parcelled out in 'penny packets', became a millstone round the Republic's neck (by contrast, the Nationalists were quick to perceive the difficulties involved in making the basic unit the brigade, the result being that they switched to the far more effective structures that characterised all the armies of the earlier conflict.
2. Whether or not the Nationalists deserve to be labelled as fascists is a moot point. If fascism is understood as a revolutionary creed that owed its origins to the fear and rage rampant among the lower middle classes in the wake of the First World War, then the answer is clearly 'no': while individuals can be found who match the stereotype, the Falange Española y de las Juntas de Ofé(n)siva Nacional-Sindicalista

(the nearest political movement Spain possessed to a fascist party) had become a tool of authoritarian conservatism, if indeed, it had ever been more than that. As a result, the term will not be used to describe them in this work, though it is accepted that, to contemporary observers such as the foreign volunteers who detrained at Atocha that rainy November morning, such nuances were immaterial: in their eyes, the Nationalist were fascists and that was that, a position which it is possible to adopt even today if fascism is identified as nothing more than the use of a combination of xenophobia, nationalism, violence and political hysteria whose only aim is to avert revolution and/or frustrate social change.

3. J. Sommerfield, *Volunteer in Spain* (London, 1997), pp. 90–1. What does not come over from this quote is that Sommerfield and his fellows were utterly exhausted after a two-day journey that involved a lengthy train journey from Albacete to Alcazar de San Juan, an 11-hour overnight trip by truck from Alcazar de San Juan to Alcalá de Henares, a further period of wandering in the area immediately to the east of Madrid in search of various units of the brigade that had gone astray, and, finally, another train, this time for the short ride between the suburban township of Vallecas to Atocha. See P. Stansky and W. Abrahams (eds), *Journey to the Frontier: Two Roads to the Spanish Civil War* (Boston, 1966), pp. 372–4.

4. Stansky and Abrahams (eds), *Journey to the Frontier*, p. 376. For a very similar version of affairs, see the account of the fighting in Madrid penned by John Cornford in a letter to his girlfriend Margot Heinemann, reproduced in M. Sperber (ed.), *And I Remember Spain: a Spanish-Civil-War Anthology* (London, 1974), pp. 29–30.

5. *Cit.* S. Alvarez (ed.), *Historia política y militar de las brigadas internacionales: testimonios y documentos* (Madrid, 1996), pp. 91–2. The Casa de Campo is a broad expanse of wooded hills on what was then the western fringes of the Spanish capital. Until the coming of the Second Republic in 1931, it had been the private hunting reserve of the royal family, but in that year it had been taken over by the government of Madrid as a species of city forest.

6. See G. Tremlett, *The International Brigades: Fascism, Freedom and the Spanish Civil War* (London, 2020), p. 91.

7. G. Cox, *The Defence of Madrid* (London, 1937), p. 66; See also D. Ibárruri, *El único camino* (Paris, 1965), pp. 466–7.

8. M. Chaves Nogales, *Los secretos de la defensa de Madrid*, ed. A. Múñoz Molina (Seville, 2017), p. 68. Setting aside the reference to the Nationalists reaching the University City, a falsehood clearly borrowed from Marty's original report, the figure of 3,500 men is a serious exaggeration. Though its composition was later altered, at the time of its arrival in Madrid the brigade consisted of just three infantry battalions – the German Edgar André (510 men), the French Commune de Paris (435 men) and the Polish Dombrowski (511 men). In addition, there was a small cavalry squadron of just 46 men and a detachment of 27 artillerymen, though the latter had not yet been equipped with any guns. J.L. Alcofar Nassaes, *'Spansky': los extranjeros que lucharon en la Guerra Civil Española* (Barcelona, 1973), pp. 197–9.

9. A. Barea, *The Forging of a Rebel*, ed. N. Townson (London, 2001), p. 595.

10. H. Cardozo, *March of a Nation* (London, 1937), pp. 181–5.

11. For a general discussion, see P. Preston and H. Graham (eds), *The Popular Front in Europe* (London, 1987).

12. For Stalin's difficulties in respect of the outbreak of the Civil War, see I. Deutscher, *Stalin* (rev. edn, London, 1966), pp. 415–16. Also useful is D. Kowalsky, 'Operation X: the Soviet Union and the Spanish Civil War', *Bulletin of Hispanic Studies*, XCI (January, 2014), pp. 159–78.

13. Alvarez (ed.), *Historia política y militar de las Brigadas Internacionales*, pp. 60–1; V. Brome, *The International Brigades* (London, 1965), pp. 14–17. The exact sequence of events is not entirely clear. However, what does seem to be the case is that the impetus for the formation of the International Brigades did not come from Moscow, the idea rather originating in the Communist parties of France and other countries and being ever more loudly pressed upon Stalin, the latter remaining dubious about the idea on diplomatic grounds until well into August. For a general discussion, see D. Kowalsky, 'The Soviet Union and the International Brigades, 1936–1939', *Journal of Slavic Military Studies*, XIX, No. 4 (December, 2006), pp. 681–704.

14. So obvious was the power-ploy that the formation of the International Brigades represented that it was immediately picked up on by the Republican government. Headed by the Socialist leader Francisco Largo Caballero, this initially strove to ensure that the new units were subordinated to the Republican high command. Defeated in this respect, it then tried to insist on a table of organisation that would have provided for brigades of six battalions apiece, three of them composed of native Spaniards and three of them of foreigners, the aim clearly being to provide some means of countering Communist moves to use the International Brigades for political purposes; needless to say, this plan, too, fell by the wayside. For all this, see G. Cardona, 'Las Brigadas Internacionales y el Ejército Popular', in M. Requena Gallego (ed.), *La Guerra Civil Española y las Brigadas Internacionales* (Cuenca, 1998), pp. 71–81.

15. Initially at least, there may have been some attempt on the part of the Party to block the recruitment of non-Communists: such was certainly the experience of Glasgow volunteer Tommy Nicholson. See P. Darman, *Heroic Voices of the Spanish Civil War: Memories of the Spanish Civil War* (London, 2009), p. 23. This practice was soon abandoned on account of the need to reflect the policy of 'Popular Front', but the presence alongside Communists of, for example, members of the Labour Party or men of no formal political affiliation is misleading: according to one study, such figures were frequently closely associated with the Party through such groups as hiking and cycling clubs or front organisations such as the National Union of Unemployed Workers, the consequence being that the Communist hold on the Brigades was even stronger than the bare figures suggest. See F. Raeburn, 'Politics, networks and community: recruitment for the International Brigades re-assessed', *Journal of Contemporary History*, LV, No. 4 (October, 2020), pp. 79–44.

16. In units recruited from nationals of countries with systems of conscription such as France, Italy and Yugoslavia, the number of men with military training was probably quite high. In the British and American units, however, the rate was much lower – no more than 40 per cent for the former and 34 per cent from the latter – while, setting aside the Irish, many of whom had fought in the Easter Rising or the Irish Civil War, such was the age structure of the recruits that fewer than half the men concerned could have heard shots fired in anger. See L. Morris, 'English-speaking units of the International Brigades in the Spanish Civil War, 1936–1939: image and reality', University of Liverpool MA thesis, 2013, pp. 32–3.

17. The role of unemployment in the recruitment of the International Brigades has been much debated. With regard to the British battalion, it is now generally accepted that the number of jobless was about one quarter of the whole, but, if still significant, this figure is much smaller than that which is often implied. Moreover, there is a corollary which it is all too easy to overlook. In the words of Liam Morris, 'At least seventy-five per cent of the volunteers were employed at the time of their departure to Spain and thus walked away from a stable source of income at a time when unemployment was rife in order to fight a foreign war that they had no guarantee of returning from.' Morris, 'English-speaking units of the International Brigades', p. 25. For examples of men finding themselves targeted as potential recruits, see MacDougall (ed.), *Voices from the Spanish Civil War*, p. 308, and W. Gregory, *The Shallow Grave: a Memoir of the Spanish Civil War* (London, 1986), p. 19.

18. *Cit.* MacDougall, *Voices from the Spanish Civil War*, p. 87.

19. By far the best guide to the organisation of the International Brigades is that provided in Alcofar Nassaes, *'Spansky'*, pp. 197–355 *passim.* See also Esdaile, *Spanish Civil War*, pp. 355–7.

20. R.D. Richardson, 'The defence of Madrid: mysterious generals, Red-Front fighters and the International Brigades', *Military Affairs*, XLIII, No. 4 (January, 1979), pp. 178–85.

21. F. Ryan (ed.), *The Book of the XV Brigade: Records of British, American, Canadian and Irish Volunteers in Spain, 1936–1938* (Madrid, 1938), p. 305.

22. *Ibid.*, p. 301.

23. W. Rust, *Britons in Spain: the History of the British Battalion of the XVth International Brigade* (London, 1939), pp. 17, 37, 73, 88.

24. *Cit.* Brome, *International Brigades*, p. 96.

25. D. Ibárruri, *They Shall Not Pass: the Autobiography of La Pasionaria* (London, 1966), pp. 258–9.

26. Anon., '"I saw the bright ones arrive": idealism, alienation, and persistence in the personal legacies of Australian involvement in the Spanish Civil War', <https://libcom.org/library/i-saw-bright-ones-arrive-idealism-alienation-persistence-personal-legacies-australian-in>, accessed 4 January 2020.

27. A.H. Landis, *Death in the Olive Groves: American Volunteers in the Spanish Civil War* (New York, 1989), p. 223.

28. R. Colodny, *The Struggle for Madrid* (New York, 1958), pp. 68–70.

29. M. O'Riordan, *Connolly Column: the Story of the Irishmen who Fought for the Spanish Republic, 1936–1939* (Dublin, 1979), p. 50.

30. W. Alexander, *British Volunteers for Liberty: Spain, 1936–39* (London, 1982), p. 16.

31. 'Interview with Steve Fullerton', *cit. Scottish Labour-History Society Journal*, No. 11 (1977), p. 22; J. Gurney, *Crusade in Spain* (London, 1974), p. 36; Gregory, *Shallow Grave*, p. 178.

32. *Cit.* P. Toynbee (ed.), *The Distant Drum: Reflections on the Spanish Civil War* (London, 1976), p. 141.

33. Gregory, *Shallow Grave*, p. 82.

34. T. Wintringham, *English Captain* (London, 1939), p. 139.

35. For Hemingway's experience's in Madrid, see D. Boyd-Hancock, *I am Spain: the Spanish Civil War and the Men and Women who Went to Fight Fascism* (Brecon, 2012), pp. 109–209.

36. For Britten and Auden's intellectual travails, and, more particularly, their struggles with the idea that they ought to be fighting with the British battalion, see R. Stradling, *History and Legend: Writing the International Brigades* (Cardiff, 2003), pp. 74–91.

37. P. Elstob, *The Armed Rehearsal* (London, 1964), pp. 277–8.

38. J. Cook, *Apprentices of Freedom* (London, 1979), p. 7.

39. Brome, *International Brigades*, p. 30.

40. Tremlett, *International Brigades*, pp. 9–10. In fairness to Tremlett, his book is a mine of information and very much necessary reading, but his failure to present the obvious conclusion that cries out from the catalogue of misfortune that he details, namely that the Brigades achieved nothing of any military value and above all served as a vehicle for the advancement of the interests of Stalinist Communism, is, at best, extremely unfortunate.

41. G. Zaagsma, *Jewish Volunteers, the International Brigades and the Spanish Civil War* (London, 2017), p. 19.

42. Baxell, *Unlikely Warriors*, p. 193. As an example of the scorn with which the POUM and the Anarchists – the forces held to be responsible for the Barcelona violence – were held among the volunteers in general, we might cite the letters written by Abraham Lincoln battalion soldier Paul Sigel. Thus, 'For almost a year the Consejo de Aragón controlled Catalonia. Soldiers went out to fight in the morning, fought their usual number of trade-union hours, and then went back home in the evening. Disunity: no organization, no discipline at all. Trotskyites, certain Anarchists and people who used their name, filled store-houses with arms [and] munitions … that were sorely needed at the front. Armed bands took over towns in or near the war zones [and] "stuck-up" gasoline trucks … Trotskyites played football with the Fascists in no-man's land.' *Cit.* C. Nelson and J. Hendricks (eds), *Madrid, 1937:*

Letters of the Abraham-Lincoln Brigade from the Spanish Civil War (New York, 1996), p. 315.

43. Gurney, *Crusade in Spain*, pp. 99–124.

44. *Cit.* Macdougall, *Voices from the Spanish Civil War*, p. 43.

45. In fairness, it has to be said that some such counter-attack did take place: as will be shown in due course, it features in the memoir of his service in Spain written by Frank Thomas, a young Welshman who had volunteered for the Spanish Foreign Legion in search of adventure and fought at Madrid, Boadilla and Jarama alike.

46. H. Thomas, *The Spanish Civil War* (3rd edn, London, 1977), p. 593.

47. R.D. Richardson, *Comintern Army: the International Brigades and the Spanish Civil War* (Lexington, Kentucky, 1982), p. 88.

48. *Ibid.*, p. 180.

49. P. Preston, *The Spanish Civil War: Reaction, Revolution and Revenge* (London, 2006), pp. 14–16.

50. P.N. Carroll, *The Odyssey of the Abraham Lincoln Brigade: Americans in the Spanish Civil War* (Stanford, California, 1994), pp. 187–8.

51. *Ibid.*, pp. 100–2.

52. See R. de la Cierva, *Brigadas Internacionales, 1936–1996: la verdadera historia – mentira histórica y error de estado* (Madridejos, 1997). For a good example of the Nationalist régime's desire to 'talk up' the International Brigades, see Luis Bolín's ludicrous claim that the number of volunteers amounted to 125,000. L. Bolín, *Spain: the Vital Years* (London, 1997), p. 213.

53. Esdaile, *Spanish Civil War*, p. 293.

54. E. Hooton, *Spain in Arms: a Military History of the Spanish Civil War, 1936–1939* (Oxford, 2019), pp. 54–5.

Chapter 2

1. Baxell, *Unlikely Warriors*, pp. 94–7. The number of men in this first batch of volunteers is often given as twenty, but this total included a German named Jan Kurzke; two New Zealanders resident in Britain in the persons of a graduate of the University of Cambridge named Griffith Maclaurin who was currently running a left-wing bookshop and electrician Steven Yates; an Australian named Joseph Stevens; and also three Irishmen, of whom two had come straight from Ireland and the third from self-imposed exile in Australia. British-born recruits, then, appear to have numbered just fourteen men. For full details, see R. Baxell, *British Volunteers in the Spanish Civil War* (London, 2004), p. 54.

2. That the XI Brigade got little in the way of training is established by the recollections of Bernard Knox. Thus, 'Our British section was assigned … to the French battalion, where we ended up in the *compagnie mitrailleuse* … but for the rest of October and

all through October, we had no machine-guns, not even rifles. Since we couldn't train with weapons, our days were spent practising close-order drill.' *Cit.* Darman, *Heroic Voices of the Spanish Civil War*, p. 58.

3. For the campaign of the Army of Africa in Andalucía and Extremadura, see Esdaile, *Spanish Civil War*, pp. 89–92. Prior to the uprising, Franco had been the commander of the garrison of the Canaries, but, having first secured the islands for the rebel cause, he had been picked up by a Dragon Rapide that had been chartered in Britain and flown to Morocco to take command of the insurgent forces there.

4. For the Nationalist advance on Madrid, see G. Hills, *The Battle for Madrid* (London, 1974), pp. 61–71, 83–92.

5. Tremlett, *International Brigades*, p. 98.

6. Sommerfield, *Volunteer in Spain*, pp. 113–17. Meanwhile, for a detailed account of the fighting of 13 November, see Alcofar Nassaes, *'Spansky'*, pp. 220–1.

7. The legend, however, would have it otherwise. For a good example of the genre, here is Delperrie de Bayac: 'On the night of the 14th [*sic*] the XI International Brigade was brought up … to counter-attack in the University City. The commander of the Commune de Paris [battalion] said to his men, "The Arabs are afraid of cold steel, so let's go after them with the bayonet." Immediately the Frenchmen threw themselves into the attack. Commanded by Marcel Sagnier, No. 1 Company got into the Faculty of Philosophy and Letters. The battle raged in the classrooms, in the lecture theatres, in the corridors. When the ground floor had been taken, the Internationals moved on to the floors above. Neither one side nor the other faltered. Insults and jeers flew to and fro. Legionaries and Moors rolled grenades down the stairwells, whilst the Internationals responded by loading bombs into the lifts and pressing the button.' J. Delperrie de Bayac, *Las Brigadas Internacionales* (Madrid, 1978), p. 107.

8. *Cit.* Sperber (ed.), *And I Remember Spain*, pp. 29–30.

9. Sommerfield, *Volunteer in Spain*, pp. 141–53. The general inefficacy of the shelling does not mean that there were no casualties: for example, John Cornford was wounded when a shell burst in the lecture hall which he was occupying. Meanwhile, the ravine mentioned by Sommerfield is probably the re-entrant on the northern edge of the Parque del Oeste by which the Avenida de Seneca descends in the direction of the Manzanares.

10. If the English-speaking section in the Commune de Paris had been lucky, their casualties had not been insignificant: of the original twenty men, four – Maclaurin, Yates, Symes and ex-Guardsman Fred Jones – were dead and another – Cornford – wounded.

11. Also attached to the British section were exiled Latvian Communist Arnold Jeans (one assumes this was a *nom de guerre*); Bill Scott, a bricklayer from Dublin and IRA militant who had fought in the anti-government forces in the Irish Civil War; a stray American called Jerry Fontana; and an Australian drifter by the name of Richard Whatley. The number is sometimes given as fourteen rather than twelve, but this

includes one man who was in fact wounded on the Aragón front in October and a second who transferred from the Commune de Paris. For a full list, see Baxell, *British Volunteers*, p. 57.

12. *Cit.* Baxell, *Unlikely Warriors*, p. 109.
13. *Cit.* MacDougall, *Voices from the Spanish Civil War*, pp. 14–15. The XII Brigade was commanded by Mata Zalka, like his XI-International-Brigade counterpart, Manfred Stern, a Hungarian who had been taken prisoner by the Russians in the First World War and enlisted in the Red Army, and consisted of the Italian Garibaldi battalion, the German Thaelmann battalion and the French André Marty battalion, a company of engineers and a battery of three 75mm guns. Alcofar Nassaes, 'Spansky', pp. 214–16.
14. E. Romilly, *Boadilla* (London, 1937), pp. 103–4.
15. *Cit.* Baxell, *Unlikely Warriors*, p. 109.
16. K.S. Watson, *Single to Spain* (London, 1937), pp. 121–2.
17. *Cit.* Alcofar Nassaes, 'Spansky', p. 224.
18. Having got separated from their fellows, the three deserters – Watson and two men named Phillip Norman and John Donovan (sometimes misremembered as Mulligan) – encountered one another that night in the small village from which the attack had originally been launched, and made a mutual decision to wash their hands of the Civil War. Thus: 'We decided to quit … Things looked all washed-up: the last few days had made a very bad impression on us: we felt tired and beaten. No-one knew quite how to quit: between us and the nearest port lay 300 miles of motor road … This gave rise to a fierce argument: I was for going … to Madrid and resigning there, Norman and Mulligan [*sic*] … for making for Valencia. We agreed to part company.' Watson, *Single to Spain*, pp. 135–6. Watson was doubtless speeded on his way by an aerial attack he experienced the next day. As he later wrote, 'The scream of a 200-kilo bomb ended in a crushing roar: a crater was torn in the earth. Men ran for cover in all directions; a pack of dogs rushed round and round in a mad circle of terror … Ambulances raced across the rough track, first-aid men rushed over. Twenty men had been hit. Some of them were unrecognisable: the bomb splinters had torn them with a macabre humour. One boy lay on his back, thrashing the air with his leg: where the other should have been was a quivering bloody stump. In the fork of a tree, another was tightly wedged: he was alive and moaning … [but] a blue-red tangle of intestines hung from his stomach … A boy, not more than sixteen, lay grinning at the blue sky as though at a remembered joke, the top of his head … taken off as one opens an egg. Those who were past aid were shot: it was the greatest mercy the ambulance men could have shown.' *Ibid.*, pp. 128–9. In general, however, aerial attacks of a tactical nature were more frightening than they were harmful. Here, for example, is Phil Gillan: 'Fascist planes coming over was a regular feature at that time … On at least three occasions they … [strafed] our lines, but … the amount of casualties was negligible.' *Cit.* MacDougall, *Voices from the Spanish Civil War*, p. 17.
19. *Cit.* MacDougall, *Voices from the Spanish Civil War*, pp. 15–16.

20. Romilly, *Boadilla*, pp. 145–6.
21. *Ibid.*, pp. 165–6.
22. *Ibid.*, pp. 250–1.
23. *Cit.* Stansky and Abrahams (eds), *Journey to the Frontier*, pp. 385–6. The original St Étiennes having been replaced, the machine guns were now more reliable but no less unwieldy Russian Maxim M1910s.
24. Romilly, *Boadilla*, pp. 279–82. Confusingly, originally in the XII International Brigade, the Thaelmann battalion had in the first week of December been transferred to the XI International Brigade.
25. By way of tribute to the seven British volunteers concerned, it is worth quoting the words of journalist Geoffrey Cox. Thus, 'On the whole the British lads were truly admirable. Particularly the earlier people, they were all sincere people. There was no doubt the occasional adventurer among them, [but] they were decent, responsible chaps who wanted to stand up against what they felt was a force that was wrong. ... people who put their lives on the line for an ideal.' *Cit.* Darman, *Heroic Voices of the Spanish Civil War*, pp. 84–5.
26. J. Monks, *With the Reds in Andalusia* (London, 1985), p. 6.
27. F. Copeman, *Reason in Revolt* (London, 1948), p. 82.
28. M. Levine, *Cheetham to Cordova* [sic]: *a Manchester Man of the Thirties* (Manchester, 1984), p. 35.
29. So bad was the Chauchat that it is widely regarded as the worst machine gun ever put into production.
30. Monks, *With the Reds in Andalusia*, pp. 14–15.
31. *Ibid.*, p. 15.
32. *Cit.* O'Riordan, *Connolly Column*, pp. 59–60.
33. *Cit.* Cook, *Apprentices of Freedom*, p. 40.
34. Monks, *With the Reds in Andalusia*, p. 16.
35. Baxell, *Unlikely Warriors*, p. 117. The source on which this claim is based being a report by some anonymous Party functionary, it cannot be wholly trusted, for the fiasco at Lopera rendered it necessary to seize on anything that could in any way mitigate the pain of defeat. That said, Nathan emerges from the memoir material as a genuinely attractive character. To quote the usually sceptical Jason Gurney, 'George Nathan had made such a good reputation for himself in command of the English company of the [Córdoba] front that he had now been appointed Chief-of-Staff of the newly-formed XV Brigade. He is the only personality serving with the International Brigades who emerges as an authentic hero figure ... He was always immaculately clean and well turned out in the Spanish regular-army uniform ... as befitted the totally dedicated military professionalism which was the basis of his life ... He had the most tremendous stamina and ... an excellent and ready sense of humour, together with enormous charm. Probably his greatest merit was his magnificent air of authority and decision: his self-assurance was so complete that he never felt the need to shout or to

give orders in anything other than a quiet and normal voice … All this may seem to be too good to be true, but … Nathan emerges from the history of these events as the only person who was universally admired.' Gurney, *Crusade in Spain*, pp. 93–5.

36. *Cit.* Cook, *Apprentices of Freedom*, p. 41.

37. M. Arthur, *The Real Band of Brothers: First-Hand Accounts from the Last British Survivors of the Spanish Civil War* (London, 2009), pp. 229–30.

38. Levine, *Cheetham to Cordova*, p. 36.

39. *Ibid.*

40. For detailed accounts of Lopera, see <http://nidosdeametralladora.tripod.com/batalla.htm> and <http://rutasimprescindibles.blogspot.com/2013/06/la-guerra-civil-en-jaen.html>, both accessed 7 November 2019. The dead included nine of the fifty Irishmen, namely Tommy Wood, Mick May, Tony Fox, Mick Nolan, Jim Foley, Leo Green, Henry Bonar, Frank Conroy and Johnny Meehan, while several others, among them Joe Monks, Donal O'Reilly, Jack Nalty, Gerry Doran and Bill Beattie, were seriously wounded. See <http://www.turtlebunbury.com/history/history_irish/history_irish_spanishcivilwar.htm>, accessed 8 November 2019.

41. *Cit.* Levine, *Cheetham to Cordova*, p. 36. For the Battle of Lopera, see Stansky and Abrahams (eds), *Journey to the Frontier*, pp. 388–9; Alcofar Nassaes, *'Spansky'*, pp. 282–4.

42. See, for example, <http://www.international-brigades.org.uk/content/homage-volunteers-who-fought-andalusia-april-2016>, <https://www.ideal.es/jaen/20100130/provincia/memoria-brigadas-20100130.html> and <http://www.international-brigades.org.uk/content/lopera-honours-its-international-brigaders>, accessed 7 November 2019.

Chapter 3

1. For a useful summary, see R. Baxell, 'Myths of the International Brigades', *Bulletin of Hispanic Studies*, XCI, Nos 1–2 (January, 2014), pp. 11–24.

2. For a biography of Macartney, see <https://spartacus-educational.com/SPmacartney.htm>, accessed 4 January 2020.

3. The Nationalist order of battle is worth giving in some detail on account of the insight it provides into the organisation of Franco's forces after six months of the war. Composed of five of the eight infantry brigades of Luis Orgáz's so-called División Resforzada de Madrid (i.e. the troops deployed on the Madrid front), together with its one-and-only cavalry brigade, the forces engaged in the Battle of Jarama are best envisaged as a de facto First-World-War-style corps, and its six brigades as divisions, and all the more so as the two regiments, each of three battalions, which made up each infantry brigade were not regiments in any usual sense of the word but rather conglomerates – brigades indeed – made up either of independent battalions drawn from such forces as the Foreign Legion

or constituent battalions of regiments of the regular army or Moorish auxiliaries. That said, this was still very much an army in miniature: in the First World War, infantry divisions had three brigades rather than two and infantry brigades four battalions rather than three.

4. Persistent claims that the attackers also numbered two battalions of German machine-gunners should be dismissed as fantasy: there were no such troops in Spain. Setting aside the Condor Legion's 16 FLAK18s, neither was there any significant German or Italian contribution in terms of artillery, the only guns in the Nationalist array sent by Hitler and Mussolini being 25 37mm PAK36 anti-tank guns and 20 65mm C.65/17 M1913 infantry guns. With regard to the aerial component assigned to the Jarama offensive, the Condor Legion contributed 25 Ju52 bombers, 23 He51 fighters, 1 Messerschmidt Me109, 1 Heinkel He112 and 6 He70 reconnaissance aircraft; the Legionary Aviation 18 Fiat CR3s; and the Nationalists 22 Ju52s and 6 Romeo Ro37 ground-attack aircraft. In all, then, we have a total of 96 aircraft. R. Permuy López and A. Mortera Pérez, *Histórica 36/39, No. 3: la batalla de Jarama* (Madrid, n.d.), p. 16.

5. J.M. Martínez Bande, *La lucha en torno a Madrid* (Madrid, 1984), p. 100.

6. Even worse off in terms of its state of preparation than the other three units, the Abraham Lincoln battalion did not reach the front until 16 February.

7. Martínez Bande, *La lucha entorno a Madrid*, p. 102. Charged with covering an ever widening expanse of territory, Asensio Cabanillas could only spare one of his two 'regiments', namely that commanded by Major Pedro Pimentel, for the San Martín sector. Still worse, meanwhile, the units concerned – the second battalion of the Tenerife infantry regiment, the newly formed Seventh Tabor de Regulares de Melilla and the Sixth Bandera of the Spanish Foreign Legion – were far from the best troops in the Nationalist array, the Moors and Spanish regulars being little more than raw recruits and the Moorish *tabor*, like all its fellows of the same type, also composed of a mere two rifle companies and a machine-gun section instead of the usual three rifle companies and one machine-gun company. That said, Asensio did enjoy the services of 4 65mm guns, 8 75mm guns, 4 105mm guns, 5 37mm anti-tank guns, a company of engineers and a company of 11 PzKpfw I tanks.

8. For the rifle companies' machine guns, see Gurney, *Crusade in Spain*, pp. 78–9.

9. *Cit.* Ryan, *Book of the XV Brigade*, pp. 41–2.

10. Gregory, *Shallow Grave*, p. 45. A wholly verifiable episode, the dogfight witnessed by the battalion typifies the situation that pertained in the skies above the battlefield. Thus, while the Nationalists had a considerable numerical superiority in terms of actual aircraft – in all, the Republicans committed no more than sixty-three planes to the fighting of which all but six were I15 or I16 fighters and the remainder Polikarpov R5 light bombers – their Fiat and Heinkel fighters were no match for the Republican Polikarpovs. In consequence, slow and unprotected as they were, the Nationalist bombers had to abandon daytime operations in favour of pointless

night attacks on Madrid and other targets, while their fighters avoided combat wherever possible and, in the case of the Italians at least, were ordered not to cross the front line. Given that losses were extremely limited – the two fighters, both of them Condor-Legion He51s, shot down over the British battalion, and a Fiat that was lost the next day – it was a dismal showing that completely belies the usual picture of Nationalist air superiority. That said, the Republicans completely failed to take advantage of the situation. Also available close at hand were the twenty-three Tupolev SB2 bombers that had been sent to Spain from Russia prior to the assault on Madrid. Fast enough to outrun the He51s, if not the CR32s, and based on airfields just minutes away from the front line, these planes might have wrought havoc had they been used en masse against the advancing Nationalists, but the commanders of the Republican air force appear to have been just as scared of the Nationalist anti-aircraft guns and, with the exception of a single raid on the road from San Martín de la Vega to the nearby bridge over the Jarama – the admittedly very precious bombers were therefore instead sent on irrelevant pin-prick raids of no more than five aircraft apiece against such irrelevant targets as Toledo and Talavera. That being the case, with the R5s not only few in numbers but very vulnerable to ground fire, the bulk of the task of ground attack had to be left to the I15 and I16s, but, armed only with machine guns, these were unable to make much of a difference. J. Salas Larrazábal, *Air War over Spain* (London, 1974), pp. 119–23; M. Alpert, *Franco and the Condor Legion: the Spanish Civil War in the Air* (London, 2019), pp. 103–5.

11. *Cit.* Ryan, *Book of the XV Brigade*, p. 64.
12. Copeman, *Reason in Revolt*, pp. 89–90.
13. *Cit.* Toynbee, *Distant Drum*, p. 125.
14. Gregory, *Shallow Grave*, pp. 45–7.
15. *Cit.* Darman, *Heroic Voices of the Spanish Civil War*, p. 100.
16. *Cit. ibid.*, p. 96.
17. As had been the case ever since the International Brigades went into action, the personal weapon of the bulk of the volunteers was the Moisin-Nagant M1891 rifle. Often called 'Mexicanskies' on account of the fact that the first examples to reach the Republican zone had been manufactured in the United States for the Tsarist government only to be sold on to Mexico following Russia's exit from the First World War, the Moisin-Nagant was essentially a perfectly serviceable weapon, but it was calibrated so as to take account of the weight of the bayonet: this last being an item which the volunteers invariably lost or threw away, the latter quickly found that they literally could not shoot straight, some men also complaining that the bolt was extremely stiff and the weapon prone to jamming, although such malfunctions were probably as much as anything the result of the use of ammunition fabricated from recycled cartridges. MacDougall, *Voices from the Spanish Civil War*, pp. 135–6; B. Clark, *No Boots to my Feet: Experiences of a Britisher in Spain, 1937–1938* (Shelton, 1984), p. 28.

18. *Cit.* Ryan, *Book of the XV Brigade*, p. 50.
19. Gurney, *Crusade in Spain*, p. 106.
20. *Cit. ibid.*, p. 66. One of the problems on Casa-Blanca Hill was the magnetic attraction of its isolated farmstead: believing that the compound offered safety, many of Overton's men crowded into it, only to discover, much too late, that it was being used as an aiming point by the Nationalist machine guns and artillery alike.
21. Gregory, *Shallow Grave*, pp. 47–8.
22. *Cit.* MacDougall, *Voices from the Spanish Civil War*, p. 61.
23. *Cit.* Darman, *Heroic Voices of the Spanish Civil War*, p. 100.
24. Gurney, *Crusade in Spain*, p. 110.
25. D. Hooper, *No Pasarán! A Memoir of the Spanish Civil War* (London, 1997), p. 20. According to Copeman, the leading role in this episode was played not by Fry, who he had blamed for the problem with the ammunition and elbowed aside as incompetent, but rather himself. That Copeman was with the machine guns at this point seems probable enough, but, at the very least, his words come over as being distinctly over-blown. See Copeman, *Reason in Revolt*, pp. 92–3.
26. Gurney, *Crusade in Spain*, p. 114.
27. Gregory, *Shallow Grave*, pp. 50–1.
28. MacDougall, *Voices from the Spanish Civil War*, p. 25.
29. *Cit. ibid.*, p. 37.
30. Baxell, *Unlikely Warriors*, pp. 171–2. At this distance, it is almost impossible to judge the veracity of the charges levelled at Overton, all that can be said being that the evidence is highly ambiguous.
31. Gurney, *Crusade in Spain*, p. 121.
32. *Ibid.*, p. 123.
33. Copeman was by all accounts a redoubtable figure. To quote Gurney, 'Fred Copeman, [a] great bull of a man, clearly visualised himself as a divinely-appointed leader by virtue of his great strength – he had been a heavy-weight boxer in the Navy – although he was almost illiterate. Throughout his life he had used his fists to put himself in charge of any group of men he found himself among. He was completely without physical fear and seemed almost entirely indifferent to physical injury ... Nominally in command of a machine-gun section over on the right flank, he had abandoned them to their own devices ... giving completely inconsequential orders to everybody in sight and offering to bash their faces if they did not comply.' Gurney, *Crusade in Spain*, p. 112.
34. No contemporary account of this attack has been found, but, according to Hughes, it was spear-headed by Nationalist tanks including a number of T26s captured in the fighting round Madrid, but there is no mention of any such machines taking part in the Battle of Jarama in other sources, while the whole story seems rather doubtful. See B. Hughes, *'They Shall Not Pass!' The British Battalion at Jarama, the Spanish Civil War* (Oxford, 2011), pp. 165–71.

35. *Cit.* Ryan, *Book of the XV Brigade*, p. 58.

36. R. Stradling (ed.), *Brother against Brother: Experiences of a British Volunteer in the Spanish Civil War* (Stroud, 1998), p. 95. For Jack Edwards' very brief account, see Arthur, *Real Band of Brothers*, p. 159. Meanwhile, the tale of the so-called 'great rally' is recounted in Hughes, *'They Shall Not Pass!'*, pp. 172–8, and Baxell, *Unlikely Warriors*, pp. 154–7.

37. Stradling (ed.), *Brother against Brother*, p. 97.

38. Martínez Bande, *La lucha en torno a Madrid*, pp. 112–24. That said, the Republican high command noted that the four International Brigades involved in the battle had fought extremely well. In the words of an anonymous report written by an officer of the general staff dated 26 April 1937: 'The behaviour … of XI, XII, XIV and XV International Brigades was highly satisfactory at every point at which they were engaged … In support of this opinion, one has only to cite the fact that the units concerned between them lost 2,800 men.' *Cit. ibid.*, p. 275.

Chapter 4

1. *Cit.* Ryan, *Book of the XV Brigade*, p. 139.

2. For Guadalajara, see J.F. Coverdale, 'The Battle of Guadalajara, 8–22 March 1937', *Journal of Contemporary History*, IX, No. 1 (January, 1974), pp. 53–76.

3. For a concise account of the Bilbao campaign, see Esdaile, *Spanish Civil War*, pp. 184–206.

4. Hills, *Battle for Madrid*, pp. 143–6.

5. The commander of the Fifteenth Division was the same Galiscz who had been at the head of XV Brigade at the beginning of the Battle of Jarama, the officer concerned having been promoted to the rank of general of division in the latter days of that action.

6. J. Modesto, *Soy del Quinto Regimiento* (Barcelona, 1978), p. 158.

7. The anti-tank gun supplied to the XV Brigade was the Russian 45mm M1930. More than capable of knocking out any tank possessed by the Nationalists, these were much admired by their crews. In the words of one enthusiastic Scottish gunner, 'The guns … fired both armour-penetrating … and high-explosive shells. They … could be used against strong points – machine-gun posts – as well as against tanks. They had … telescopic sights on them [with] which you could pin-point your target over a … distance of maybe up to two kilometres'. *Cit.* MacDougall, *Voices from the Spanish Civil War*, p. 200.

8. Copeman, *Reason in Revolt*, pp. 122–3. The battalion commissar was erstwhile *Daily Worker* Barcelona correspondent Walter Tapsell, of whom one volunteer remarked, 'God! What a good man he was!' Hooper, *No Pasarán!*, p. 34. Apart from Escuadero, the company commanders, meanwhile, were Alec Cummings, Joe Hinks and Bill Meredith.

9. That said, a number of survivors of the Battle of Jarama slipped away from Mondéjar rather than face going into action again. See Baxell, *Unlikely Warriors*, p. 225.
10. F. Thomas, *To Tilt at Windmills: a Memoir of the Spanish Civil War* (East Lansing, Michigan, 1996), p. 19.
11. *Cit.* H. Francis, *Miners against Fascism: Wales and the Spanish Civil War* (London, 1984), p. 277.
12. *Cit.* Cook, *Apprentices of Freedom*, p. 86.
13. *Cit.* Arthur, *Real Band of Brothers*, p. 91.
14. Unlike anything seen in the First World War, the infiltration tactics favoured by Rojo were feasible because of the complete absence of anything like the continuous lines of trenches seen in France and Belgium. With the front line no more than a chain of widely separated fortified villages and other outposts, such tactics were easy to implement, while the battlefield of Brunete, in particular, was cloaked in groves of ilex and pine that did not get in the way of movement but, for all that, provided excellent cover.
15. Chapeyev was a particularly lauded hero of the Russian Civil War. Meanwhile, the other units in Copeman's command were the Abraham Lincoln battalion and a second American unit called the George Washington battalion. Baxell, *Unlikely Warriors*, p. 221. Copic, it seems, was not well liked. While those volunteers who remained loyal to the Party line to the end spoke highly of him, Jason Gurney could hardly be more scathing. Thus, 'Vladimir Copic … was the most consistently disliked and mistrusted of all the "Russians" in Spain … An utterly unprincipled brute who would swear that black was white if it suited his convenience … he was an oily little bastard, and I hated him'. Gurney, *Crusade in Spain*, p. 96.
16. Brunete housed a small field hospital, and its capture therefore saw a number of Nationalist nurses fall into Republican hands, including two sisters of the prominent Duque de Larios.
17. Thomas, *To Tilt at Windmills*, pp. 34–5.
18. E. Lister, *Memorias de un luchador* (Madrid, 1977), pp. 257–8. Manning one of the tanks concerned was a young Republican soldier named Alvaro Cortes Roa. For him the battle was above all an inferno of heat. 'The tanks that we had got now had been fitted with a new device for observing the battlefield and aiming the gun in the form of a periscope: in my view, this was much better than the old visor: one could see far more … and obtain much greater accuracy. Some had a second periscope for the loader as well, whilst others had been fitted with a machine gun on top of the turret for use against aircraft as well as another projecting from its rear … All of these improvements were important, but nothing had been done to ensure a decent supply of fresh air or a means of extracting all the fumes from the cordite, the oil and the gasoline. Still worse, however, there was no device to keep the temperature in the interior of the tanks at a reasonable level when they were closed down for battle: it was like being in an oven.' A. Cortes Roa, *Tanquista desde mi tronera* (Madrid, 1989), pp. 145–6.

19. Copeman, *Reason in Revolt*, pp. 126–7.
20. Gregory, *Shallow Grave*, pp. 69–70.
21. *Cit.* Cook, *Apprentices of Freedom*, p. 86.
22. *Cit.* Darman, *Heroic Voices of the Spanish Civil War*, p. 108.
23. Cortes Roa provides a dramatic account of the experiences of the Republican tank crews. Thus, 'As soon as a tank appears … all the furies of hell … converge upon it … On all sides, then, there is nothing but fire, smoke, shrapnel and great gouts of earth. … Meanwhile, sweating feverishly, the drivers are frantically … zig-zagging from side to side in the hope of impeding the enemy's aim … With so much movement, however … the task of their comrades in the turrets above their heads also becomes very difficult as the latter have to constantly struggle … just to keep their weapons pointing at the enemy … Occasionally, a hit is obtained, and whenever this happens the successful tank heads straight for the gap in the enemy defences, and does all that it can to increase the damage … But, all too often, the crew perceives that they are alone, that they have advanced too far, that the infantry … have not been able to keep up … either because they have been pinned down by the enemy's fire or because the tank has been too fast for them. If such is, indeed, the case, there is nothing for it but to retire.' Cortes Roa, *Tanquista desde mi tronera*, pp. 149–50.
24. At the mention of the capture of Villanueva de la Cañada, memoirs of the veterans of the British battalion almost invariably retell a story to the effect that, as the defence finally melted away, a number of Nationalist soldiers tried to escape under cover of a human shield of women, children and old men. However, while the capacity of the Falangists involved to act in such a fashion is difficult to doubt, it appears that the incident was either completely fabricated or based on a tale that grew enormously in the telling. See Stradling, *Writing the International Brigades*, pp. 131–48. Even some of the veterans confessed to a degree of scepticism, Frank Thomas, for example, writing as follows, 'This tale has become part of the legend of Brunete: I have not seen anyone who saw it happen.' Thomas, *To Tilt at Windmills*, p. 36. Of course, arriving at the truth is now impossible, but one potential interpretation of events is that, with their situation going from bad to worse, a group of Nationalist soldiers attempted a break-out in company with a number of friendly civilians, only to run into the British battalion and spark off a fire-fight in which most of them, soldiers and civilians alike, were shot down. A very useful means of covering up the killing, however inadvertent, of at least some of the civilians, tales of the defenders employing them as human shields were soon doing the rounds, while it is possible that the story of the shoot-out on the road to Brunete also became conflated with memories of a much darker incident, namely the summary execution of an unknown number of Nationalist prisoners that is either hinted at or openly admitted in several of the personal accounts. Baxell, *Unlikely Warriors*, p. 226.
25. Lister, *Memorias de un luchador*, pp. 256–8.

26. Copeman, *Reason in Revolt*, pp. 132–3. Many of the deserters mentioned by Copeman may in reality have rather been stragglers, but even so the comment is extremely telling.

27. Initially, the Republicans enjoyed air superiority at Brunete, the only Nationalist aircraft in a position to help the defenders being one wing of Fiat Cr32 fighters and another of Romeo Ro37 ground-attack aircraft, both of them drawn from the Italian 'Legionary Aviation'. However, very soon a variety of units had either been relocated to airfields in the vicinity of the Madrid front or tasked with joining the battle by means of regular raids from their bases in the vicinity of Burgos and Vitoria. Among the new arrivals were not just new bombers – the Heinkel He111 and the Savoia-Marchetti SM79 that were a great improvement on the lumbering Junkers and Savoias of 1936 – but the first examples of the deadly Messerschmidt Me109, a very fast and manoeuvrable monoplane that was superior to both the I15 and the I16. Had it just been a case of the new bombers, the Republican flyers might have coped reasonably well. But the Messerschmidt was a deadly foe, the result being that the Nationalists increasingly had control of the air. Alpert, *Franco and the Condor Legion*, pp. 149–55.

28. J.M. Martínez Bande, *La ofénsiva sobre Segovia y la batalla de Brunete* (Madrid, 1972), p. 160.

29. Copeman, *Reason in Revolt*, pp. 134–5.

30. See Darman, *Heroic Voices of the Spanish Civil War*, p. 116.

31. *Cit.* MacDougall, *Voices from the Spanish Civil War*, p. 205.

32. See Cook, *Apprentices of Freedom*, p. 87.

33. Martínez Bande, *La ofénsiva sobre Segovia y la batalla de Brunete*, p. 162.

34. *Cit.* Darman, *Heroic Voices of the Spanish Civil War*, pp. 111–12. If many casualties were never evacuated, even those who did reach safety found themselves in over-crowded hospitals manned by personnel who were ever more hard-pressed. To quote Phelps, 'The constant flow of ambulances and wounded gave us little respite. We didn't know much about what was going on: it was kept from us, really … The heat was terrific and in the theatre it brought millions of flies: they settled on the wounds and instruments and everything! We had no Flit so I used to spray them with ethyl chloride. Day after day we only finished operating in the early hours of the morning with only a few hours rest before the spell … Once we were left in the dark: the main lights were cut off … while three operations were in progress. Two surgeons had the use of the only two flashlights in the place. The third surgeon had just begun sewing up and I held my cigarette lighter for him.' *Cit.* Arthur, *Real Band of Brothers*, pp. 93–5.

35. *Cit.* Ryan, *Book of the XV Brigade*, p. 142.

36. Copeman, *Reason in Revolt*, pp. 136–7.

37. Along with the Falangists, the Carlists were one of two mass-movements dedicated to the overthrow of the Second Republic that had emerged out of the Spanish Right's

hatred of the latter's reforms and fear of revolution. Particularly powerful in Navarre and the Basque provinces, they were associated with ultra-Catholicism and support for the branch of the Spanish royal family that had thrice risen in revolt against the ruling Isabelline dynasty in the course of the nineteenth century.

38. The clash did not occur face-to-face but rather over the telephone via an unfortunate staff officer who was faced with toning down 'the most ugly words in our language … the vilest remarks that anyone could possibly make'. *Cit.* A. Cervera Gil, *Ya sabes mi paradero: la Guerra Civil a través de las cartas de los que la vivieron* (Barcelona, 2005), p. 211.

39. For a detailed account of the Nationalist counter-attack, see Martínez Bande, *La ofé11siva sobre Segovia y la Batalla de Brunete*, pp. 178–98.

40. Gregory, *Shallow Grave*, pp. 73–4.

41. Alexander, *British Volunteers for Liberty*, pp. 127–9; Hills, *Battle for Madrid*, pp. 161–2.

42. *Cit.* Ryan, *Book of the XV Brigade*, pp. 164–5. Tapsell's reference to the presence of Spanish soldiers with the battalion is one of the very few occasions in the literature when this issue is referred to prior to the Battle of Belchite.

43. Baxell, *Unlikely Warriors*, pp. 234–5. In fairness, it is worth pointing out that the British battalion clearly performed much better than its counterparts in XIII International Brigade: so bad was the disintegration of this unit that a number of fugitives hijacked a column of trucks and took off in the direction of Madrid, only to be detained by a force of Assault Guards (an erstwhile force of paramilitary police that had in large part thrown in its lot with the Republic and was now used as shock troops), a considerable number of those concerned later being executed by firing squad.

44. Hills, *Battle for Madrid*, pp. 164–5. Franco has been much criticised for his decision to counter-attack – regaining Brunete and the other villages that had fallen to the enemy was in military terms of little consequence, after all – but in fact the decision rested on the very sound principle that, a substantial Republican army having in effect offered itself up to destruction, it was best to take advantage of the opportunity. Meanwhile, defeat though it was, in one sense the Battle of Brunete made an important contribution to the defeat of fascism. Thus, the military situation that developed at Stalingrad in the autumn of 1943 was all but a carbon copy of the one that had developed before Madrid in the winter of 1936, while the Brunete offensive bore a strong resemblance to the one which finally cut off the German VI Army off on the banks of the Volga. Given the fact that so many Soviet commanders of the Second World War rotated through Republican Spain, it is therefore difficult to believe that precedent and plan alike were forgotten. For detailed accounts of the battle, see Hills, *Battle for Madrid*, pp. 147–66, and Martínez Bande, *La ofensiva sobre Segovia y la batalla de Brunete*, pp. 103–201, while the role of the International Brigades is recounted, sometimes at the level of the individual battalion, in C. Vidal,

Las Brigadas Internacionales (Madrid, 1998), pp. 179–99; Delperrie de Bayac, *Brigadas Internacionales*, pp. 249–59; Landis, *Death in the Olive Groves*, pp. 39–57; Baxell, *British Volunteers*, pp. 82–6. Finally, for the role and experience of the rival air forces, see Salas Larrazábal, *Air War over Spain*, pp. 173–7.

Chapter 5

1. *Cit.* B. Doyle, *Brigadista: an Irishman's Fight against Fascism* (Dublin, 2006), p. 55.
2. R. and E. Frow (eds), *Bill Feeley: Singer, Steel-Erector, International Brigader* (Manchester, n.d.), p. 13.
3. Thomas, *To Tilt at Windmills*, p. 45.
4. Alexander, *British Volunteers for Liberty*, p. 143.
5. *Ibid.*
6. Gregory, *Shallow Grave*, p. 95.
7. *Cit.* MacDougall, *Voices from the Spanish Civil War*, p. 179.
8. *Cit. ibid.*, pp. 147–8.
9. For all this, see Baxell, *Unlikely Warriors*, pp. 162–70.
10. Gurney, *Crusade in Spain*, pp. 183–4.
11. These figures are derived from a report submitted to Moscow by the Comintern's then chief representative in Spain, Palmiro Togliatti, on 29 August 1937, the latter's view being that 'the Albacete base must be energetically purged'. Meanwhile, it is not just the over-staffing of the Albacete base that raises eyebrows: in all, Brunete is shown to have cost the International Brigades over half the men who had actually fought in the battle including 2,658 dead, 696 missing (most of them deserters) and 4,787 wounded or evacuated from Spain. For this report, see R. Radosh *et al.* (eds), *Spain Betrayed: the Soviet Union in the Spanish Civil War* (Newhaven, Connecticut, 2001), pp. 253–9.
12. *Ibid.*, p. 183. As an example of the contempt in which the rear-area staff were viewed, one might cite a ditty that was sung by the Americans and British to the tune of the theme from the popular hit musical *The Road to Mandalay*. Thus, 'See them strolling in the evenings to the grog-shops for their wine, for they are the brave defenders of the Albacete line.' *Cit.* C. Eby, *Between the Bullet and the Lie: American Volunteers in the Spanish Civil War* (New York, 1969), p. 97.
13. *Cit.* Darman, *Heroic Voices of the Spanish Civil War*, p. 106. One issue that has sometimes been claimed as having been of some importance in the growing disillusionment was the 'civil war within a civil war' that broke out in Barcelona between the Anarchists and forces loyal to the central government and/or the Communist Party in May 1937 and the subsequent suppression of the dissident Marxist group known as the POUM. However, except in the case of a few individuals, the news of the 'May Days' and their sequel in reality seems to have had little impact,

the British volunteers in the first instance having access to little information other than that with which the Communists chose to provide them, and, in the second, being pre-disposed to believe the Communist line that the Anarchists were doing little to support the war effort. See Baxell, *Unlikely Warriors*, pp. 193–4.

14. There were plenty of non-Communists in the ranks of the political commissariat of the People's Army as a whole, but the fact that the International Brigades constituted an independent entity ensured that the Party could nominate all the men it wanted without let or hindrance and, still more so, ensure that all the key roles were kept in its hands.

15. MacDougall, *Voices from the Spanish Civil War*, p. 144.

16. *Cit.* Baxell, *Unlikely Warriors*, p. 245.

17. Gregory, *Shallow Grave*, p. 88.

18. R. Felstead, *No Other Way: Jack Russia and the Spanish Civil War – a Biography* (Port Talbot, 1981), pp. 78–83.

19. Gregory, *Shallow Grave*, p. 76. The 'mistakes' recognised at these meetings did not, alas, extend to such matters as the battalion's failure to overcome the insignificant garrison of Villanueva de la Cañada on the first day of the battle. According to Gregory, at least, discussions rather centred on such matters as the lack of adequate supplies of drinking water.

20. *Cit.* Baxell, *Unlikely Warriors*, p. 235.

21. Baxell, *Unlikely Warriors*, pp. 235–7. According to one of the two accounts put forward by Copeman, at the meeting Cunningham demanded 'a change in attitude to the rank and file of the battalion … the withdrawal of the older volunteers and … political education in conformity with the principles for which these men had gone to Spain', whereas 'the counter-argument which came through the alternate shouting and threatening was for a stricter Communist control'. As for the decision that was taken to plump for himself and Tapsell, he suggests that it was because the two of them adopted a quieter and more conciliatory line than most of the other people present, thereby projecting an impression of balance and disinterestedness. See Copeman, *Reason in Revolt*, pp. 138–9. However, in an interview held in the Imperial War Museum's sound archive, he claims that Pollitt had long since become jealous of Cunningham and decided that he alone was the right man for the job. See Darman, *Heroic Voices of the Spanish Civil War*, pp. 124–5. That Pollitt hated Cunningham was all too plausible, but why he was so set on Copeman is rather more puzzling: it was scarcely as if the latter had shown himself to be a malleable figure.

22. Hooper, *No Pasarán!*, pp. 31, 34. Hooper's recollections being extremely garbled, to say the least, the order of these phrases has been re-arranged so as to render these remarks more lucid. However, the sense remains completely unchanged.

23. For an example of a volunteer who was disgusted with Tapsell, we might cite Manchester volunteer Walter Greenhalgh. Thus, 'Tapsell definitely made a hash of things. I know for a fact that he caused a tremendous amount of despair among those

who survived the battle of Brunete … A lot of the men were new … and there was
Tapsell telling them that the … military command [was] useless, that they weren't
revolutionary enough and … that there should be full co-operation between all
ranks … I went to George [Aitken] and said the way things were going on, every
lad in the battalion [would] go home because he was telling them … that they were
being driven to the slaughter like cattle. So Tapsell was arrested, and, of course,
the next thing there was a political struggle … because it would have been too …
dangerous for Tapsell to have been put on a proper charge for disaffecting the troops.'
Cit. Darman, *Heroic Voices of the Spanish Civil War*, pp. 118–19.

24. A connected issue which also caused much upset was the manner in which Party
    trusties were regularly pulled out of Spain so that they could undertake tasks back
    in their home countries. Wounded at Quinto, for example, John Roberts – 'Jack
    Russia' – to his friends was dispatched home to Wales so that he could contest the
    council seat he occupied at Caerphilly. Felstead, *No Other Way*, p. 112.

25. *Cit.* Cook, *Apprentices of Freedom*, pp. 95–6.

26. For details of Daly's life, see O'Riordan, *Connolly Column*, pp. 80–1.

27. *Cit.* Baxell, *Unlikely Warriors*, p. 266.

28. J.M. Martínez Bande, *La gran ofénsiva sobre Zaragoza* (Madrid, 1973), p. 101.

29. The best guide to the personnel of the International Brigades at this or any other time
    is the tables contained in Vidal, *Brigadas Internacionales*, pp. 413–77. Thoroughly
    laudatory biographies of Copic, Nelson and other figures can be found in Ryan, *Book
    of the XV Brigade*, pp. 190–214.

30. Landis, *Death in the Olive Groves*, p. 71. After the fighting was over, two members
    of the anti-tank battery wandered into the cemetery to look around to find a scene of
    utter devastation criss-crossed with enemy trenches and strewn with human bones.
    See MacDougall, *Voices from the Spanish Civil War*, p. 214.

31. *Cit.* Brome, *International Brigades*, p. 218. At both Jarama and Brunete, fear of
    Nationalist anti-tank guns and the difficulties of operating in close co-operation with
    infantry had generally dissuaded the Republican tank crews from doing anything more
    than hanging back and engaging the enemy, more or less ineffectually, at long range.

32. *Cit.* Ryan, *Book of the XV Brigade*, pp. 248–9.

33. *Cit. ibid.*, pp. 71–2.

34. *Cit.* Darman, *Heroic Voices of the Spanish Civil War*, p. 158.

35. For Porroche's account, see <http://www.quintodeebro.com/historia/historia_1937_
    relato_pascual_porroche.htm>, accessed 18 August 2019.

36. See Ryan, *Book of the XV Brigade*, p. 250.

37. *Cit. ibid.*, p. 254. Judging from another eyewitness account cited by Richard Baxell,
    the right wing of the battalion may have attempted to make a flanking move across
    the flat ground to the south-east of the Nationalist positions, but, even more exposed
    than their comrades to the left, the men concerned showed no more enthusiasm for
    pressing home their advance than they did. Baxell, *Unlikely Warriors*, p. 267.

38. Gregory, *Shallow Grave*, p. 79.
39. Felstead, *No Other Way*, p. 99.
40. The figure of three dead is derived from Baxell, *British Volunteers*, p. 89. In his later *Unlikely Warriors*, Baxell does not mention this figure. For the incident with the white flag, see O'Riordan, *Connolly Column*, p. 81.
41. *Cit.* Darman, *Heroic Voices of the Spanish Civil War*, p. 103.
42. *Cit.* Brome, *International Brigades*, p. 220.
43. *Ibid.*
44. *Cit. ibid.*
45. I. Puig (ed.), *Personal Memories of the Spanish Civil War in Catalan and English* (Lampeter, 1999), pp. 73–5.
46. If there were significant gaps in the ranks, this can only have been due to straggling or desertion: according to the roll of honour put together after the war by the International Brigades Association, Daly and Guerin were the only British volunteers to fall in the Belchite campaign out of the 200 men who took part, while, unknown though they are, losses among the latter's 200 Spanish counterparts are unlikely to have been much higher. See Alexander, *British Volunteers for Liberty*, pp. 263–76.
47. *Ibid.*, p. 150.
48. Well-educated and articulate, the 'anti-tanks' gave plenty of witness to the fighting at Belchite. Here, for example, is Bill Alexander: 'The fascists had been completely surrounded and were holding the church as a strong-point. It was in the centre of a whole system of inter-connecting houses with holes battered between the walls so they could retreat. We took our guns right … up behind the big sand-bag barricades which the fascists had left behind, poked our muzzles through and fired … directly at the church. This undoubtedly played a role in the final fascist surrender.' *Cit.* Darman, *Heroic Voices*, p. 124.
49. Gregory, *Shallow Grave*, p. 84.
50. *Cit.* Francis, *Miners against Fascism*, p. 28.
51. *Cit.* Ryan, *Book of the XV Brigade*, p. 256.
52. See 'Las posiciones defénsivas de Quinto (Aragón)', <http://www.griegc. com/2017/07/01/hola-mon/>, accessed 7 July 2020.
53. Baxell, *Unlikely Warriors*, p. 270. Surprisingly enough, the transfer of the International Brigades to the authority of the regular army seems to have been accepted without demur by the representatives of the Comintern and even by some key figures in the volunteers' command structure. Thus, if there is one thing that is absent from the documents that they generated, it is triumphalism. Far from being a magnificent fighting force, the International Brigades are rather described as being beset by problems of every kind including indiscipline, low morale and poor-quality leadership, the abolition of their autonomy therefore coming over as, above all, an attempt to stem what looked more and more like a slide into irrelevance and disintegration. Interestingly, particular alarm was expressed at the manner in which

the Brigades were being sent into battle far more frequently than other units of the Republican army, the inference being that keeping them in being had become far more important than the glory that was to be derived from employment at the front. See, for example, Vital Gayman, 'Confidential Report on the Situation of the International Brigades at the End of July 1937', *cit.* Radosh *et al.* (eds), *Spain Betrayed*, pp. 241–8.

Chapter 6

1. Part of XV Brigade since its formation in February 1937, the Dimitrov battalion had been sent to the rear on account of the heavy casualties it had suffered in clearing the streets of Quinto and Belchite.
2. See Alexander, *British Volunteers for Liberty*, pp. 152–4. Once again, the British battalion failed to distinguish itself, the fact that only three men were killed suggesting that the volunteers made little attempt to press home their advance. Still more damningly, as at Quinto, two of the fallen were the acting battalion commander, Harold Fry, who, it will be remembered, had been taken captive at the Battle of Jarama, but, after release as part of a prisoner exchange, had insisted on returning to Spain, where he had promptly taken over from O'Daire, and John Robert's replacement as battalion commissar, Mansfield volunteer Eric Whalley, both of whom appear to have been shot down at the very start of the action while trying to inspire the rank and file to advance.
3. *Cit.* Darman, *Heroic Voices of the Spanish Civil War*, p. 120. Here, too, is Fred Copeman. As he wrote of the situation that he encountered on his return to Spain in the wake of the crisis meeting of the British politbureau, 'Within our own brigade, a British versus American struggle had now set in: the Americans were struggling for military control as an indirect road to political power. In the end, they gained both.' Copeman, *Reason in Revolt*, p. 143.
4. Hooper, *No Pasarán!*, p. 33.
5. *Cit.* Darman, *Heroic Voices of the Spanish Civil War*, p. 124.
6. *Cit.* MacDougall, *Voices from the Spanish Civil War*, p. 117.
7. Alexander, *British Volunteers for Liberty*, p. 160. The fact that anything was achieved at all is somewhat surprising. While Copeman was sincere in his devotion to the cause, he was beginning to have many doubts about his Communist masters and so incorrigible in his suspicion of the upper echelons of the Brigade's command that he managed to alienate Tapsell, and that notwithstanding the latter's own repeated criticisms of the leadership. See Baxell, *Unlikely Warriors*, pp. 275–6.
8. Baxell, *Unlikely Warriors*, pp. 278–80.
9. J.M. Martínez Bande, *La batalla de Teruel* (Madrid, 1974), pp. 60–98; D. Alegre Lorenz, *La batalla de Teruel: guerra total en España* (Madrid, 2018), pp. 89–102. If the reasons why the Republicans chose Teruel as a target or, indeed, chose to

launch a fresh offensive at all, are clear enough, the background to the attack was, to put it mildly, extremely complicated. Thus, just as Belchite had in part been about smashing the power of the Anarchists, so Teruel was aimed at the erosion of Communist influence. Thanks to the massive numbers of new adherents it had gleaned by championing the cause, however temporarily, of the beleaguered bourgeoisie and peasantry (here defined – correctly – as small owner occupiers and tenant farmers), its association with Russian aid and, last but not least, its strong position in the Republican army and total control of the political commissars, the Communists had acquired a very powerful position in the loyalist zone. By the middle of 1937, it had become clear to Juan Negrín and Horacio Prieto, the moderate Socialists who headed the government, that they were not to be trusted, and so Teruel was set up in such a way as to ensure that the Communists could not capitalise on its success.

10. As with other such instances, the leading British historian Paul Preston is inclined to be critical of the decision to counter-attack: 'The sound advice of the senior German and Italian officers in Spain was to abandon Teruel and go ahead with the planned operation to cut off Madrid. His own staff … also believed that he should not let himself be diverted from his original plans. However, his determination to bring the Republic to total humiliating annihilation did not admit of allowing the enemy such successes. The capture of Madrid would have hastened the end of the war, and, possibly, with Rojo [the Republican chief-of-staff] having thrown everything into the Teruel offensive, at little cost. In contrast, to snuff out the move against Teruel had little strategic significance, and might, and indeed did, take a bloody toll. However, to Franco its attraction was that it provided the opportunity to destroy a large body of the Republic's best forces.' P. Preston, *Franco: a Biography* (London, 1995), pp. 292–3. The key sentence here is the last one, however. While the case for Franco wanting a long war is, at best, unproven, and that for the capture of Madrid ending the war downright dubious, the destruction of the People's Army was a guaranteed road to victory.

11. For the siege of the Nationalist strongholds, see Martínez Bande, *La batalla de Teruel*, pp. 105–20, 139–61. Rey d'Harcourt, Polanco and the other prisoners were at first spared, but on 7 February 1939 the colonel, the bishop and forty-two other survivors of the battle were summarily executed by their guards as they were being evacuated to France in the wake of the fall of Barcelona.

12. *Ibid.*, pp. 176–7; Alegre Lorenz, *La batalla de Teruel*, pp. 251–4.

13. Arthur, *Real Band of Brothers*, p. 161. Another driver was Australian Lloyd Edmunds: 'The snow was feet thick (one day the temperature was sixteen below zero) and we went with tow ropes on the back of each truck so that when a truck slid off the road, we could pull it back again without a waste of time … Each night we let the water out of the radiator so as not to freeze, but we had so much trouble in the mornings that we took it in turns to stay up all night and run each truck for five or ten minutes each hour to keep them warm.' *Cit.* A. Inglis (ed.), *Lloyd Edmonds: Letters from Spain* (Sydney, 1985), p. 76.

14. Alexander, *British Volunteers for Liberty*, p. 163.

15. Martínez Bande, *La batalla de Teruel*, p. 175.

16. Thomas, *To Tilt at Windmills*, p. 73. Among the Nationalist pilots was José Larios, 'On 19 January 1938, one of our biggest and most concentrated raids of the war took place over the Teruel battlefield. Around 400 bombers and fighters swept backwards and forwards during the whole day and 110 tons of high explosives were dropped over vital targets. We were briefed … to escort the Junkers, Savoias, Heinkel 51s and Romeos: this meant that we would be flying in wide circles over the target area, some of us at the same level of the bombers, the rest high above them … The patrols lasted from two to two and a half hours from take-off to landing: we were over the lines between sixty and ninety minutes. It was a strain on the neck muscles to continually swivel one's head around in all directions, especially above and behind, two most vulnerable spots, but it was the best way to keep alive … During this period we were flying two or three patrols daily.' J. Larios, *Combat over Spain: Memoirs of a Nationalist Fighter Pilot, 1936–1939* (London, 1974), pp. 160–1. Impressive as the Nationalist showing in the air was, however, it is worth noting that its efficacy lay not so much in the power of its bombs, but rather its paralysing moral effect. To quote Bill Feeley, 'Personally, I felt nothing but contempt for the airmen's … efforts to kill us. It is possible that, at one time or another, Hitler's mighty Condor Legion might have killed a Republican soldier, but, if they did, I never heard of this singularly unlucky or careless person.' Frow and Frow (eds), *Bill Feeley*, p. 21.

17. See Alpert, *Franco and the Condor Legion*, pp. 164–5. Salas Larrazábal, *Air War over Spain*, pp. 209–18.

18. *Cit.* Alegre Lorenz, *La batalla de Teruel*, p. 261.

19. Clark, *No Boots to my Feet*, pp. 51–2.

20. Alexander, *British Volunteers for Liberty*, pp. 165–6.

21. *Cit.* MacDougall, *Voices from the Spanish Civil War*, p. 247.

22. *Ibid.*, p. 155.

23. Alexander, *British Volunteers for Liberty*, p. 166.

24. *Cit.* Frow and Frow (eds), *Bill Feeley*, p. 16.

25. Alegre Lorenz, *La batalla de Teruel*, p. 251.

26. Thomas, *To Tilt at Windmills*, p. 74

27. For a discussion of the battalion's casualties, see Baxell, *Unlikely Warriors*, p. 283.

28. *Cit.* Darman, *Heroic Voices of the Spanish Civil War*, p. 133.

29. Baxell, *Unlikely Warriors*, p. 284.

30. Martínez Bande, *La batalla de Teruel*, p. 228. In his memoirs, Lee includes a detailed account of the Battle of Teruel, but, while this is certainly worth reading, it is almost certainly not based on personal experience: quickly spotted as the epileptic he was, Lee was kept away from the front and instead employed in propaganda activities in Barcelona.

31. L. Lee, *A Moment of War* (London, 1991), p. 158.
32. *Cit.* Martínez Bande, *La batalla de Teruel*, p. 207.

Chapter 7

1. For a detailed account of the operations of the Condor Legion in the first days of the battle, see R. Proctor, *Hitler's Luftwaffe in the Spanish Civil War* (Westport, Connecticut, 1983), pp. 191–5.
2. In brief, sent up to defend the area of Codo, the XI Brigade was quickly overwhelmed and forced to retreat on Hijar and Alcániz, eventually being all but wiped out in the vicinity of Calaceite, and the XII, XIII and XIV overwhelmed in a series of combats that enveloped them as soon as they entered the line. Vidal, *Brigadas Internacionales*, pp. 262–73; Delperrie de Bayac, *Brigadas Internacionales*, pp. 282–92.
3. *Cit.* Arthur, *Real Band of Brothers*, pp. 184–5.
4. *Cit.* Cook, *Apprentices of Freedom*, p. 113. The George Fletcher mentioned here is the same Fletcher who Doyle reports as having been shot in the hand. As we shall see, he was soon to become the battalion's temporary commander.
5. *Cit.* MacDougall, *Voices from the Spanish Civil War*, p. 222. There is something studiedly vague about this account, and it is therefore difficult not to suspect that Sloan hung back rather than accompany the guns to the new position, only to be rounded up by Merriman as a straggler.
6. Clark, *No Boots to my Feet*, pp. 60–1.
7. *Cit.* Darman, *Heroic Voices of the Spanish Civil War*, p. 159.
8. *Cit.* MacDougall, *Voices from the Spanish Civil War*, p. 223.
9. *Cit. ibid.*, p. 261.
10. *Cit.* Baxell, *Unlikely Warriors*, p. 110.
11. Gregory, *Shallow Grave*, pp. 102–6. As Gregory implies, a major role was played by both the Condor Legion and the Legionary Aviation whose aircraft strafed the endless columns of troops and refugees in the most unmerciful manner, ranged at will across the Republican lines of communication and pounded such targets as Lérida and Tortosa.
12. Clark, *No Boots to my Feet*, p. 73.
13. *Cit.* MacDougall, *Voices of the Spanish Civil War*, p. 225.
14. Gregory, *Shallow Grave*, p. 106. The fall of Caspe brought to an end what is generally regarded as the first phase of the Nationalist offensive. For a general account of the fighting of the period 9–17 March, see J.M. Martínez-Bande, *La llegada al mar* (Madrid, 1975), pp. 25–68, while events at Caspe in particular are described by S. Melguizo Aísa, *Brigadas Internacionales en el frente de Caspe, marzo de 1938: aproximación arqueológica a través de dos fosas de combatientes* (Zaragoza, 2018), pp. 15–17. Finally, confirmation of the stubborness which the International-Brigaders

displayed comes from Peter Kemp, a student at the University of Cambridge who had resisted the lure of Communism and instead come out to Spain to fight for Franco, who later admitted that his company of the Spanish Foreign Legion lost three-quarters of its strength in the course of taking the town. Baxell, *Unlikely Warriors*, p. 392.

15. Baxell, *Unlikely Warriors*, p. 312.
16. Doyle, *Brigadista*, p. 62.
17. Baxell, *Unlikely Warriors*, pp. 313–14.
18. Gregory, *Shallow Grave*, p. 108. For a more general account, see Baxell, *British Volunteers*, pp. 98–9.
19. *Cit.* Arthur, *Real Band of Brothers*, p. 188. Doyle's memory is clearly at fault in respect to the enemy armour. Thus, the reference to the enemy tank whose commander shot Tapsell having a turret implies that the vehicle concerned was either a German Panzer I or a captured Russian T26, but the Italians only had the turretless L3 tankette.
20. *Cit.* Cook, *Apprentices of Freedom*, p. 115.
21. *Cit.* Darman, *Heroic Voices of the Spanish Civil War*, p. 136.
22. Frow and Frow (eds), *Bill Feeley*, p. 17.
23. *Cit.* MacDougall, *Voices of the Spanish Civil War*, p. 268.
24. Alexander, *British Volunteers for Liberty*, p. 179.
25. Gregory, *Shallow Grave*, p. 110.
26. For all this, see J.M. Martínez Bande, *La Batalla del Ebro* (Madrid, 1978), pp. 87–97. Not only was the Army of the Ebro an ostensibly powerful force in military terms, but it was also one that was overwhelmingly Communist: Modesto, Lister, Vega and Tagueña were all long-standing Communists, and the first three, in addition, stars of the Party's war effort, while the same applied to all the commissars above divisional level as well as all the divisional commanders.
27. M. Tagüeña Lacorte, *Testimonio de dos guerras* (Barcelona, 2005), pp. 205–6.
28. Martínez Bande, *Batalla del Ebro*, pp. 84–5.
29. Alpert, *Franco and the Condor Legion*, pp. 179–80.
30. Frow and Frow (eds), *Bill Feeley*, pp. 20–1.
31. Alexander, *Volunteers for Liberty*, pp. 201–4.
32. G. Wheeler, *To Make the People Smile Again: a Memoir of the Spanish Civil War* (Newcastle upon Tyne, 2003), p. 61; Gregory, *Shallow Grave*, p. 116.
33. *Cit.* Arthur, *Real Band of Brothers*, p. 138.
34. Thomas, *To Tilt at Windmills*, p. 117. Thomas writes as follows of the battery's new armament, 'At the moment we are dissecting the "Baby". It's a shame to have to put up with one little gun like this after the three beauties. This one had two high wheels, about three feet six inches in diameter, [and] a tiny barrel three feet long. It fires a midget shell one and one half inches in diameter and six inches or so in length. Rumour has it [that] the shells are pulled back on a string after firing.' *Ibid.*, p. 105. An educated guess would be that the weapon concerned was a Russian 37mm Rosenberg M1915 infantry gun.

35. Wheeler, *To Make the People Smile Again*, p. 65.

36. *Ibid.*, pp. 67–8.

37. Many International-Brigade accounts are insistent that the summit was crowned with a ring of trenches and pill boxes and surrounded by a belt of barbed wire. However, visits to the site have revealed no evidence of concrete defences of any sort, while it is in any case highly unlikely that a position so far removed from the front line that had been in the hands of the Nationalists for so little time would have had the expense in labour and materials represented by the construction of concrete fortifications lavished upon it. As the hill had also been given a garrison – a battalion of the Foreign Legion – only a very short time before the arrival of the Republicans, it seems likely that the defenders had recourse to little more than hastily dug scrapes in the rocky ground and a few coils of barbed wire.

38. Wheeler, *To Make the People Smile Again*, p. 69.

39. Clark, *No Boots to my Feet*, pp. 107–9.

40. *Cit.* MacDougall, *Voices from the Spanish Civil War*, pp. 299–200. Fullarton's luck did not last, however: later that same day, he was wounded in the abdomen and evacuated to the rear.

41. Gregory, *Shallow Grave*, pp. 124–6.

42. Martínez Bande, *Batalla del Ebro*, p. 162.

43. Wheeler, *To Make the People Smile Again*, p. 77.

44. Alexander, *Volunteers for Liberty*, p. 27.

45. *Cit.* MacDougall, *Voices from the Spanish Civil War*, p. 320.

46. *Cit. ibid.*, p. 241.

47. Gregory, *Shallow Grave*, p. 129.

48. *Cit.* Darman, *Heroic Voices of the Spanish Civil War*, p. 152.

49. *Cit.* MacDougall, *Voices from the Spanish Civil War*, p. 318.

50. *Cit.* Toynbee, *Distant Drum*, pp. 135–8.

51. Wheeler, *To Make the People Smile Again*, p. 115.

52. Gregory, *Shallow Grave*, p. 130.

53. Wheeler, *To Make the People Smile Again*, p. 114.

54. Gregory, *Shallow Grave*, pp. 131–2.

55. For the formation of the new anti-tank battery, see Thomas, *To Tilt at Windmills*, p. 151.

56. Wheeler, *To Make the People Smile Again*, p. 118.

57. *Cit.* MacDougall, *Voices of the Spanish Civil War*, p. 166.

58. Frow and Frow (eds), *Bill Feeley*, p. 22.

59. Gregory, *Shallow Grave*, p. 134. Gregory claims that he and his men assisted in the destruction of three enemy tanks that were knocked out as they closed in on the defenders, but it seems likely that these rather fell victim to the new anti-tank battery.

60. Alexander, *British Volunteers for Liberty*, p. 215.

61. There is considerable disagreement as to how much the British volunteers knew about this agreement before the action of 23 September. Thus, Gregory insists

that he and his fellows knew nothing about what was planned, while Alexander is equally adamant the decision was known to all. See Gregory, *Shallow Grave*, p. 132; Alexander, *British Volunteers for Liberty*, p. 212.

62. *Cit.* Baxell, *Unlikely Warriors*, p. 350.
63. *Cit.* Arthur, *Real Band of Brothers*, p. 192.
64. The key text for the revisionist case is M. Seidman, *Republic of Egos: a Social History of the Spanish Civil War* (Madison, Wisconsin, 2002), but see also J. Matthews, *Reluctant Warriors: Republican Popular-Army and Nationalist-Army Conscripts in the Spanish Civil War, 1936–1939* (Oxford, 2012).
65. L.A. Kirschenbaum, *International Communism and the Spanish Civil War: Solidarity and Suspicion* (Cambridge, 2015), pp. 113–14.
66. Gregory, *Shallow Grave*, p. 19.
67. Darman, *Heroic Voices of the Spanish Civil War*, p. 223.
68. For a very down-beat assessment of the International Brigades in military terms, see Kirschenbaum, *International Communism and the Spanish Civil War*, pp. 103–7.
69. Thomas, *To Tilt at Windmills*, p. 156.

Conclusion

1. Alexander, *British Volunteers for Liberty*, p. 216.
2. For Clifford's defence of the military worth of the International Brigades, see A. Clifford, *Fighting for Spain: the International Brigades in the Civil War* (Barnsley, 2020), pp. 228–31.

Bibliography

Primary Sources

Alvarez, S. (ed.), *Historia política y militar de las Brigadas Internacionales: testimonios y documentos* (Madrid, 1996)

Arthur, M., *The Real Band of Brothers: First-Hand Accounts from the Last British Survivors of the Spanish Civil War* (London, 2009)

Barea, A., *The Forging of a Rebel*, ed. N. Townson (London, 2001)

Cardozo, H., *March of a Nation* (London, 1937)

Cervera Gil, A., *Ya sabes mi paradero: la Guerra Civil a través de las cartas de los que la vivieron* (Barcelona, 2005)

Chaves Nogales, M., *Los secretos de la defensa de Madrid*, ed. A. Múñoz Molina (Seville, 2017)

Clark, B., *No Boots to my Feet: Experiences of a Britisher in Spain, 1937–1938* (Shelton, 1984)

Copeman, F., *Reason in Revolt* (London, 1948)

Cortes Roa, A., *Tanquista desde mi tronera* (Madrid, 1989)

Cox, G., *The Defence of Madrid* (London, 1937)

Darman, P., *Heroic Voices of the Spanish Civil War: Memories of the Spanish Civil War* (London, 2009)

Doyle, B., *Brigadista: an Irishman's Fight against Fascism* (Dublin, 2006)

Frow, R. and E. (eds), *Bill Feeley: Singer, Steel-Erector, International Brigader* (Manchester, n.d.)

Gregory, W., *The Shallow Grave: a Memoir of the Spanish Civil War* (London, 1986)

Gurney, J., *Crusade in Spain* (London, 1974)

Hooper, D., *No Pasarán! A Memoir of the Spanish Civil War* (London, 1997)

Ibárruri, D., *El único camino* (Paris, 1965)

Ibárruri, D., *They Shall Not Pass: the Autobiography of La Pasionaria* (London, 1966)

Inglis, A. (ed.), *Lloyd Edmonds: Letters from Spain* (Sydney, 1985)

Larios, J., *Combat over Spain: Memoirs of a Nationalist Fighter Pilot, 1936–1939* (London, 1974)

Lee, L., *A Moment of War* (London, 1991)

Levine, M., *Cheetham to Cordova* [sic]*: a Manchester Man of the Thirties* (Manchester, 1984)

Lister, E., *Memorias de un luchador* (Madrid, 1977)

MacDougall, I. (ed.), *Voices from the Spanish Civil War: Personal Recollections of Scottish Volunteers in Republican Spain, 1936–1939* (Edinburgh, 1986)

Modesto, J., *Soy del Quinto Regimiento* (Barcelona, 1978)

Monks, J., *With the Reds in Andalusia* (London, 1985)

Nelson, C., and Hendricks, J. (eds), *Madrid, 1937: Letters of the Abraham-Lincoln Brigade from the Spanish Civil War* (New York, 1996)

Puig, I. (ed.), *Personal Memories of the Spanish Civil War in Catalan and English* (Lampeter, 1999)

Romilly, E., *Boadilla* (London, 1937)

Rust, W., *Britons in Spain: the History of the British Battalion of the XVth International Brigade* (London, 1939)

Ryan, F. (ed.), *The Book of the XV Brigade: Records of British, American, Canadian and Irish Volunteers in Spain, 1936–1938* (Madrid, 1938)

Sommerfield, J., *Volunteer in Spain* (London, 1997)

Sperber, M. (ed.), *And I Remember Spain: a Spanish-Civil-War Anthology* (London, 1974)

Stansky, P., and Abrahams, W. (eds), *Journey to the Frontier: Two Roads to the Spanish Civil War* (Boston, 1966)

Stradling, R. (ed.), *Brother against Brother: Experiences of a British Volunteer in the Spanish Civil War* (Stroud, 1998)

Tagüeña Lacorte, M., *Testimonio de dos guerras* (Barcelona, 2005)

Thomas, F., *To Tilt at Windmills: a Memoir of the Spanish Civil War* (East Lansing, Michigan, 1996)

Toynbee, P. (ed.), *The Distant Drum: Reflections on the Spanish Civil War* (London, 1976)

Watson, K.S., *Single to Spain* (London, 1937)

Wheeler, G., *To Make the People Smile Again: a Memoir of the Spanish Civil War* (Newcastle upon Tyne, 2003)

Wintringham, T., *English Captain* (London, 1939)

Secondary Sources

Alcofar Nassaes, J.L., *'Spansky': los extranjeros que lucharon en la Guerra Civil Española* (Barcelona, 1973)

Alegre Lorenz, D., *La batalla de Teruel: guerra total en España* (Madrid, 2018)

Alexander, W., *British Volunteers for Liberty: Spain, 1936–39* (London, 1982)

Alpert, M., *The Republican Army in the Spanish Civil War* (Cambridge, 2013)

Alpert, M., *Franco and the Condor Legion: the Spanish Civil War in the Air* (London, 2019)

Baxell, R., *British Volunteers in the Spanish Civil War* (London, 2004)

Baxell, R., *Unlikely Warriors: the British in the Spanish Civil War and the Struggle against Fascism* (London, 2012)

Baxell, R., 'Myths of the International Brigades', *Bulletin of Hispanic Studies*, XCI, Nos 1–2 (January, 2014), pp. 11–24

Bolín, L., *Spain: the Vital Years* (London, 1997)

Boyd-Hancock, D., *I am Spain: the Spanish Civil War and the Men and Women who Went to Fight Fascism* (Brecon, 2012)

Brome, V., *The International Brigades* (London, 1965)

Carroll, P.N., *The Odyssey of the Abraham Lincoln Brigade: Americans in the Spanish Civil War* (Stanford, California, 1994)

Cierva, R. de la, *Brigadas Internacionales, 1936–1996: la verdadera historia – mentira histórica y error de estado* (Madridejos, 1997)

Clifford, A., *Fighting for Spain: the International Brigades in the Civil War, 1936–1939* (Barnsley, 2020)

Colodny, R., *The Struggle for Madrid* (New York, 1958)

Cook, J., *Apprentices of Freedom* (London, 1979)

Coverdale, J.F., 'The Battle of Guadalajara, 8–22 March 1937', *Journal of Contemporary History*, IX, No. 1 (January, 1974), pp. 53–76

Davies, G., *'You are Legend': the Welsh Volunteers in the Spanish Civil War* (Cardiff, 2018)

Delperrie de Bayac, J., *Las Brigadas Internacionales* (Madrid, 1978)

Deutscher, I., *Stalin* (rev. edn, London, 1966)

Eby, C., *Between the Bullet and the Lie: American Volunteers in the Spanish Civil War* (New York, 1969)

Elstob, P., *The Armed Rehearsal* (London, 1964)

Esdaile, Charles J., *The Spanish Civil War: a Military History* (Abingdon, 2019)

Esdaile, Charles J., 'Recent writing on the military history of the Spanish Civil War', *European History Quarterly*, L, No. 2 (April, 2020), pp. 331–44

Felstead, R., *No Other Way: Jack Russia and the Spanish Civil War – a Biography* (Port Talbot, 1981)

Francis, H., *Miners against Fascism: Wales and the Spanish Civil War* (London, 1984)

Gray, D., *Homage to Caledonia: Scotland and the Spanish Civil War* (Edinburgh, 2008)

Hills, G., *The Battle for Madrid* (London, 1974)

Hooton, E., *Spain in Arms: a Military History of the Spanish Civil War, 1936–1939* (Oxford, 2019)

Hughes, B., *'They Shall Not Pass!' The British Battalion at Jarama, the Spanish Civil War* (Oxford, 2011)

'Interview with Steve Fullerton', *cit. Scottish Labour-History Society Journal*, No. 11 (1977)

Kirschenbaum, L.A., *International Communism and the Spanish Civil War: Solidarity and Suspicion* (Cambridge, 2015)

Kowalsky, D., 'The Soviet Union and the International Brigades, 1936–1939', *Journal of Slavic Military Studies*, XIX, No. 4 (December, 2006), pp. 681–704

Kowalsky, D., 'Operation X: the Soviet Union and the Spanish Civil War', *Bulletin of Hispanic Studies*, XCI (January, 2014), pp. 159–78

Landis, A.H., *Death in the Olive Groves: American Volunteers in the Spanish Civil War* (New York, 1989)

Martínez Bande, J.M., *La oténsiva sobre Segovia y la Batalla de Brunete* (Madrid, 1972)

Martínez Bande, J.M., *La gran oténsiva sobre Zaragoza* (Madrid, 1973)

Martínez Bande, J.M., *La batalla de Teruel* (Madrid, 1974)

Martínez Bande, J.M., *La llegada al mar* (Madrid, 1975)

Martínez Bande, J.M., *La Batalla del Ebro* (Madrid, 1978)

Martínez Bande, J.M., *La lucha en torno a Madrid* (Madrid, 1984)

Matthews, J., *Reluctant Warriors: Republican Popular-Army and Nationalist-Army Conscripts in the Spanish Civil War, 1936–1939* (Oxford, 2012)

Melguizo Aísa, S., *Brigadas Internacionales en el frente de Caspe, marzo de 1938: aproximación arqueológica a través de dos fosas de combatientes* (Zaragoza, 2018)

Morris, L., 'English-speaking units of the International Brigades in the Spanish Civil War, 1936–1939: image and reality', University of Liverpool MA thesis, 2013

O'Riordan, M., *Connolly Column: the Story of the Irishmen who Fought for the Spanish Republic, 1936–1939* (Dublin, 1979)

Permuy López, R., and Mortera Pérez, A., *Histórica 36/39, No. 3, la batalla de Jarama* (Madrid, n.d.)

Preston, P., *Franco: a Biography* (London, 1995)

Preston, P., *The Spanish Civil War: Reaction, Revolution and Revenge* (London, 2006)

Preston, P., and Graham, H. (eds), *The Popular Front in Europe* (London, 1987)

Proctor, R., *Hitler's Luftwaffe in the Spanish Civil War* (Westport, Connecticut, 1983)

Radosh, R. *et al.* (eds), *Spain Betrayed: the Soviet Union in the Spanish Civil War* (Newhaven, Connecticut, 2001)

Raeburn, F., 'Politics, networks and community: recruitment for the International Brigades re-assessed', *Journal of Contemporary History*, LV, No. 4 (October, 2020), pp. 79–44

Requena Gallego, M., (ed.), *La Guerra Civil Española y las Brigadas Internacionales* (Cuenca, 1998)

Richardson, R.D., 'The defence of Madrid: mysterious generals, Red-Front fighters and the International Brigades', *Military Affairs*, XLIII, No. 4 (January, 1979), pp. 178–85

Richardson, R.D., *Comintern Army: the International Brigades and the Spanish Civil War* (Lexington, Kentucky, 1982)

Salas Larrazábal, J., *Air War over Spain* (London, 1974)

Seidman, M., *Republic of Egos: a Social History of the Spanish Civil War* (Madison, Wisconsin, 2002)

Stradling, R., *History and Legend: Writing the International Brigades* (Cardiff, 2003)

Thomas, H., *The Spanish Civil War* (3rd edn, London, 1977)

Tremlett, G., *The International Brigades: Fascism, Freedom and the Spanish Civil War* (London, 2020)

Vidal, C., *Las Brigadas Internacionales* (Madrid, 1998)

Zaagsma, G., *Jewish Volunteers, the International Brigades and the Spanish Civil War* (London, 2017)

Index